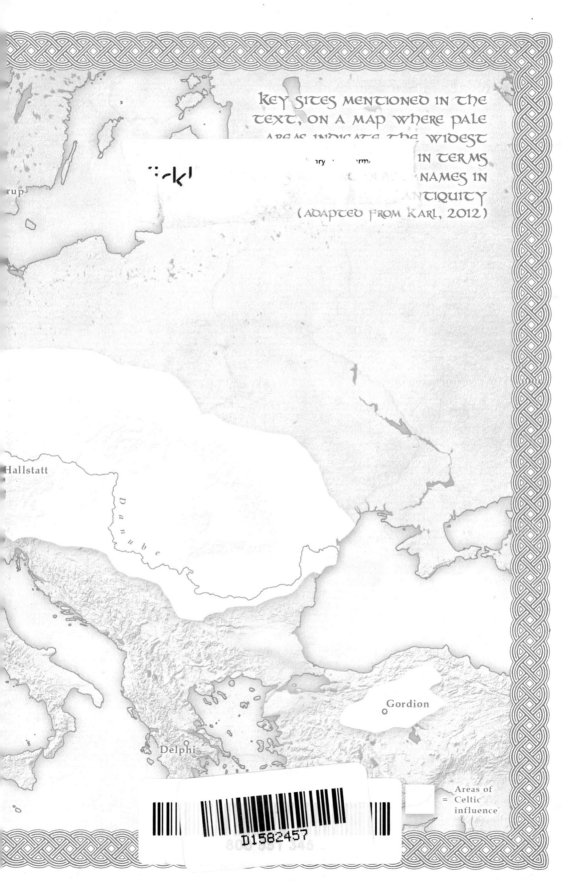

KEY SITES MENTIONED IN THE
TEXT, ON A MAP WHERE PALE
AREAS INDICATE THE WIDEST
⋯ry ⋯rm⋯ IN TERMS
⋯ NAMES IN
⋯TIQUITY
(ADAPTED FROM KARL, 2012)

rup

⸫⸫ckl

Hallstatt

Danube

Gordion

Delphi

Areas of
= Celtic
influence

Praise for Alice Roberts

'Clear-spoken and enthusiastic' *Telegraph*

'The Celts are here and all around us, even today. The Romans might have tried to snuff them out, but the flames were not wholly extinguished. Alice's book will make them easier to find' Neil Oliver

'She is a gift to broadcasting because she, like physicist Professor Brian Cox, is enthusiastic, easy on the eye and can explain complicated ideas with simplicity' *Radio Times*

'Roberts's lightness of touch is joyous, and celebratory' *Observer*

'The biggest gap in biology is that between DNA (which is just chemistry) and living creatures. Somewhere, the answer must reside in the embryo and in this book Alice Roberts has set out to find it. With wit and enthusiasm, she succeeds' Steve Jones – Geneticist and author of *The Single Helix*

'Alice Roberts is our preeminent science storyteller' Adam Rutherford – Geneticist, broadcaster and author of *Creation*

'Television's top osteoarchaeologist' *Mirror*

About the author

Alice Roberts is an anthropologist, osteoarchaeologist broadcaster, author and Professor at the University of Birmingham. She has presented *Coast*, *The Incredible Human Journey* and *Digging for Britain* on BBC2, and appeared as an expert on *Time Team*. She writes a regular column for the *Observer* and is passionate about various aspects of anthropology including human health, evolution and history. Her previous book *The Incredible Unlikeliness of Being* was shortlisted for the Wellcome Book Prize. She lives in the West Country with her husband, two children and a large variety of spiders.

Also by Alice Roberts

The Incredible Unlikeliness of Being:
Evolution and the Making of Us

Evolution: The Human Story

The Incredible Human Journey

The Complete Human Body

Don't Die Young:
An Anatomist's Guide to Organs and Your Health

THE CELTS

SEARCH FOR A CIVILIZATION

ALICE ROBERTS

Based on the BBC series
The Celts: Blood, Iron and Sacrifice

HERON
BOOKS

First published in Great Britain in 2015 by Heron Books
an imprint of

Quercus Publishing Ltd
Carmelite House
50 Victoria Embankment
London EC4Y 0DZ

An Hachette UK Company

Published by arrangement with the BBC.
The BBC logo is a trademark of the British Broadcasting Corporation
and is used under licence. BBC logo © BBC 1996

Map illustrations © 2015 Jamie Whyte
Chapter title illustrations © Victor Ambrus
Images © BBC and Alice Roberts unless otherwise stated

A CIP catalogue record for this book is available
from the British Library

HB ISBN 978 1 78429 332 1
EBOOK ISBN 978 1 78429 334 5

10 9 8 7 6 5 4 3 2 1

Typeset by Hewer Text UK Ltd, Edinburgh
Printed and bound in Great Britain by Clays Ltd, St Ives, plc

The ocean is in flood, the sea is full, delightful
    is the home of ships,
The wind whirls the sand around the estuary,
Swiftly the rudder cleaves the broad sea.

Extract from an early Celtic poem
Song of the Sea

CONTENTS

CELTIC TIMELINE

BC

4500	Approximate beginning of the Neolithic in Britain, with farming adopted alongside hunting and gathering, and the first pottery
3200	Approximate beginning of the Bronze Age in Europe, with metalworking in the Aegean; earliest writing appears in the form of pictograms
2500	Approximate beginning of Bronze Age in Britain and Ireland
2300	Amesbury archer buried near Stonehenge
2200	Completion of Stonehenge (approx.)
2000	Domestication of the horse (approx.)
1800	First large-scale copper mines dug in Britain
1800–1500	Early precursors of alphabetic script appear in Bronze Age inscriptions in Egypt and Palestine
1500	Metal hoards appear in Britain and Ireland
1400	Gold bar torcs originate in Ireland
1300	Approximate beginning of Urnfield culture in central Europe
1200	Phoenician alphabet develops
1200	Iron production starts in Anatolia

1200–1150	Late Bronze Age collapse in the Eastern Mediterranean region. This is also the period which forms the setting of the *Iliad* and the *Odyssey* epic poems, written down some four centuries later
1200–1000	Bronze Ballintober swords manufactured in the British Isles
1100	Increasing use of iron across Europe
800	Approximate date for the composition of the *Iliad* and the *Odyssey*
800	Approximate date of the transition from Bronze to Iron Age in central and western Europe; gradual phasing in of the use of iron between 800 and 500 BC in the British Isles
753	Traditional date for the founding of Rome
750	Urnfield culture replaced by Hallstatt culture (approx.)
740	Greek script develops from Phoenician script
700–600	Earliest Tartessian inscriptions in southwest Portugal
700–600	Etruscans and Greeks establish trading posts in Mediterranean – including Greek colony of Massalia
653	Rise of Persian Empire
650	Land along the Danube becomes increasingly heavily farmed with irrigation channels dug in the area of Heuneburg
600	Mud-brick walls built at Heuneburg
583	Bettelbühl Princess buried
540	Destruction of the mud-brick walls at Heuneburg
530–500	Hecataeus of Miletus pens his Periegesis highlighting the Celtic cities of the Mediterranean
500	Transition from Halstatt to La Tène culture in central Europe

500–400	Glauberg Prince burial
499–449	Persian wars with the Greeks
470/469	Birth of Socrates
450–400	Heuneburg fort abandoned, also Mont Lassois and Burgundy
430–400	Herodotus writes his *Histories*
387	Celts, led by Brennus, sack Rome
338	Greece under Macedonian rule
336	Alexander becomes king of Macedonia
335	Alexander the Great receives Celtic ambassadors in the Balkans
334	Celts and Romans sign treaty of Senones in northern Italy
331	Alexander the Great defeats Darius III of Persia in the Battle of Gaugamela, completing his conquest of Persia
325	Pytheas of Massalia voyages to Britain
323	Death of Alexander the Great at Babylon
300–200	Traditional date for the manufacture of the Gundestrup cauldron (though recent analysis suggests it may date to as late as 300 AD)
280	Celts ally with Thracians and attack Macedonians
278	King Nichomedes I of Bithynia encourages Celts to settle in Galatia in Turkey
277	Four thousand Celtic mercenaries employed by Ptolemy II of Egypt
263	First Punic War between Rome and Carthaginian army including 3,000 Celts
233	King Attalus I of Pergamum commissions the statue of The Dying Gaul (later copied by the Romans) to commemorate his victory over the Galatians

383   Roman troops withdrawn from the north and west of Britain

410   Traditional date for the end of Roman rule in Britain as Emperor Honorius rejects British request for military assistance to resist Germanic attacks, and Rome is sacked by the Germanic Visigoths

519   Cerdic crowned the first Anglo-Saxon king of Wessex, according to the *Anglo-Saxon Chronicle*

1100   The first known copy of the Irish *Book of the Dun Cow*

1350–1410 The *White Book of Rhydderch* and the *Red Book of Hergest* – earliest Welsh manuscripts containing the stories of the Mabinogion

FOREWORD

A few years ago, while filming an item for the BBC television series *Coast*, I spent some time on the enigmatic tidal island of St Michael's Mount, in Cornwall. A local, one who had relearned the Cornish language, told me the old name for the island was *Karrek Loos Yn Koos* – meaning 'the grey rock in the woods'.

The Cornish language – one of the so-called Celtic languages of the British Isles – therefore has roots that reach all the way down to a time when St Michael's Mount was surrounded, not by waves, but by trees. Given that folklore has it that the Phoenicians called the place 'Ictis', and moored their ships there during the millennium before the birth of Christ while they loaded precious cargoes of Cornish tin, the time of 'the grey rock in the woods' must be distant indeed.

Language is a crucial part of the story of these islands. Trapped in the Celtic language, like a bug in amber, is a memory of a mysterious time – a time when these homelands of ours looked and sounded very different. If we could go there now, we would be aliens – unwanted foreigners in our own country.

During 2015, Alice and I had the privilege of travelling in search of that mysterious and foreign past, and its inhabitants. It was a journey that took us around Britain and also far from home. We travelled through Austria, France, Germany, Italy, Portugal, Spain, Switzerland and Turkey in search of traces and echoes of the people who inhabited Europe in the long-lost centuries and millennia before Rome cast its instantly recognizable shadow across the continent.

Romans are part of this story too. Look for Celts and, as often as not, you have to scrape away Roman rubble and dust before you see the people you're looking for. Those Romans seem to squat everywhere – cuckoos in the nest.

I will admit right now that I have always found the ancient Romans hard to love. As an archaeology student, I was drawn to prehistory – to the long ages before the advent of written records, which seem to make everything too easy. For me, the Romans represented the arrival of the modern world. Apart from anything else, they were bureaucrats, administrators, accountants, keepers of books. I preferred, and prefer, to try and make sense of the world before the coming of the written word – the world the Romans sought to dominate and to remake in their own image.

The Romans certainly wrote about the Celts. Much of what we know (or think we know) about Celtic civilization is an image glimpsed through Roman eyes. To those Romans who encountered the Celts in Gaul, Germania, Britannia and elsewhere, the Celts were always foreign and often downright frightening. They were also their most stubborn foes.

For me, therefore, the search for the Celts was made in the hope of understanding just what it was that had made these pre-Roman Iron Age peoples so alien, foreign and disturbing to those tiresome empire builders with their pen-pushers and their armies of uniformed, identikit soldiers that marched in time, like marionettes.

An old Sanskrit, or perhaps Arabic proverb expresses the thought that, 'My enemy's enemy is my friend'. Given that the Celts were such worthy enemies of those damned Romans – and vehemently opposed to everything the invaders stood for – they surely have to be my friends.

For me, the journey in search of those old pals came at just the right time. A few months before the start of the project, I sat up all night watching the results of the referendum on Scottish independence. There was a febrile atmosphere in Scotland in the weeks leading up to the vote, and the temperature has run high since. The night of the referendum itself was one of the longest I can remember enduring.

As a nation, and as individual private citizens, we were made to consider and to reconsider our notions of identity. Who are the British? Who are the Scots? Who were they in the past? Who are they now?

While the process of self-analysis went on, we were invited to consider characters and events from our nations' shared pasts. Much was made of the oppressive nature and behaviour of England's Edward I – how he had sought to deny the Scots their independence and make them subject to his rule. Much was made, too, of the legacies of William Wallace and Robert Bruce. I swear there are folk living in Scotland in the twenty-first century who think *Braveheart* is the news.

To me, too, the time when several families of Norman-French descent fought each other for control of the land of the Scots seems like recent history – one of many veneers stretched thin across the rocks of the place – but for different reasons.

My fascination with Scotland – and indeed with the whole of the British Isles and the European mainland beyond – lies in the great depth of the countries' histories. The Romans made a colony of Britannia in 43 AD and, in time, saw fit to draw a line across the long island, separating the mostly-settled south from the always-troublesome north. Hadrian's Wall was built out of necessity. Rome's soldiers needed something hard to stand behind and so they strung their great white wall from west to east – from the Solway Firth to the mouth of the River Tyne.

It was an arbitrary line – one that made sense only to military commanders. It was drawn the best part of 2,000 years ago by strangers from a strange land – and yet Scots and English have fought about it ever since, as though it was their own idea.

At least the Romans had a reason to hold that line – and that reason was the Celts.

While hunting Celts at home and elsewhere, I preferred to think about Calgacus. He is the first named 'Scot' – and certainly a Celt. We know his name because the son-in-law of a Roman general wrote it down (or, more likely, made it up).

It was Agricola who had headed north to subdue the Celtic Caledonian tribes. Tacitus wrote *De vita et moribus Iulii Agricolae* – 'About the life and character of Julius Agricola' – to heap praise upon his wife's father. Part of the sucking up required ensuring the great general was challenged by worthy foes, and Calgacus – literally, 'the swordsman' – certainly fitted the bill.

It is from the mouth of Calgacus that we hear the immortal words about the Caledonians being 'the last of the free . . . shielded before today by the very remoteness and the seclusion for which we are famed . . . Romans . . . Robbery, butchery, rapine . . . they create a devastation and call it peace'.

Sometime in the autumn of 84 AD, Agricola found Calgacus and his thousands waiting in the shadow of a great glen, a place remembered by Tacitus as 'Mons Graupius' – the Grampian Mountain. That mysterious Celtic swordsman, whoever he was, if ever he was, delivered his soliloquy, launched his attack and disappeared into history. The Caledonians fought bravely that day but were ultimately overwhelmed, just like all the others.

The following day, wrote Tacitus: 'An awful silence reigned on every hand; the hills were deserted, houses smoking in the distance, and our scouts did not meet a soul.'

All across Europe, the Romans left a smoking ruin of the Celtic world. It had been a civilization and a society made of thousands of years of history. The Celts were descended from peoples who had, thousands of years before, made a science out of the study of the night sky, of the cosmos, and, indeed, of their place within it.

Whatever those Celts knew, whatever they had learned – the science and all the rest of it – they would not relinquish it without a fight.

The task for Alice and I has been to try and understand those dispossessed former landlords of ours.

Along the way, we have reached out at the shadows they left behind, and which we glimpse from the corners of our eyes. So much has been speculated about them, so much misremembered and made myth, that it can even be hard to accept they were ever real. Their very names feel strange in our mouths – Boudica . . . Brennus . . . Vercingetorix – so that sometimes they seem as fanciful and hard to believe in as Asterix and Obelix.

Sometimes, in the presence of their mortal remains, the truth of them seems momentarily close by. The same effect is to be had from the sight and the feel of the things they made – the jewellery, the artworks, the weapons.

In *Letters from Iceland*, W. H. Auden and Louis MacNeice wrote:

> To all clay-bound or chalk-bound, stiff or scattered,
> We leave the values of their periods,
> The things which seemed to them the things that mattered.

I feel I know exactly what they meant – that the ancient dead had their own values, different values, and that our modern sensibilities force us to struggle to understand what it was that 'mattered' about the things they left behind, and which we find from time to time.

In this struggle for understanding, Alice is a powerful ally. In her words, the Celts come back to life, to be appreciated as the real flesh-and-blood people they once were. Perhaps they were not too different from ourselves; maybe they are made separate only by time and by their hugely different circumstances.

I always find it hard to keep them in plain view. Mostly they are revealed to me only for moments. But, above all else, Alice is a scientist and it seems to me she sees them more clearly than I do. In any event, her words frame them perfectly.

The Celts are here and all around us, even today. The Romans might have tried to snuff them out, but the flames were not wholly extinguished. Alice's book will make them easier to find.

Neil Oliver

INTRODUCTION

SETTING OUT

I'm about to set sail on an adventure that will take me right across Europe, from its wild, western Atlantic coasts to its eastern edge and beyond. It's a journey that will take me back, deep into the past, into mysterious prehistory, in search of ancestors who still help us to construct our identities today – especially those of us who live near that storm-beaten Atlantic fringe. I'm going to explore a world where battles were fought with the mighty Mediterranean empires of Greece and Rome, where warriors were worshipped as gods, and where princes and princesses were buried with dazzling gold treasure. It's a world shrouded in mystery, where watery places held sacred significance – where swords and shields were thrown into rivers, huge cauldrons sunk in lakes, and the bodies of kings, slain as sacrifices, were consigned to bogs. I'm going in search of the Iron Age ancestors we call the Celts; I want to find out more about their lives, their art, their technology, their knowledge and beliefs. But I'm also setting out to discover how, in just the last ten years, our understanding of the Celts has been shaken to its foundations. The way we see the Celts is being completely transformed by a radical new theory.

The Celts are fascinating and enigmatic. They have been described as the first civilization of Europe, living to the north and west of the Alps. But one of the reasons I find them so intriguing is that they exist right on the edge of history, and we're still struggling to understand them and to find out who they really were.

They are the first northern European ancestors we know by name – but even the name is a problem. 'Celts' was a word used by the Greeks and Romans to refer to the barbarians (as they saw them) of central and western Europe. Some archaeologists have suggested that we shouldn't even use this name – that it's an unhelpful way of lumping together lots of disparate, ancient populations that were never really linked in any meaningful way. But other experts continue to use 'Celts' as a term to describe the people of central and western Europe, who do seem to have been united by some aspects of culture – most importantly, perhaps, by language. I think that's a reasonable definition, so let's start by using the term 'Celts' in this way, even if we decide later that the name shouldn't be applied quite so widely – if at all. This debate is part of the enigma; right from the outset, the Celts are proving difficult to define.

Even once we've cautiously accepted this working defin-ition of the Celts, they're still tricky to pin down. We must piece together their story from fragments, glimpses and half-remembered images and tales. They are Iron Age people – their story spans most of the first millennium BC, from the end of the Bronze Age to the arrival of Romans in Celtic lands. They left virtually no written records, but they made stunning art, knew the secrets of metallurgy and had their own myths and religion.

The further you go back in time, the more history starts to fade. It gets sparser; you find occasional reports of mysterious people from far-flung and almost mythical places, and then . . . history runs out completely. We come up against the very definition of prehistory – people living in that distant past didn't write down anything about their understanding of the world, their rituals or their feelings. They didn't even write down anything about their everyday lives – their day-to-day existence, their families, their societies, their daily trans-actions. They didn't write down anything. And so you're left looking around for clues – objects, bones, the traces of walls and ditches – in fact, any physical traces that might give you a chance of finding out what people were like, and what they were doing with their lives. Archaeology drags up this evidence for us from deep underground or underwater – from ploughed fields, bogs, graves and riverbeds.

Some of that archaeological evidence reveals mundane but important details of day-to-day life in Iron Age Europe. But among those fragments of material culture are items that provide us with a wonderful, visceral, tangible link to those ancestors – including jewellery, decorated cauldrons and furniture, and sculpture. This ancient art is quite different from its modern counterpart. Celtic art has evolved consider-ably over time. Modern Celtic art, with flowing, organic lines, stylized animals and complicated knotwork, draws its inspir-ation largely from the illuminated pages of mediaeval manu-scripts and from carved stone crosses. In fact, it's that Christian art of Britain and Ireland in the seventh and eighth centuries AD which was first described – in the mid-eighteenth century – as 'Celtic art'. But it does seem that this mediaeval expression of Celtic art was itself a reimagining of an ancient style. The Iron Age 'original' is – to me – much more interesting, strange and visually arresting.

Together with these physical traces of the Celts themselves, we have indirect clues, including the persistence of stories, which, though changed by the passage of time, have recognizably ancient roots. The wonderful, strange and vibrant myths of the Celts have come down to us through the Irish and Welsh tales that were part of an ancient oral tradition, and which were finally committed to paper in the Middle Ages. Those stories give us a glimpse of Iron Age society, and still have the power to excite and thrill us today.

And there are contemporary historical accounts to turn to – not penned by the Celts themselves, of course, but by their literate neighbours. The Greeks and Romans met the Celts – initially, on voyages of discovery and, later, in the context of military campaigns – and wrote about them. Greek and Roman writers offer us precious glimpses of the Celtic world, providing us with compelling portraits of the inhabitants of that barbarian hinterland beyond their civilized frontiers.

Through the eyes of the classical historians, geographers and generals, the Celts appear from that prehistoric mist. We learn about their predilection for human sacrifice and head-hunting, their penchant for wearing trousers and their barbaric habit of drinking undiluted wine. Plato described the Celts as warlike and hard drinking, while Aristotle wrote that they would send their children outside with few clothes on, to harden them up, and that they would punish men who grew too fat. But we also glimpse individual characters. There's the fearless Celtic warrior, striding naked into battle, wearing only paint on his body and a gold torc around his neck. We see the warrior returning from the latest bloody battle, the heads of his enemies dangling from his horse's neck. We see the white-robed Druid harvesting mistletoe in the moonlight; fierce women, painted from head to toe in blue woad; and the warrior queen, riding in her chariot, her cloak billowing.

These images are indeed compelling – but how much can we trust such visions of the Celts? We must remember that each and every one of these accounts was written from the perspective of an outsider. I wonder how much they are coloured by a need and a desire to portray the Celts as barbaric, strange and almost the stuff of myths – or whether there might be a grain of truth in them.

I want to get closer to the real Celts, to know who they were and how they lived. I want to test those classical reports against the physical evidence uncovered by archaeologists. I also want to know more about the threads that connect us, today, with the Celtic past – the wonderful stories, beautiful art and, of course, modern Celtic languages. These three different aspects of culture appear to represent ideas that have survived through the centuries and millennia: echoes of an ancient – but not forgotten – past.

Language provides a crucial link with the past and, on the Atlantic fringe of Europe, there are living languages that form the basis of the modern Celtic identity – in Scotland, Wales, Ireland and Brittany. Cornish, spoken until very recently, was also a Celtic language. The similarities between these languages suggest that they came from a 'common ancestor'. There's something really intriguing about these languages and their ancient heritage, something that connects us with

'CELTIC
ORIGIN'

'celticised'

'celticised'

'celticised'

N

Areas of
Celtic
Influence

THE TRADITIONAL VIEW
OF CELTIC EXPANSION AND
MIGRATION SAW THE CELTS
ORIGINATING IN CENTRAL EUROPE
AND THEN SPREADING OUTWARDS,
TO THE EAST, SOUTH AND WEST
(ADAPTED FROM KARL, 2012)

'CELTICISED'

CELTICISED

the very distant past and seems important in our understanding of our regional and national identities today.

Although the Celtic languages are now restricted to the western fringe of Europe, place names right across Europe preserve a memory of a much more diffuse Celtic past. The Welsh word for water, *dwr*, is echoed in the names of rivers right across Europe – the Adur in Sussex, the Dwrdy in France, the Oder in Germany, the Turie in the Czech Republic and the Tur in Hungary. The Celtic languages spring as a branch from the large Indo-European language family – which includes Sanskrit, Greek and English.

The traditional story of the Celts sees them starting out in central Europe, then spreading east, south and west, carrying their distinctive material culture – and their language – with them. This model was based on nineteenth-century archaeology, interpreted in the light of the classical accounts. By the end of the twentieth century, archaeological evidence that didn't fit with the standard model was already stacking up and, in the past ten years, another significant challenge has appeared from the study of ancient Celtic languages. Under the old paradigm, Celtic languages reach the Atlantic fringe of Europe late in the story, eventually evolving into modern Welsh, Scots Gaelic, Irish and Breton. But the new challenges to this old view lead us to question that idea of a relatively recent arrival of Celtic in the west. Could it be possible that the Celtic language was here, on the Atlantic fringe of Europe, much earlier – perhaps even before the Iron Age? Linguistics provides us with clues, delving into the links between modern and ancient languages. And it's becoming clear that the traditional story of Celtic origins and spread is not just too simple – it's wrong.

Culture (including language) and genes do not travel around the world in a tightly bound package. If people are moving around plenty and sharing ideas, culture can spread without any significant permanent migrations or invasions taking place. On the other hand, genetics should be able to tell us about large shifts in population, and perhaps even about more subtle movements – migrations of just a few people, perhaps – which could have led to large cultural changes. Celtic languages help to underpin a strong sense of Celtic identity today, but is there a genetic link as well – right back to prehistoric populations in this north-western corner of Europe? In England, did the arrival of the Anglo-Saxons wipe out Celtic genes as well as Celtic language? Genetics may still have some way to go before it can provide full answers to these questions – if, indeed, it ever can – but it can certainly begin to provide us with another perspective on who the Celts were – and are.

Research from fields as diverse as history, archaeology, linguistics and genetics is providing us with new and surprising insights. We can turn to evidence that takes us right inside the Celtic world, bringing us closer to the ancient Celts and their experience of life in Iron Age Europe. But, as our picture of the Celts is becoming more rich and detailed, the standard model of Celtic origins is starting to fray around the edges. In fact, it's worse than that – the emerging new picture turns our old understanding of the Celts on its head.

Celtic studies is undergoing a paradigm shift, providing us with a whole new perspective on the European Iron Age. In the process of re-examining the evidence, while old theories are being torn down and new ones are being constructed, we'll get a chance to see the Celts as never before. We'll get a clearer, brighter and more truthful picture of our prehistoric ancestors.

To understand why the picture is changing so radically, we need to go right back to the evidence – to look at the archaeological discoveries, the histories and the new insights from linguistics. It will be useful to explore sites and discoveries that were important to the traditional view of Celtic origins and spread, but then we'll need to dig deeper and go further afield, to see just how new evidence and new perspectives have shaken up that old story. Starting in what used to be thought of as the centre of the Celtic world – in central Europe – I'll then track the story of the Celts as far east as Turkey, and along the western Atlantic fringe of Europe, in Britain, Ireland, France and Iberia.

I know that this journey in search of the Celts is going to be far from straightforward. I know that the trail will twist and turn, and also that I'll be wading into an extremely controversial area. Indeed, my friend, the historian, Neil Oliver, has called it a 'C-word'. The Celts are dangerous – too slippery to hold; too hot to handle. I don't care. I want to grasp the Celts, their culture and their origins, and I'm prepared to get my fingers burned. If I manage to unravel some of this mystery, it will be worth it. These are our ancestors, and it's time to find them.

WHAT'S IN
A NAME?

REIMAGINING THE CELTS

The Hochdorf Prince

In 1968, the state archaeologist of Badem-Wurttemburg in south-west Germany was alerted to a large quantity of stone being ploughed up in a field near the village of Hochdorf an der Enz. This site, perhaps unpromising at first, would turn out to be one of the most astonishing Celtic discoveries of the twentieth century.

On closer inspection, it became clear that this pile of stone was the remains of an ancient burial mound. Centuries of ploughing had reduced the mound to such an extent that it had become merely a slight rise in the field – no longer an obvious and imposing feature in the landscape. The mound had already suffered considerable plough damage, and it would only get worse, so the decision was made to excavate. But they didn't rush into it.

Ten years later, in 1978, the dig started. The archaeologists found layers and layers of stone protecting an underlying burial chamber. In fact, it was a double chamber. There was an outer chamber, 7.4 metres by 7.4 metres, containing an inner chamber, almost 5 metres by 5 metres, and the gap between them was filled with 50 tonnes of stone. Whoever had constructed this grave had done it extremely well, with a clear intention of deterring anyone from attempting to rob it. But, in the end, it was really the plough that had saved this burial mound, diminishing it and disguising it in the landscape.

When the archaeologists reached the inner chamber, they found its contents completely intact – it hadn't been robbed, like so many of the other, more obvious burial mounds in the area. Inside, they discovered a tomb, containing a wealth of treasure and the mortal remains of a man who quickly became known as the Hochdorf Prince.

The Hochdorf Prince may not have risen to the global notoriety of Tutankhamun, but, for those searching for the Celts, he is just as significant a discovery. Analysis of his skeleton revealed him to be about forty years old. And he was tall. It's estimated that he would have stood about 1.85 metres (6 feet, 1 inch) tall.

But it wasn't his physical stature that revealed his high status; it was the grave goods placed in his tomb – most notably, a long, bronze couch. It was about 2.75 metres long – enough room for four people to sit comfortably beside each other. It was made of bronze sheets riveted together, and the back panels curved forwards to form the sides. The back of the couch was decorated with a hammered design, with a central panel depicting three pairs of warriors engaged in single combat, waving their swords at each other. The two outer panels each depicted a figure riding in a four-wheeled wagon, pulled by two stallions. The couch was supported on bronze feet, complete with castors, each in the form of a small female figurine. These caryatids held up their arms to carry the couch, each with a bronze pot on her head, which neatly helped her to bear the load. Their faces were simple, with eyebrows and nose in relief, and tiny inlaid eyes, but no mouth. Their bodies were covered in small, drilled holes, which had been filled with coral inlay. And each of these caryatids was sitting astride a single wheel. Together, these unicyclists formed castors for the couch to move on.

To see this treasure, I had to visit the Depository Store of Stuttgart Museum. This is where some of the grave goods from the Hochdorf tomb were being held – before being returned to the Museum itself to become part of a new exhibition, later in 2015.

The Hochdorf tomb didn't just contain images of wagons, it also held a life-size, four-wheeled cart, its wooden frame and wheels completely encased in strips of iron, together with harnesses for two horses. Perhaps this was the means by which the body of the prince had been brought to his final resting place.

The Depository Store also held another impressive find from the prince's tomb – an enormous bronze cauldron, big enough to hold 500 litres. The cauldron was Greek, it bore three handles and was decorated with three beautiful bronze lions, sitting couchant around its rim. One lion was more crudely modelled than the others – it appeared to be a later replacement – a Celtic copy of a Greek embellishment. Pollen analysis of the residue inside the cauldron has revealed that it was filled with mead when it was placed in the grave. The archaeologists found a horizontal tidemark about two thirds of the way up on its interior surface, marking the original level of the mead. But there was also a lower tidemark, at an angle, showing that the wooden stand of the cauldron must have collapsed, tipping the cauldron, before the chamber finally fell in and crushed it.

Along with this huge cauldron of mead, far too much just for his personal consumption, the prince had been buried with a range of other items that suggested he was fully intending to hold parties in the afterlife. On his wagon were placed goblets and a set of nine gilded plates, and nine large drinking horns had been hung around the chamber. While the horns themselves had rotted, the gold bands decorating them had been preserved in the tomb. Some of these bands were so wide in diameter that the horns they encircled must have been truly huge. Too large, in fact, to have come from domesticated bulls. Those horns must have come from aurochs – the huge wild cattle that still roamed Europe during the Iron Age.

When the cauldron, the iron-clad chariot and the magnificent bronze couch were discovered by the archaeologists, they were all badly crushed and damaged. The timber structure forming the inner chamber had collapsed and rotted away centuries before, leaving the tonnes of overlying stone unsupported. But hours of painstaking work have allowed the artefacts, including the wonderful couch, to be restored almost to their former glory. The bronze of the couch and cauldron, now green with verdigris, would have been polished and shining, almost like gold, when they were placed in the tomb.

Despite the efforts of the conservators, the green verdigris has formed its own patterns, like lichen, over the seat of the couch. But, looking carefully, it's possible to discern a particular texture to some of this oxidized surface: it was clearly woven – a trace of textile that had once covered the couch. All the large objects in the Hochdorf Prince's grave had been draped with cloth, almost as if they were shrouded, like the body itself. The grave had also been full of flowers. Inside his shroud of coloured fabrics, the prince himself seems to have been fully clothed, and wearing what can only be described as fabulous jewellery. He was dripping with gold.

The gold objects from the Hochdorf tomb were kept under lock and key in Stuttgart Museum itself, and so I reluctantly tore myself away from the extraordinary couch and drove across town to meet curator Thomas Hoppe, who had removed the Hochdorf Prince's gold from its vault and laid it out in a lab for me to examine.

The treasure was quite breathtaking. There, laid out on a black cloth, were the golden objects that had lain close to the prince's body. There was a wide neck-ring, made of gold sheet, beaten into ribs and hammered with a design that looked, at first glance, like an abstract, geometric pattern. 'But look at it closely,' said Thomas, 'and you see that the repeating, stamped motif is a rider on a horse.' The stamp was tiny, but Thomas was right: miniature equestrians rode around the neck-ring. There was also a reddish gold armband and two gold fibulae, or 'safety pin' brooches, which appeared to have been damaged. 'The pins have been deliberately bent back to prevent them being used again,' said Thomas.

A bronze dagger, which may well have been used by the prince in life, had been encased in thin sheet gold, with a stamped, geometric design, for the grave. The hilt of the dagger looked particularly unusual. It ended with a finial, shaped like a miniature trident. These 'antenna daggers' seem to signal high status in this time and place. About ten kilometres away from Hochdorf, a sandstone statue of an Iron Age Prince was discovered, complete with hat, torc – and antenna dagger. But, on its own, the bronze antenna dagger seems to have been not quite resplendent enough for this prince's tomb. Even the hilt and its finial had been encased in gold.

The prince's broad, bronze belt plaque had also been gilded; once again, the gold sheet was covered with a stamped design. But perhaps most extraordinary of the whole collection were the prince's shoes. I should qualify that – his leather shoes had long since rotted away when the archaeologists excavated his grave, but what remained were bands of gold sheet that had decorated the tops of the shoes and looped down to the toes.

Of course, what all this treasure is telling us is that this man from Hochdorf was no ordinary individual. Whatever we choose to call him now – chieftain or prince – it doesn't really matter; we know beyond a shadow of a doubt that he came from the upper echelons of his society. He had certainly been used to the finer things in life, enjoying a particularly lavish lifestyle. And when he died, he was buried in his finery and lay surrounded by luxury.

But alongside all those emblems of status and wealth were objects that were much more ordinary, and extremely personal. The Hochdorf Prince was also buried with his comb and his razor, a pouch with three fish hooks, an iron knife and a quiver full of arrows. Looking at this collection, I felt that he'd packed an overnight bag, with some extra survival essentials (quiver and fish hooks), and then everything he needed for a full-on feast (a huge cauldron of mead, goblets, horns and plates), should the afterworld turn out to be a thoroughly convivial place.

We must remember, however, that the dead don't bury themselves. The Hochdorf Prince may well have had those expectations of feasting into the afterlife, and the people who buried him may have found solace in this belief. But the pomp and wealth associated with his burial was also a clear indication of the status of those close to the dead prince. Only an incredibly wealthy family could afford to commit such riches to the tomb – to gild his belt, his dagger and his shoes and to dispose of such a weight of gold into the ground. In reality, that wealth may have been hard won, but such a profligate show of affluence would suggest that the riches and power of this family were endless and boundless, and perhaps even God given.

As well as incredible wealth, the grave goods accompanying the Hochdorf Prince speak of connections far beyond his small chiefdom in Germany. He has a Greek-style cauldron, which was probably made in southern Italy, then part of the empire of Greater Greece, or Magna Graecia. He has everything he needs for a feast – including a couch. If you were to feast in the Greek style, you did it reclining on couches. The bronze couch looks like it may have been locally made, but with clear Italian influences. This man was well connected with the Mediterranean empire to the south; he had imported actual, material objects from Magna Graecia, as well as adopting some of their exotic ideas.

In the first millennium BC, it's all too easy for our attention to be drawn to the Mediterranean empires of Greece and then Rome. The achievements of those civilizations are undeniably impressive, and we can find the philosophical roots of our modern science, maths, medicine and legal systems there, as well as important influences on art, music and literature. It's sometimes hard not to view the rest of Europe, beyond the margins of those empires, as uncivilized and stuffed full of rough, barbarous, warlike tribes who didn't even bother to write anything down – at least, not until they eventually became assimilated into the Roman Empire and learned a bit of Latin.

But the Hochdorf Prince, who was buried in the sixth century BC, doesn't seem to be a barbarian. Far from it. He may not have been literate, but he was certainly cultured. The objects that accompanied him to the grave reveal a rich and complex culture, which blended distinctive local elements with influences from much further afield. The grave goods from his tomb represent a particular material culture known to archaeologists specifically as 'late western Hallstatt'. This fits into the umbrella of 'Celtic culture'.

This seems a bit odd. Why should we imagine that our Hochdorf Prince was a Celt? The German archaeologists I met seemed to have no problem with this terminology. They were happy to describe him as a Celt. I suddenly became aware that this name meant something very different in Germany compared to what it meant in Britain. In Germany, it's pretty much synonymous with the Iron Age – with the people and culture of that period. In Britain, it may be used in a similar way in archaeological contexts, but of course it's also used to describe modern populations in Ireland, Scotland and Wales, where Celtic languages are still spoken. I was encountering a riddle that had been puzzling historians and archaeologists for centuries. The use of the term 'Celt' is different in different places, and carries different meanings. What – if any – connection does the 'Celtic' Hochdorf Prince have with the 'Celtic' Iron Age people of Britain and Ireland?

This question takes us back to the nineteenth century, when archaeology began to emerge from its antiquarian origins as a distinct discipline. The idea of 'race', based first and foremost on physical characteristics – and deeply flawed in itself – started to gather cultural attributes as well. It was possible to define a race not only by the shape of its people's skulls, but also by the type of art, pottery and metalwork they made, by their particular burial rites and by their political organization. It's an attractively neat idea, this package of biological and cultural characteristics. Sometimes the cultural package works fairly well. If you ignore local physical characteristics, you could pick anyone from the ancient Roman Empire and call them 'Roman' and that means something, culturally and politically. Most 'Romans' had never been to Rome, yet they can be classified as Romans because they were part of the empire clearly ruled over by the great city state. But the Celts had no such empire, nor any central leadership structure or citizenship, nor indeed any consistent cultural signature. So how did this disparate group of people come to be grouped together under one name at all?

It's a tricky question to answer, but a good place to start is in the etymology of the word 'Celtic'.

Edward Lhuyd's Glossographia and 'Celtic' Languages

In 1707, the Welsh antiquarian scholar, Edward Lhuyd, did something that would have a profound effect on the way that people living on the edges of north-western Europe would see themselves. He popularized the term 'Celtic'.

As Keeper of the Ashmolean Museum in Oxford, he decided that he would write a book about the 'languages, histories and customs of the original inhabitants of Great Britain', and that he would call it *Archaeologia Britannica*. He spent the last few years of the seventeenth century travelling around Scotland, Ireland, Cornwall and Brittany, listening carefully to the language spoken in each place. He also drew on historical sources and the writings of previous antiquarians, and he published his studies in 1707, in a book entitled *Glossography*. He intended it to be the first volume of his *Archaeologia*, but he died just two years later, leaving the rest unpublished.

Lhuyd identified similarities between the Irish, Welsh, Cornish and Breton languages. Previous scholars, as early as the sixteenth century, had spotted these connections and used the term 'Gallic' to describe those languages. In a book published in 1703, a Breton named Paul-Yves Pezron made the explicit link between the Celts described by the classical writers and these surviving 'Celtic' languages. Edward Lhuyd followed Pezron, calling this group of languages 'Celtic'. But the relationships between the languages were complex. Gaulish and Irish seemed particularly close, while Welsh, Cornish and Breton formed another cluster. Lhuyd interpreted these patterns as reflecting ancient migrations: first, a wave of Spanish Celts arrived to settle in Ireland, and then a second wave came from Gaul into Britain. His interpretation clearly drew inspiration from – and helped to reinforce – traditional stories about the peopling of Britain and Ireland. Some of these tales had been collected centuries before by Nennius, a Welsh monk writing in the early ninth century.

Archaeologist Simon James sees Lhuyd's *Glossography* as fundamental to our ideas about what 'Celt' and 'Celtic' mean today. And, instead of some unbroken link back to prehistoric ancestors, he sees the modern Celtic identity as something relatively recent. In his book, *The Atlantic Celts*, he says, 'The Welsh, Scots, Irish and other peoples have only come to describe themselves and their ancestors as Celts since the eighteenth century.'

Well, that's a reality check for anyone who, like me, considers themselves to have Celtic roots. My Welsh ancestors would, I'm sure, be turning in their graves to hear such a thing.

But perhaps the modern Celts had just forgotten their common heritage, and needed Lhuyd to remind them. Through language, then, Lhuyd had identified a shared culture that still seemed to bind together these places on the north-western edge of Europe. And while he may have come up with the adjective 'Celtic', he didn't invent the name 'Celt'. Long before Lhuyd put pen to paper, people were writing about 'Celts' – and a land called 'Celtica'.

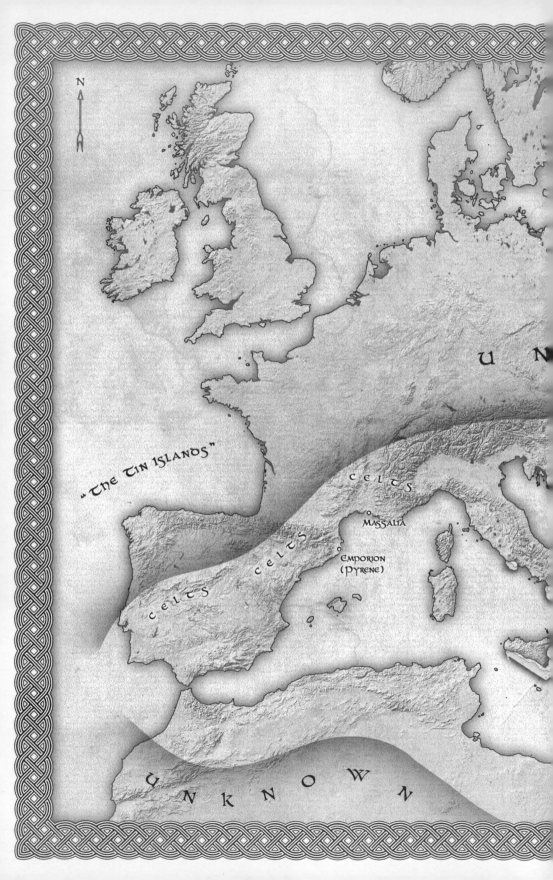

N

U N

"The Tin Islands"

CELTS

MASSALIA

CELTS

EMPORION
(PYRENE)

CELTS

U N K N O W N

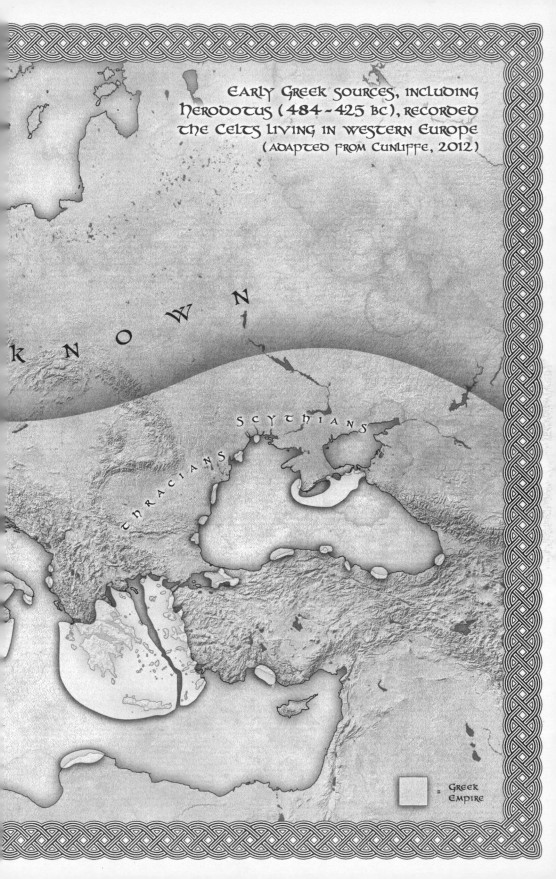

EARLY GREEK SOURCES, INCLUDING
HERODOTUS (484~425 BC), RECORDED
THE CELTS LIVING IN WESTERN EUROPE
(ADAPTED FROM CUNLIFFE, 2012)

K N O W N

S C Y T H I A N S

T H R A C I A N S

= GREEK
EMPIRE

'Celtica' and the 'Celts'

The earliest mention of the Celts and their territory takes us back to the late sixth century BC, and the first known Greek historian, Hecataeus of Miletus. He travelled widely and wrote about his travels, the countries and people he encountered, in his *Periegesis* (literally: 'A Tour Around'). The original book is lost, but many fragments of it are quoted in later works, particularly in Stephanus of Byzantium's *Ethnika*, dating to the sixth century AD. And so we know that Hecataeus identified two Celtic cities in Europe: Narbon, which evolved into modern Narbonne, in the south of France, and the enigmatic Nyrax, which has no obvious modern counterpart. Hecataeus also mentioned that the city of Massalia (modern-day Marseilles), which was a Greek colony in ancient Liguria, lay close to 'Celtica', or the land of the Celts. It's clear that this 'Celtica' refers to a large area, with cities within it. The inhabitants of cities had their own local identities – for instance, Hecataeus referred to the inhabitants of Narbon as Narbaioi – but their broader ethnic identity was Celtic.

Just how far did this land of the Celts extend? Further clues appear in writing just a century later, in the *Histories* of Herodotus of Halicarnassus, dating to the late fifth century BC. Herodotus wrote about yet another Celtic city, close to the source of the Ister – which we know as the Danube:

> This . . . river has its source in the country of the Celts near the city Pyrene, and runs through the middle of Europe, dividing it into two portions. The Celts live beyond the pillars

of Hercules, and border on the Cynesians, who dwell at the extreme west of Europe. Thus the Ister flows through the whole of Europe before it finally empties itself into the Euxine [Black Sea] . . .

This paragraph has long confused historians, as it seems to offer a number of contradictions. We're introduced to two groups of people: the Celts and their neighbours, the Cynesians (in Greek, '*Kunetes*'). But scholars have suggested that these Kunetes were also a Celtic tribe, living in what is now southern Portugal, as the name looks Celtic.

As for the mysterious city of Pyrene, its name suggests that it might have lain close to the Pyrenees. It might be another name for the Greek colony of Emporion (modern Ampurias), founded from Massalia in the early sixth century BC, on the north-eastern coast of Spain, where the Pyrenees dip down to the sea. But that's a long way from the origin of the Danube, which forms at the confluence of two rivers in the Black Forest of Germany. It's possible that 'Pyrene' has nothing to do with the Pyrenees at all – it could even be a descriptive Greek name for a town, invoking fire and perhaps metal-working. Whatever the true location of Pyrene, Celtica suddenly seems to look like a very large place, stretching from south-west Iberia to the Alps, and right through to the Danube Valley of central Europe.

The wide expanse of the Celtic lands is emphasized by another ancient Greek historian, Ephorus, who wrote an ambitious *Universal History* in the fourth century. Although the original has been lost, we're lucky that Ephorus was extensively quoted by a later Greek writer, Strabo, who lived from the first century BC into the first century AD. From Strabo, we learn that Ephorus divided the world and its inhabitants broadly into four parts (presumably with the Greeks occupying the centre), inhabited by Scythians in the north, Indians in the east, Ethiopians in the south and Celts in the west. While Strabo sees the Pyrenees as a natural border between Celtica and Iberia, he acknowledges that Ephorus, writing a few centuries earlier, saw Celtica extending much further south-west, right into Spain: 'Ephorus, in his account, makes Celtica so excessive in its size that he assigns to the Celtic regions most of what we now call Iberia'. But Strabo's Celtica was still expansive, even without Iberia, and he uses Celti, or 'Celts', as a collective term for a whole bunch of people – including such exotic-sounding tribes as the Tectosages, Trocmi, Tolistobogii, Prausans, Veneti, Osismii and the less exotic Belgi.

Strabo also tells us that this collective term, 'Celti', originally came from the name of one particular tribe, called Celtae, who lived in what we know as southern France, around modern-day Narbonne. In what sounds like a particularly painful affliction, Strabo calls this territory 'Narbonitis'. He writes:

This, then, is what I have to say about the people who inhabit the dominion of Narbonitis, whom the men of former times named 'Celtae'. It was from the Celtae, I think, that the Galatae as a whole were by the Greeks called 'Celti' – on account of the fame of the Celtae, or it may also be that the Massiliotes, as well as other Greek neighbours, contributed to this result, on account of their proximity.

This passage from Strabo suggests that the name 'Celtae' was Celtic in origin – used to describe a tribe living around Narbonne, and presumably what they called themselves, as well as the name that the Greeks used for them. But how did that term come to mean something much bigger? Strabo says it could have been 'on account of the fame of the Celtae' – but does that mean it was just the Greeks who expanded the term to include other tribes, or did those tribes themselves adopt the identity of these famous Celtae? Strabo thinks that it could just have been because this particular tribe happened to live close to Greeks living in the colony of Massilia (Marseilles). These Greeks knew their neighbouring tribe by name, and simply extrapolated this to take in north-western European tribes across a much larger region.

Just to add to the confusion, Strabo also says that 'Celti' is a term the Greeks used for the people he knows as Galatae (Galatians). There's other evidence of these terms being closely related, if not synonymous. Back in the fourth century BC, Aristotle wrote a little about the Celts, mentioning their priests, the Druids, and he lumped the Celts together with Galatians. Around the same time, a Greek comic poet called Sopater of Paphos wrote a long parody entitled *Galatae*, about the Celts.

Later writers continue to use the two names interchangeably, but, in the first century BC, Diodorus of Sicily makes a distinction between Celts and Galatians. The Celts live in the south-west, in an area which extends north of Massalia, into the Alps and south of the Pyrenees. The Galatians live further north, from the coast, through the Hercynian Mountains (the Black Forest region of Germany) and further east, as far as

Scythia. But Diodorus also notes that the Romans lump Celts and Galatians together and call them all 'Galli' – or Gauls.

Another classical historian, but this time one with a very personal vested interest in the land occupied by the Celtic tribes, was also writing in the mid-first century BC: Julius Caesar. In *De Bello Gallico*, Caesar defines the extent of Celtic lands more precisely than any before him – but, of course, his scrutiny of Celtic politics and geography was motivated by more than just idle curiosity. For Julius Caesar, Gallia, or Gaul, lay west of the Rhine and comprised three territories, each inhabited by a different group: the Belgae, the Aquitani and the Celtae:

> Gaul as a whole consists of three separate parts; one is inhabited by the Belgae, another by the Aquitani, and the third by the people we call Gauls, though in their own language they are called Celts. In language, customs, and laws these three peoples are quite distinct. The Celts are separated from the Aquitani by the river Garonne and from the Belgae by the Marne and the Seine.
>
> *De Bello Gallico* 1.1

Gaul corresponds roughly to modern Belgium, France and the western part of Switzerland. The territory of the Belgae maps roughly on to modern Belgium, but extends further west, as far as modern-day Calais. In Caesar's definition, the Celts themselves occupy most of the rest of what is now France, while the Aquitani live in the south-west corner of France. But clues that the Gauls were not limited to France in antiquity come from the names of other tribes; in the north-western corner of Spain, a tribe called the Gallaeci gave their name to the region we now know as Galicia.

Over five centuries, then, we have records of the Celts (or Gauls, or Galatians) of Europe. These written records emanate from a literate Mediterranean culture that is attempting to define its barbarian neighbours to the north and west; this is very much an outsiders' view of the Celts. But, crucially, it's all we have to go on, in terms of written history.

These three names – Celts, Gauls, and Galatians – sometimes seem to coincide in meaning. At other times, they are used to differentiate between different levels of ethnic groupings: Celts within the larger territory of Gaul; Celts as a group of tribes in the west, and Galatians as a group of tribes in the east; Celts and Galatians as essentially the same and referring to anyone living across a huge territory, maximally defined as stretching from Iberia to central Europe – and beyond.

Although these shifting definitions seem, on one level, to be confused and confusing, we're getting snapshots of the political situation in Europe over more than 500 years – from that Mediterranean perspective. Perhaps the problem with pinning down the Celts as a defined group is that, if they do represent some sort of political unit, it's a very different one to the Greek and Roman empires. At its most diffuse, this could have been a collection of tribes which shared some common elements of culture, including similar languages, and who traded and fought with each other. It's really not surprising that the Celts are so hard to define, given the shifting boundaries, changing identities and differing relationships with the Greek and Roman empires over those centuries.

Although using 'Celts' in its narrower sense, referring to a tribe called Celtae, Caesar reveals something important about this particular name. He writes of these Celts: *'qui ipsorum lingua Celtae, nostra Galli appellantur'* – which translates as, 'those who in their own language are Celts, in ours are called Gauls.' So it's clear that the Celts, at least in this more restricted sense, in that part of Gaul, called themselves 'Celts'. In fact, our word 'Celts' comes from the Greek word Κελτοί (Keltoi), which may be a Greek version of a Celtic word – Galos, meaning 'brave warrior'.

It seems quite likely that the alternative names used by the classical writers, *Galatai* and *Galli*, may have come from the same – Celtic – root. Perhaps the Greeks were being respectful when they referred to their north-westerly neighbours as Galatai – 'warriors', in their own language. Or perhaps it was less deferential in tone, and they were really labelling the Celts as 'that belligerent lot'. But it's also possible that the word 'Galatai' isn't Celtic at all, and actually has its roots in Greek. *Galaktos* means 'of milk' in ancient Greek – so was this a term that the olive-skinned Mediterraneans coined for those pale, 'milk-white' tribespeople in the north-west?

As for the origin of the term 'Galli', that simply appears to be a Latin version of the Greek 'Galatai'. When Galatai becomes Latinized to Galli, a pun is created – it also means 'cockerel'. And, even with my negligible knowledge of football, I know that the mascot of the French football team is a rooster. It's not a coincidence. The Gallic rooster has adorned the French strip since 1909, but it's been the unofficial mascot of the French nation for centuries – since Roman times, in fact.

There's a curious omission from all these accounts that define the widest extent of the Celtic world in the eyes of the Greeks and Romans: not one of them includes either Britain or Ireland as a land known to be inhabited by Celts. There seems to be a fundamental disconnect between the principal areas where Celtic languages are still spoken today and the extent of Celtic lands described in antiquity. In fact, the only overlap seems to be Brittany – firmly identified as within the territory of Celtica by Julius Caesar, and with the Breton language included in Lhuyd's Celtic language family.

Just because the Greeks and Romans didn't explicitly include Britain and Ireland in Celtic Europe doesn't mean they weren't Celtic. But neither does it mean we should assume they were Celtic. In the earliest classical records, they are described as places quite separate from Celtica.

Some time around 325 BC, the Greek geographer, Pytheas, set sail from Massalia, heading west, through the Pillars of Heracles, then following the Atlantic coast to the north. Pytheas' original record of his trip – *On the Ocean* – is lost, but fragments of it are preserved in later works, including Strabo's *Geographica*, Diodorus Siculus' *History* and Pliny's *Natural History*. Although Strabo refers to Pytheas, it's certainly not in the manner of a trusted source. Strabo was deeply sceptical about Pytheas' account; he accuses Pytheas of being an 'arch-falsifier' – of deliberately fabricating his material. He is particularly doubtful about Pytheas' description of Thule – a country in the extreme north. And yet, Pytheas' observations now ring true.

Pytheas is said to have described places in the far north where the night became so short that the sun rose again, just a short time after setting. And in Thule, on the summer solstice, he claimed there was no night. This is the first recorded description anywhere of the midnight sun. Pytheas also told of a *'mare concretum'*, where land and sea were bound together, which could not be crossed on foot or by boat. I've visited Greenland in early spring, and this sounds just like the ice mélange, or sikkussaq – icebergs trapped in the winter sea ice – that fills the frozen fjords. Was Thule indeed Greenland? Some think so, but others have suggested Orkney, Shetland, Faroe, Norway and Iceland as possibilities.

Pytheas tells us that Thule was six days' sail from 'Brettanike' (Βρεττανικη), or Britain – and, unlike Thule, there is much less doubt about the identity of this island. This is Britain, as we know it. Before Pytheas set off on the northernmost leg of his trip, from Britain to Thule, he had sailed from Celtica to Britain. He tells us that this journey also took six days; he seems fond of this duration. Strabo is doubtful of this detail, pointing out that the eastern extremity of Britain, known as Cantium (modern-day Kent), is visible from Celtica, from around 'the mouths of the Rhine' and therefore much closer than six days' journey. Well, now it's my turn to be sceptical, as, while I know that it's possible to see the white cliffs of Dover from the coast around Calais, I don't think anyone has ever seen Kent from the Netherlands. And, you never know, poor old Pytheas could have started off way down the west coast of France, with the wind against him.

Whatever his misgivings about Pytheas' veracity, Strabo agrees that Britain is separate from Celtica. So the Britons, it seems, were not Celts – at least as far as the Greek geographers were concerned.

Although Pytheas has often been described as the 'discoverer' of Brettanike (at least as far as classical civilization was concerned), it seems that there were earlier sailors who already had a good knowledge of the islands lying at this north-west corner of Europe. The Roman poet, Avienus, who lived in the fourth century AD, wrote a poem called *Ora Maritima*, which was apparently based on a *periplus*, or mariners' handbook, dating back almost a millennium, to the sixth century BC. Like Pytheas, the author of the *periplus* had set out from Massilia and sailed around the Atlantic coast of Spain and France, up to Ireland and Britain. In Avienus' poem, as in Pliny's *Natural History*, the name for Britain appears as 'Albion'. But Avienus provides another clue that Albion may in fact have been Celtic: he says that the country of the Celts lies beyond the Oestrumnides – a group of islands, or perhaps a peninsula, which may refer to Cornwall, the Scilly Isles or Brittany.

When Pytheas and Avienus described Britain and Ireland, which, for them, lay close to the edge of the known world, it's clear that there was far more than just idle curiosity motivating the journeys of discovery. (There always is, we're tempted to reflect – whether we're talking about later European voyages to the Americas, or our contemporary efforts to reach other planets). Britain and Ireland were economically significant. They contained important sources of metal – especially copper, in Ireland, and tin, in Cornwall. Back in the fourth century BC, Herodotus wrote about the Cassiterides – although he admits he knows nothing about them: 'But concerning those [islands] in Europe that are furthest away, towards evening . . . I have no knowledge of the Cassiterides, where our tin is brought from.'

Modern scholars have identified the Cassiterides variously as Cornwall, the Iberian peninsula, the Scilly Isles, or now-submerged islands in the Bay of Biscay.

And so we have a variety of names for what we now call Britain: Albion, Brettanike and, possibly, the Cassiterides. The last, even if does refer to Cornwall, doesn't tell us anything about the local language, as it's simply a description, in Greek – 'the tin islands'. 'Albion' is unhelpful, too, as it could be either a Celtic or a Greek name. But 'Brettanike' is not a Greek name. It looks very much like a Celtic name. Avienus also writes about Ireland, which he calls the 'Holy Isle' of the ancients, but names it 'Ierne', which linguists believe is probably an early Celtic name, too, perhaps meaning 'fertile land'. This suggests that, at the very least, there was a linguistic connection between the inhabitants of Brettanike and the continental Celts.

When the Roman historian, Tacitus, came to write about the life of his father-in-law, the general Gnaeus Julius Agricola, at the end of the first century AD, he made an important observation. He recognized that the inhabitants of Britain and Ireland were similar to each other, and that they were also similar to the Celts living on the continent. Tacitus says that there is both a linguistic and a religious connection between Gaul and Britain. In a more subjective vein, he notes a similarity in the character of the Gauls and the British: 'there is the same boldness in challenging danger, and, when it is near, the same timidity in shrinking from it.'

So, despite what the classical authors say about the bound-aries of Celtica, the shared language and religion noted by Tacitus, and the very names 'Brettanike' and 'Ierne', suggest that the inhabitants of Britain and Ireland did indeed have a cultural identity, which we can perhaps call 'Celtic', in common with their near neighbours in western continental Europe.

Sifting through these classical sources, pulling together the mentions of Celts, Gauls and Galatians, together with places which sound Celtic, like Brettanike and Ierne, we can tentatively define a swathe of Europe that represents the widest extent of Celtic lands, from the beginning of the eighth century BC through to the first century BC. It's huge. It stretches from the Atlantic coasts of Europe, through central Europe to the Balkans and into Anatolia. But what does it actually mean to circumscribe this huge expanse of land? Was there really a shared language, culture and ethnic identity, right across this vast territory? And, if so, how – and where – did it start?

These are tricky questions. The historical sources offer clues, but archaeology provides us with the chance to examine material culture, and to see how these widespread lands might have been linked by similarities in styles of pottery, metalworking and burial practice. I suppose what we're looking for is a hallmark of Celticity: a particular type of material culture, which we'll assume – just for now – went along with the Celtic language.

It's tempting to think that the earliest mentions of the Celts by the classical writers may give us a clue to the origins of the Celtic people, their culture and their language. From Hecataeus, we learned that, in the sixth century BC, the land of Celtica was close to Massalia (Marseilles). From Herodotus, we received the information that the Celts lived around the headwaters of the Danube. Putting these together, we can suggest a continental 'homeland' for the Celts, stretching from east-central France, into Switzerland, south-western Germany and Austria. From there, we can imagine the Celts spreading out over time, in waves of invasion, taking their culture and their language with them. Eventually, they would reach the islands on the north-west edge of Europe. This also fits with Edward Lhuyd's theory that his two groups of Celtic languages had reached Britain and Ireland as two waves of invasion from the continent.

In the nineteenth and twentieth centuries, archaeologists began to reach for the physical, material evidence of the Celtic people described in the classical histories. All that time, no one seemed to remember that Herodotus had mentioned Celts in Iberia. Everyone seemed very sure indeed that the Celts had started out in west-central Europe and spread out from there. They also seemed very sure that Celticity originated and spread as a package – people, material culture and language.

In the nineteenth century, the source of Celtic culture seemed to have been found, right in the heart of the proposed homeland, with the discovery of a spectacular site called Hallstatt, in Austria.

IRON, SALT AND WINE

BUILDING A BIG SOCIETY AND THE THIRST FOR RESOURCES

△ Eye in the sky – Filming at the Iron Age hill fort of Heuneburg

The Hochdorf Prince – skeleton of the sixth-century BC burial found in an undisturbed tomb in 1978 and now in Stuttgart Museum

Museum reconstruction of the Hochdorf Prince's grave

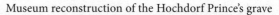

△ The magnificent bronze couch on which the prince was laid to rest

One of the unicycling castors ▷

▽ The back of the couch with images of fighting (or dancing) warriors

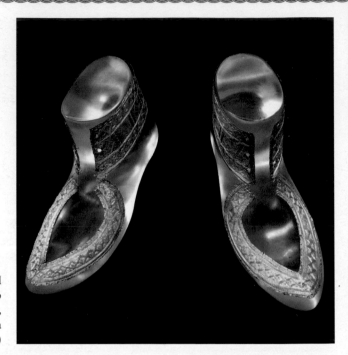

Gold treasures found
in the Hochdorf tomb
included jewellery,
shoes (right) and a
gilded belt (below)

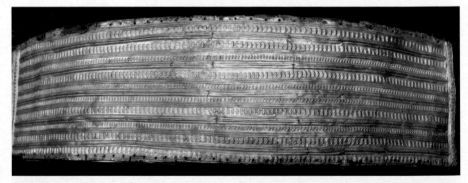

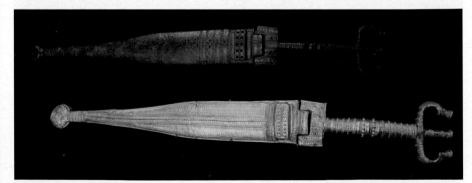

The Hochdorf Prince's bronze dagger (top) was encased in gold (bottom – the removed gold casing), probably specifically for burial

The Birth of a New Age

Salt is often archaeologically invisible. It washes away. And yet it was crucial in the development of early civilizations.

The first modern humans to reach Europe were Stone Age hunter-gatherers. But around 12,000 years later, a new way of living emerged in the eastern Mediterranean and began to spread: farming. The early farmers still used stone implements – the name for this period is the Neolithic, or New Stone Age. Storing food became vitally important, and people started to make pots, build granaries – and use salt as a preservative.

Salt became a valuable commodity – it was traded for sought-after goods like jade axes and, later on, copper axes. During the Bronze Age, salt production intensified. People grew rich from the white gold. Salt was in high demand and settlements sprang up around natural sources of salt. These sites are some of the longest continually occupied sites in Europe and they offer us crucial insights into the development of civilizations. One such community was at Hallstatt, located near to the modern city of Salzburg, in Austria.

In the mid-nineteenth century, the then director of the Hallstatt salt mines in Austria developed an interest in archaeology and embarked on the excavation of a huge cemetery near the mine. Between 1846 and 1863, Johann Georg Ramsauer and his team unearthed nearly a thousand graves, containing not only the bones of the individuals who had been buried in them, but also a vast and varied array of grave goods – swords, pottery and bronze vessels and jewellery. Imported bronze vessels allowed archaeologists to date the burials in the cemetery; most of them, including so-called 'chieftain's graves', with the most elaborate grave goods, dated to the seventh and sixth centuries BC.

The excavation of the extraordinary cemetery at Hallstatt came at a key point in the development of archaeological thinking. Since the sixteenth century, people had been describing various antiquities that seemed to predate the Roman period in central and western Europe as 'Celtic', 'Gaulish' or 'British'. But all this was done in a rather haphazard way. In the early nineteenth century, there was a concerted effort to end the vagueness of prehistoric studies. Danish archaeologists came up with a three-age model of European prehistory: a sequence comprising the Stone, Bronze and Iron Ages. Careful analysis of excavations had revealed that technology changed over time, with stone being replaced by bronze, and then bronze being replaced by iron.

When Hallstatt was excavated, it was interpreted according to this three-age model. And the link had already been made between those classical references to the Celts and the Iron Age of west-central Europe – the presumed homeland of the Celts. So Ramsauer was following the convention of his time in identifying the richly furnished graves of Hallstatt as 'Celtic'. The huge range of objects from the graves meant that archaeologists could begin to paint a detailed picture of what Celtic, or Iron Age European culture actually looked like.

Although broad cultural groupings in archaeology might be given general names like 'Iron Age', more narrowly focused types of culture are often named after the site where they were first discovered or identified. And so this impressive site in Austria was to give its name to this particular early Iron Age culture, spanning the eighth to the sixth centuries BC in central Europe. Archaeologists began to talk about a 'Hallstatt culture', based on the distinctive objects and styles found at the original site.

It wasn't just the graves at Hallstatt that contained Iron Age objects. In his salt mines, Ramsauer found more wonderful things. Salt was precious to the ancient inhabitants of Hallstatt and it formed the basis of their wealth. The same preservative properties that made salt such a sought-after commodity meant that prehistoric organic objects left in the salt mines were still more or less intact when Ramsauer's team recovered them in the nineteenth century.

So often in archaeology, we have only stone, bone, metal and pottery left to look at, while everything else tends to rot away. Anything made of wood, paper, leather or fur usually has a limited existence, as the agents of putrefaction and decay get stuck in. But if you leave a leather rucksack, a shoe or a woollen blanket in a salt mine, it can remain there, perfectly preserved, for more than two and a half millennia. Ramsauer found objects such as these, along with wood chips, which would have been used to light the mines, lengths of ropes and cord, wooden shovels and pick handles, and even food – all thousands of years old.

The name 'Hallstatt' comes from the Greek word for salt, giving us a clue, perhaps, to the very ancient origins of the mine. But recent archaeological investigations of the Hallstatt salt mines have meant that it's now possible to pin accurate dates on phases of the mine and its contents. Samples of spruce timbers in the mines have yielded radiocarbon dates going right back into the Bronze Age, to the thirteenth and fourteenth centuries BC. Dendrochronology, also known as tree-ring dating, has provided some precise dates for specific pieces of timber; so we know, for instance, that a wooden staircase found in the mines was made from a tree that was felled in 1344 BC. This makes it the oldest wooden staircase in the world, from the oldest salt mine.

The Bronze Age salt miners dug vertical shafts down into the salt-rich rock, and then branched out along horizontal galleries. In the early Iron Age, the miners got more ambitious and chipped out huge underground halls, some twenty metres wide and tall, and more than a hundred metres long, chasing the richest saliferous strata deep into the rock.

The prehistoric people of Hallstatt weren't keeping their salt to themselves – they were trading it, and it was this industry and commerce that made them rich. Or, at least, it made some of them rich. By the Iron Age, we see that wealth amply demonstrated in the cemetery.

The earliest burials at Hallstatt, like the mines themselves, date back to the Bronze Age. They are cremation burials: the body of the deceased was cremated, then the fragments of burned bone were collected and placed in a cinerary urn, which was buried in the cemetery. This type of cremation burial is not exclusive to Hallstatt – it's seen over a wide area at this time, and it's recognized by archaeologists as the 'Urnfield culture'. In fact, and not surprisingly, this culture is about much more than just funerary rituals. Across a wide area, which centres on the Alps but stretches south into Italy, west into France and east into Hungary, archaeologists have found striking similarities in the types of bronze objects being made and used, from weaponry to jewellery. All of this is recognized as part of the Urnfield culture, which lasted from about 1300 to 700 BC.

The Urnfield culture seems to take off just as the Bronze Age Minoan and Mycenaean cultures of the Mediterranean collapse. These were palace economies, where production supported, and was controlled by, powerful rulers. Each kingdom had a centre of administration – a palace – such as that at Knossos on Crete, and at Mycenae and Pylos on the Greek Peloponnese. These economies had been thriving for centuries, but something – and archaeologists fiercely debate the cause – led to their demise around the thirteenth century BC. It's difficult to work out how these two processes – the Mediterranean late Bronze Age collapse and the rise of the Urnfield culture – are linked, but the trading networks of Europe would undoubtedly have undergone a major shift as the palace economies of the Aegean crumbled, and Greece was plunged into a Dark Age.

It's tempting to see the shared Urnfield culture, extending right across the heart of Europe, as reflecting some sort of emerging political entity – perhaps an expanding tribe, conquering a swathe of territory and bringing its own culture with it. But there's really no evidence to suggest that Urnfield was this sort of mini-empire. And this flags up a very general problem with the way we describe ancient cultures, and how our attempts to classify them can produce assumptions and expectations that just don't stand up to scrutiny.

In the early twentieth century, archaeologists began to approach ancient people and their cultures using an evolutionary model. They would look to define a particular 'archaeological culture group', which they could then track through time – pinpointing its origin and showing its expansion and contraction. Cultures evolved over time like a branching tree. Archaeologists were essentially treating culture groups as though they were biological species, arranging them on an evolutionary family tree. Culture groups tended to be equated with particular ethnic groups and particular languages. So, if an archaeologist found a particular type of material culture, they would assume that this equated to a certain ethnic group, speaking a particular language. If one culture was seen to be spreading out, geographically, replacing other cultures, it was assumed that this related to the migration of an ethnic group, displacing others. But, in fact, the spread of particular aspects of culture doesn't necessarily mean a spread of people. Ideas have a life of their own. They don't stick together in neatly consistent packages. And it's also rare to find examples where the appearance of a particular 'culture group' is closely tied to a mass migration of people.

In the 1960s, a fresh approach to archaeology stressed the importance of networks of communication, where the mobility of individuals – rather than of whole populations – was crucial. Ideas could emerge anywhere and spread through the network. This concept is equally relevant whether we're looking at the Bronze Age Urnfield or the Iron Age Celts. We need to make sure that we're not slipping back into thinking of neat, tightly defined packages of language, ethnic group and material culture. We can continue to use labels like 'Urnfield' and 'Celts' but we must be incredibly wary of letting those labels define how we think about the past.

As tempting as it might be, we certainly don't need to invoke the expansion of a particular tribe to explain the spread of the Urnfield culture. Instead, this phenomenon seems to reflect a spread of ideas, which were probably jumping on the numerous bandwagons of trade links that were already thriving in the Bronze Age, as copper, tin and salt were transported across Europe. Across the wide landscape where the Urnfield culture can be identified, there is similarity and some degree of consistency, but there's also regional variation, particularly in pottery styles.

The Urnfield period seems to represent a real boom in Europe – both in terms of economics and population – and these two probably go hand in hand. Throughout this period, more and more copper is coming out of the ground, being traded and being fashioned into bronze artefacts; more and more settlements appear; more and more land is pressed into service as farmland. There's also a change happening in the way that societies are structured. It's during this period that we see two crucial developments in this area of Europe: hill forts start to appear, and some burials are very richly furnished compared with others. Archaeologists see this as evidence of a concentration of wealth and power in the hands of a few.

Whatever you may wish to call these people of high status –
aristocrats, chiefs, kings and queens, princes and princesses
– it doesn't really matter. What does matter is that we can see
the markers of their high status in their graves.

These divisions within society, with clear differences
between ordinary people and a ruling elite, continue and
intensify as we move from the Bronze Age into the early Iron
Age, and the Urnfield culture gives way to a new cultural
phenomenon, named after that salt mine where it was first
recognized: Hallstatt. There's plenty of evidence of continuity
– to some extent, Hallstatt can be seen as a natural development of that indigenous Urnfield culture. The transition from
Bronze Age to Iron Age, here in central Europe, as elsewhere,
is a smooth change – not a revolution.

Iron extraction and ironworking seem to have been
invented somewhere in Asia Minor, in the middle of the
second millennium BC, and then the practice gradually
spread westwards across Europe. The Hallstatt period saw
improvements in agriculture and the development of some
iron technology, but this happened against a background of
uninterrupted settlement and the continuation of social
trends that had emerged in the Urnfield. But here again we
come up against that old-fashioned but surprisingly persistent idea that different cultures must be made by different
ethnic groups. The people who created the Hallstatt culture
were most probably not incomers to the region. They were
simply the descendants of the people who had cremated their
dead and buried them in the Urnfields. They are no longer
Bronze Age people, but early Iron Age people – early Celts.
But let's just remember that these are all names we're

applying to them. It helps us to carve up and understand archaeology, but it really tells us nothing about what those people thought about their own ethnic identity.

As well as those themes of continuity between the Bronze Age and Iron Age, there were other important – this time, external – influences on the early Iron Age in central Europe. In eastern Europe, nomadic horsemen from the Pontic steppe, north of the Black Sea, were on the move, coming into contact with the early Celts of the Hallstatt period. Horses, already a symbol of status in the Urnfield culture, now became even more important. Trade in the Mediterranean was intensifying, and new trade connections opened up, right into the heart of central Europe. Those connections added to the existing networks that allowed ideas to travel and flourish far away from the place of their inception. Ideas from the Mediterranean started to find their way into central Europe.

In the eighth century BC, the Phoenicians, based in the eastern Mediterranean, were extending their trading empire to the west. They established a trading post at Gadir (modern Cadiz) and formed links with the important trading centre of Tartessos (modern Huelva, in south-western Spain), tapping into existing Atlantic trade in gold, copper and tin. Around the same time, the Greeks began to colonize Sicily and southern Italy, becoming neighbours of the Etruscans in northern Italy, who were hungry for Greek goods and ideas. In the seventh century BC, the Etruscans established their own trading posts in the western Mediterranean, along the coast of southern France. And then the Greeks also established colonies here, the first of these being Massalia, around 600

BC. This Greek colony was the place from which Pytheas set off on his maritime adventure into the northern Atlantic. We know, from Strabo, that this colony lay near to the territory of the Celts in the south-west. But it was also very close to the mouth of the Rhone, and that river formed an important trade route linking the Mediterranean with Celtic lands north of the Alps.

In the sixth century, the Mediterranean world entered a period of turmoil. The Phoenician cities in the Levant were subsumed into the Babylonian empire, cutting adrift the Phoenician city of Carthage, in modern Tunisia, which contin-ued its trade with the western Mediterranean. Greek cities along the Aegean coast of what is now Turkey became swal-lowed up into the expanding Persian empire. The inhabitants of one of these cities, Phocaea (modern Foca, in Turkey), left en masse and attempted to settle in Corsica, but, facing opposition from the Etruscans, eventually settled for a new home in southern Italy. Archaeologists believe that Massalia – which had originally been founded by the seafaring Phocaean Greeks – was then left somewhat isolated. It's hard to know which one drove the other, but it seems that, just as the Massiliote Greeks were starting to look around for new markets for their goods, the emerging Hallstatt elite devel-oped a need for such luxuries, to consolidate and display their high status. Trade up and down the Rhone had never been so frantic.

The Celts were clearly interested in one particular aspect of Greek culture: wine drinking. Dating to the late sixth century and into the fifth century, Greek and Etruscan amphorae, bowls for mixing wine, flagons, jugs and cups suddenly start turning up in excavations of early Celtic, Hallstatt period hill forts and in the graves of the social elite. These finds are hugely enlightening. They show that powerful people were controlling not only local production – agriculture, iron and salt – but also prestige goods that they obtained through trade. These valuable possessions were important symbols of wealth and status: only the most powerful could hope to acquire them. As long as they could maintain this monopoly, they would keep their social status.

Among the most richly furnished of all the Hallstatt burials is that of the Hochdorf Prince. His grave was discovered in southern Germany in the late sixties, around 250 miles northwest of the town of Hallstatt itself. The wonderful objects buried in the grave alongside the mortal remains of the 'prince' graphically reveal the heady heights to which the rich and powerful could ascend in this Iron Age society, and the importance of exotic prestige goods – especially items associated with drinking and feasting – in securing such high status.

The prince is also noteworthy because he was not, in any obvious way, a warrior. He wasn't even buried with a sword. The most dangerous object he had with him was his ornate antenna-style dagger. So his status in Celtic society doesn't seem to have come from any fighting prowess or his ability to shock and subjugate foes – at least, there's no evidence of this among his grave goods. With his gold, his penchant for feasting and his taste for Mediterranean luxuries, he looks like an extremely well-heeled merchant king. The Hochdorf Prince seems a long way from the belligerent and barbaric Celts described by the classical writers. Perhaps there was a lot more to the Celts than their enemies would have us believe.

The connections between trade, wealth and social status are indelibly stamped on the elite, princely graves of the Hallstatt period. But they are also represented in the most obvious expressions of such power in the landscape – the Iron Age hill forts. One of the most impressive hill forts in Europe – from an archaeological perspective, if not a purely aesthetic one – is Heuneburg, on the banks of the Upper Danube, in southern Germany.

The Giant's Castle

On a clear spring morning, just as the sun began to appear over the horizon, I walked up the grassy ramparts of Heuneburg – the 'Giant's Castle'. It is well named. Looming over the Danube River, this natural hill was sculpted by Iron Age architects. Its steep sides had been recently cleared of trees and scrub, so that its contours were clear to see. It still looks formidable today, and, in its heyday, in the early Iron Age, this was the site of a powerful Celtic citadel.

Standing at the top of the Giant's Castle, looking out to the east, I could see the Danube hugging the flank of the hill fort below me. A modestly sized river at this early point in its journey, the Danube is essential to the story of Heuneburg as it provided a hugely important route for trade and communications, flowing right through the heart of Europe. The wider landscape around the hill fort today is heavily agricultural, with small towns and forested bluffs. I could just make out the Alps on the horizon in the south-east.

The position of Heuneburg is very important – it's on a crossroads in Europe. While the Danube formed a connection from west to east, goods could also reach Heuneburg from the south and then be traded on to the north, along the Rhine. Like Hallstatt, then, Heuneburg had grown up as a centre of commerce. But, unlike Hallstatt, there was no specific commodity at Heuneburg that the local Celts were exchanging for imported goods – no salt, no metal ores. Instead, the wealth and power of Heuneburg seems to have flowed from trade itself. Its merchants could bring in raw materials – like amber, from the Baltic – and sell them on at a profit. But archaeologists have also found plenty of evidence of the work of craftsmen and artisans at Heuneburg, so they were probably trading in manufactured goods as well.

The range of artefacts discovered in the archaeological digs at Heuneburg are testament to its importance as a trading centre, and to its connections with lands far away, particularly to the south and east. Thousands of fragments of pottery have been recovered from excavations. Most of them are locally made, very ordinary Iron Age ware. But there are also fragments of more special pottery, and, among those pieces, while some represented local styles, others were most definitely imports.

I had looked at a few fragments in the Depository Store in Stuttgart. A triangular fragment of a terracotta-coloured pot bore a design, painted on in black, with scratched details added. It was typical Attic black-figure ware. It showed a warrior with a helmet, shield and spear, and two other figures, and the head of a dog. A key pattern ran around the rim, above the figures. This was a piece of pottery that had travelled here all the way from Greece. There were also Etruscan drinking cups in burnished black ware. As well as these imports, there were locally produced goblets that were clearly influenced by the Etruscan style, but combined it with a local, Celtic twist. The shape of the cups was close to, but not exactly the same as the Etruscan versions, and one bore a typically Celtic pattern, with thumb-sized impressions alternating with vertical ridges around the bowl of the cup.

There were other exotic imports, alongside the pottery. Archaeologists had found flat pieces of amber and ivory, which had once been inlaid as decoration on a wooden couch. This is extremely unlikely to have been made locally – such couches are characteristically Greek. They were not just for sitting on: they were for dining and were associated with Greek drinking parties or symposia. The Greeks would have drunk wine, but, while the more refined Celts may have copied the trend for sitting around on elaborate couches at parties, they're more likely to have had mead or beer in their cups.

It wasn't just the objects found in the archaeological excavations at Heuneburg that spoke of these wide connections across Europe. The construction of the wall itself suggested exotic influences. I met with state archaeologist Dirk Krause to find out the latest theories about this wall.

'This mud-brick construction is something very special; in fact, it is unique,' said Dirk with some pride. 'There is nowhere else north of the Alps with this type of construction.'

So where did this idea come from? Archaeologists have previously suggested that it could have been influenced by a similar style of building originating in the Greek empire. The basic construction – using air-dried mud-bricks on a stone base – was certainly used in defensive walls at Greek sites, including Eretria, Delphi and Corinth. Historians have suggested that the founding of the Greek colony at Massalia (where Pytheas sailed from), could have catalysed the spread of essentially Greek ideas to the north. While this is probably true, the colony at Massalia was founded around 600 BC, and possibly even later. This makes it too late to have influenced the initial development of the 'princely seats' – the fortified strongholds – that started to appear across the western Hallstatt zone, from eastern France into Austria, Switzerland and south-western Germany, from around 600 BC. It seems that Massalia was just too late to have inspired the building of the Mediterranean-style mud-brick wall at Heuneburg. So where had the architect got this idea?

There's an important clue on the western side of the fort, where the great limestone and mud-brick wall at Heuneburg was punctuated by large towers or bastions. This was a similar plan to fortresses that had existed in Sicily and Iberia – outposts of the Phoenician empire. The similarity has prompted archaeologists to speculate that Heuneburg might have been masterminded by a Mediterranean, possibly Phoenician, architect. But did he just happen to turn up at Heuneberg? Or had a chieftain of this Celtic stronghold travelled to the south, seen the Phoenician forts and decided to create their own, back at home, enlisting the help of a capable architect? Evidence suggests that Heuneburg's elite would certainly have had the wealth and the connections to attract such a master builder.

Commenting on the 'mad builder' of Heuneburg, German prehistorian Karl Narr points out that the fort would have been 'revolutionary for its time and place', and he sees here the mark of 'a very dominant personality – a powerful ruler of the citadel'. It was such an unusual and innovative thing to build – the locals of Heuneburg wouldn't have seen anything like it before. The mud-brick wall offered advantages over traditional timber defences: it needed less maintenance, it didn't require so much wood (which seems to have been becoming scarce in the area) and it was less vulnerable to fire. And – as Dirk pointed out – it could be painted white, making it a visually stunning landmark, an impressive feat of engineering and also a demonstration of the ability of its ruler to control resources, including human labour. Perhaps building the wall involved promises of help from allies, and so the work of construction itself may have also helped to build and cement allegiances. At least five different types of stone were brought in to lay the foundations of the walls – brought in, perhaps, from the territories of different allies. This really is where archaeology runs out; we can only ever guess at exactly how the walls and towers of Heuneberg came to be ordered, devised and built. But we can be absolutely sure that it would have been a significant event for the people living in and around the citadel, and probably for miles around.

These curious Mediterranean influences in the contents and construction of Heuneberg had already marked it out as a site of special significance in this period of the early Iron Age when another discovery was made that confirmed the site as one of the most significant in the Celtic world.

Archaeologists knew that the fort of Heuneberg, encircled by its whitewashed mud-brick wall, was reasonably large and could have contained around 2,000 permanent inhabitants. But the extent of the settlement sprawled far beyond the wall. It has long been known that there was a lower town at Heuneberg, spread over terraces on the western flank of the hill. This had a wall of its own and archaeologists have recently discovered the foundations of a huge gate into this part of the settlement. But what really shocked them were the results of a detailed survey of the surrounding landscape, carried out using LIDAR technology.

A LIDAR survey can reveal features in a landscape that are too subtle to see on the ground, and, at Heuneburg, many of the salient features had almost been ploughed out of existence. The survey revealed an extraordinary array of banks and ditches, which, in the first half of the sixth century BC, had formed the defences and trackways of an area of outer settlement that covered some one hundred hectares. Both the citadel and its lower town were densely settled, but even this exterior settlement consisted of around fifty fairly closely spaced farmsteads. This new vision of Heuneberg transforms it from a small hill fort to a much larger town, extending far beyond the acropolis, and home to at least 5,000 inhabitants.

In fact, the word 'town' may underplay the importance of the settlement. It's likely that Heuneburg was politically as well as economically important in the area, and would have been ruled by a social elite, whose impressive burial mounds lie within clear sight of the hill fort. Dirk argues that even the term 'princely seat' doesn't quite hit the nail on the head. The term 'polis' was and is used for similarly sized polities in Greece. It was also used to describe Etruscan city states, which grew up in Italy in the Archaic period, including Tarquinii (near modern Tarquinia), Veii (just ten miles north of Rome) and Orvieto (which still exists as a city in modern Umbria). If those settlements deserve the label of 'polis', Dirk believes Heuneburg should attract the same degree of recognition. It was a city: the first city north of the Alps.

This revelation transforms our understanding of the site and of Celtic history. If we start to see Heuneburg as an Iron Age city, then it's very likely that it was well known far beyond the country we now know as Germany, and especially in areas with which it had established trade links. Indeed, it's possible that it was Heuneburg that was mentioned by Herodotus in that famous extract, quoted in the previous chapter, from his *Histories* in the middle of the fifth century BC. He described a city in Celtic lands: 'The Istros [Danube] river arises among the Celts and the polis of Pyrene, cutting Europe across the middle.'

Heuneburg lies just eighty kilometres from the source of the Danube, and the new survey showed that it would have been a substantial, city-sized settlement. With strong mercantile connections with lands to the south, it's hard to imagine that this trade centre wasn't well known in Mediterranean Europe. For Dirk Krause, Heuneburg represents the best candidate for Herodotus' ancient city of Pyrene. Even if it wasn't the polis Herodotus was referring to, Heuneburg tells us something very important about the early Celts of the Hallstatt period. These people weren't just eking out an existence in small villages scattered across the landscape. They were trading across Europe, picking up ideas from distant cultures, and building cities.

Building a Big Society

I came away from Heuneburg with a sense of having visited a really special place. It can be very difficult to get away from that classical view of the Celts as barbarians – it's very powerful propaganda. But this Celtic city, built over 2,500 years ago, with its Phoenician-style ramparts and its Celtic-Etruscan-fusion-style pottery, makes us look at those Iron Age people of central Europe in a new light. They don't seem all that different from their neighbours south of the Alps and along the coasts of the Mediterranean, after all. But I still had plenty of questions. How had Heuneburg evolved into such a prestigious and important settlement? How long did it last? And how was it connected with developments across the rest of the Celtic world?

Archaeological investigations have already revealed how the settlement at Heuneburg grew up over time. During the seventh century BC, the landscape around this part of the Danube became more heavily farmed. The land was fertile and the farmers of the early Hallstatt period in this area made a good living. The population began to grow. As well as farms, small hamlet-like settlements began to appear. By the end of the seventh century BC, we can imagine that some particularly wealthy families had become politically important. A few of these families probably joined forces to instigate the development of the settlement centred on Heuneburg. Much like a mediaeval castle, the citadel may have been a seat of power – and an impressive reminder of that power, stamped on the landscape – but it was surely also designed to form an easily defendable stronghold in times of trouble.

The first fortifications of the hilltop involved traditional earthworks, probably with a timber palisade on top. But, by around 600 BC, as I had learned from Dirk, these basic defences had been replaced with the much more sophisticated Mediterranean-type mud-brick wall.

The tall and impressive fortifications at Heuneburg might almost have been expected to last forever, but in fact they lasted less than a century. Archaeologists have found evidence of two episodes of burning, before a final conflagration destroyed the wall in 540 BC. Sections of burning wall collapsed, killing and burying five children and one man, whose bones were discovered by the archaeologists. The settlement outside the citadel was also burned. Iron projectile points were discovered in this archaeological layer. Violence, rather than industrial accident, then, seems to have been the cause of the conflagration.

Immediately after this 'mud-brick wall horizon', the external settlement was abandoned. But life inside the citadel seems to have picked up and carried on pretty much as before – minus the mud-brick wall. Clearly, there were still very powerful people associated with Heuneburg, people who continued to trade with the Mediterranean world and who were given elite burials, with burial mounds thrown up close to the citadel – in fact, right on the site of the former external settlement.

Was the final burning of the mud-brick wall linked to a dynastic takeover? Perhaps. After 540 BC, the exotic-looking wall was never rebuilt. It was, instead, replaced by a traditional earthwork and timber rampart. The vision of the mastermind behind the gleaming white fort on the hill was erased from the landscape. Just a century later, in the mid-fifth century BC, the Iron Age story of Heuneburg appears to finally come to an end. The citadel and its lower town were abandoned.

The story of the rise and fall of Heuneburg is of much more than just local interest. It provides crucial insights into social and political changes that were rippling across Iron Age Europe.

It used to be thought that the first real cities north of the Alps grew up in the late Iron Age, in the second and first centuries AD. Julius Caesar described these Celtic Iron Age cities, which formed hubs for trade as well as being seats of regional power, as 'oppida'. Caesar named some twenty-eight oppida, including Bibracte (modern Mont Beuvray), Cenabaum (modern Orléans) and Geneva. But, over the last decade or so, archaeologists have found increasing evidence of Celtic city-like settlements appearing much earlier than this. Between the seventh and fifth centuries BC, in the later Hallstatt period, these cities or proto-cities popped up across a wide area. Around fifteen such sites have been identified, stretching from Mont Lassois in central France to Závist in the Czech Republic. Heuneburg sits in the middle of this range.

Dirk has convincingly argued that the recent survey showing the true extent of Heuneburg meant that the settlement should be viewed as equivalent to the Etruscan city states of the Archaic period. But this is about much more than just size. It's also about the political importance of such settlements – which takes in a much wider territory. It's been all too easy to buy that classical propaganda and distinguish between the civilized Mediterranean societies to the south and the barbarians north of the Alps. But, from as early as the seventh century BC, it looks like those 'barbarians' were busy creating their own complex social and political systems.

Each of the Hallstatt 'cities' may be seen not only as a seat of power and commerce, but also as the centre of a self-governing mini-kingdom. Suddenly, these Celts begin to look more similar to their cousins south of the Alps, especially the Etruscans, whose city states of the same period seem to have been loosely allied in a confederation. In his *History of Rome*, the historian Livy describes twelve cities of Etruria joined in a 'League'. While we'll never know if the Celtic city states were ever organized in a similar way – there are no historical records of this period in this part of the world – we can certainly imagine them united by commerce and culture. But while trade, language and religion may have formed positive links between these autonomous polities, there would have been less friendly interactions too – cut-throat competition and warfare. We need to be wary about using analogies from other times and other places, but, at the same time, we do have historical records from other parts of the world that show us what interactions between city states might have looked like.

From Homer, we learn of the battles between Aegean city states in the late Bronze Age; from Herodotus, the confederation of Greek city states that fought against Persian rule; and from Thucydides, we hear about the history of the Peloponnesian war between the city states of Sparta and Athens, and their respective allies. When we turn to look north of the Alps, these wonderful histories from the Aegean remind us of just how much we don't know about the Celtic world – which makes any insights that we can glean from archaeology even more precious.

So much about these early city states remains mysterious. Apart from the brief mention of the polis of Pyrene by Herodotus, these emerging centres of Celtic power remain beyond the boundaries of written history, accessible only through archaeology. But it's clear from recent investigations that the political complexity of Celtic society has been much underestimated. Again, this probably comes down, to a large extent, to the classical propaganda against the Celts and their barbarian friends elsewhere. Polybius, writing in the second century BC, produced a portrait of the Celts as totally chaotic and anarchic, with allies likely to end up fighting each other, and angry warriors murdering their chiefs. He claimed they had an insatiable appetite for meat and were often drunk out of their minds. In spite of that, he said, they managed to do some farming, and they were decent warriors – but they were intellectually impoverished, with no real knowledge, science or art. Polybius also tells us that the Celts were semi-nomadic, that they lived in unwalled villages and lay on beds of leaves.

But archaeology shows us that the Celtic political land-scape consisted of much more than just scattered villages with people eking out a meagre existence. While I don't doubt at all that there were plenty of people doing just such eking, it's now clear from the excavations at sites like Heuneburg that there was also a consolidation of power into larger collect-ives – minor chiefdoms were evolving into powerful political states. In this organized and stratified society, the highest echelons enjoyed a lavish lifestyle and were buried with golden treasure in their graves. Many richly furnished tombs have been discovered under mounds close to these Hallstatt city states. Such elite burials include Hohmichele and Bettelbühl, near Heuneburg, the Hochdorf Prince's burial, close to Hohenasperg, and the grave of the 'Princess of Vix', near Mont Lassois in Burgundy.

These early Iron Age city states were clearly centres of political power, associated with a ruling elite, but also centres of trade and production – with workshops or even entire craft quarters. They also served ceremonial and religious purposes: shrines, sanctuaries and processional ways have been discovered at various sites.

Perhaps it seemed, to people living in and around these city states, that this type of civilization was there to stay. But these early Celtic city states did not last; archaeological investigations across Europe show that the abandonment of Heuneburg in the fifth century BC was not an isolated occurrence. Other settlements, including Mont Lassois in Burgundy, suffered a similar fate at around the same time. It seems that the middle of the first millennium BC was a time of major economic and political upheaval in central Europe. These city states, with their well defined, centralized power structures and highly stratified societies, may have controlled large territories, but around and between those territories there were communities where social hierarchy was not as rigid, and where power was not concentrated to such an extreme extent in the hands of the few. We'll never know precisely what events led to the shift in power, but the rise and fall of the early Celtic city states appears to represent a cycle of centralization and decentralization of power in Celtic society. That cycle continued later; in the first and second centuries BC, another 'wave of centralization' swept through Celtic Europe with the emergence of a new generation of political centres: the settlements described by Julius Caesar as 'oppida'.

Heuneburg would never again be the centre of power that it had been in the sixth century BC, and yet neither was it completely forgotten. Very recent finds have suggested that later Celts were still visiting the ancient citadel. In 2010, construction work along the banks of the Danube, near Heuneburg, led to the discovery of some unexpected archaeological finds. Buried in the thick gravel, probably washed there from somewhere close by, were two bronze fibulae of a style characteristic of the late Iron Age – long after the abandonment of the citadel.

So while Heuneburg itself seems to have been abandoned at the end of the early Iron Age – the end of the Hallstatt period, around 450 BC – these fibulae suggest that, centuries later, people were still visiting what would already have been an ancient site. Perhaps the ceremonial function of the hill persisted long after its political demise. Maybe those brooches were offerings to the gods in a place that had already become a sacred monument and a shrine of the ancestors.

There must have been stories about this once-glorious citadel, and about the men and women who ruled it. Heuneburg itself is surrounded by burial mounds, which presumably contained the graves of its nobility, and which continued to be prominent features in the landscape long after the city had fallen into ruins. But while, for some, this may have been a respected place of the dead, for others, the temptation of buried treasure was too great. Most of the tumuli fell victim to grave robbers long ago. But there was one grave which escaped, and that's because it had become virtually invisible in the landscape.

The Bettelbühl Princess

In 2005, German archaeology students on a university field trip were exploring the landscape around Herbertingen, in southern Germany. On one particular day, they were field walking just half a mile to the east of the hill fort of Heuneberg, on the other side of the Danube, paying careful attention to any features or small surface finds. When they were close to the Bettelbühl stream, which runs into the Danube, one of the students spotted something glinting at his feet. Stooping to pick it up, he thought at first that it was a metal bottle-top. But in fact it was something far more exciting. It was a small gold fibula or brooch.

That same year, the university carried out a small excavation in the field where the gold fibula had been discovered. It became clear that they were dealing with an Iron Age burial mound, which had been ploughed almost completely flat, leaving just a slight rise in the landscape. Digging down only a foot or so beneath the surface of the soil, they uncovered a small grave. It contained the bones of a child who had been about three years old when she died. But she must have been no ordinary child; a second fibula, to match the first, was found in her grave, along with two gold earrings. In excavating this tiny grave, the archaeologists discovered just the corner of a larger chamber cut down into the gravelly river terrace. Further investigation uncovered the collapsed remains of a large wooden burial chamber, which must have been very similar to the chamber at Hochdorf, except this one had never been covered with layers of large stones. At Bettelbühl, the mound over the burial chamber would have been built up of earth, before it was ploughed flat.

What the archaeologists discovered in this burial mound next to the Bettelbühl stream once again challenges that lingering stereotype of the Celts as savages. The magnificent treasures, the style of burial and the individuals who were laid to rest in that chamber provide us with precious insights into the lives, society and culture of the early Celts.

The Bettelbühl burial is still being investigated, but I was granted privileged access to see the contents of the mound at the grandly named State Office for Cultural Heritage Management Baden-Wuerttemberg, in Esslingen, southern Germany. Up on the seventh floor is Dirk Krause's office, where he showed me a poster-sized print of a photo of the excavated burial chamber.

Although the roof of the chamber had collapsed down, presumably centuries ago, the damp conditions had preserved the lower timbers. The floor was built of long planks – mostly oak, but with two fir planks as well. It seems that the chamber had flooded seasonally, as the Bettelbühl river ran a little higher, and that the burials and objects inside had been disturbed by this movement of water. There were two individuals inside the chamber – one stretched out, with amber beads and gold objects lying on the remains of the body, and another lying in a corner of the chamber. In contrast with the fantastic preservation of the wood forming the chamber, the human bones were poorly preserved. This is exactly what I'd expect to see in this kind of burial environment, where the water level changes and the soil is slightly acidic. The skull of the main burial had been found a long way from the rest of the body, close to the opposite wall of the chamber. The lower jawbone had also come adrift, and was found quite separate from the skull and the rest of the body.

There are two possibilities here. Either the skull fell away from the rest of the body as the soft tissues decomposed and then floated or rolled over to the other side of the chamber, losing its jaw somewhere along the way; or the body was decapitated before being laid in the burial chamber. Dirk said that there were some examples of decapitated bodies in graves elsewhere during this period, but it was still a very unusual thing to find at this time, in this area. If you suspect that a body may have been decapitated, it's important to look carefully for cut-marks at the back of the skull or on the upper cervical vertebrae, which could help to confirm that this happened. Unfortunately, the bones of this headless individual are so poorly preserved that this type of evidence is likely to be missing. And so it remains impossible to know whether the body was decapitated, or lost its head naturally.

Five years after the burial chamber was lifted, en bloc, out of its field near the Danube, its contents were still being excavated and analysed. Once the chamber had been dug down to the level that appeared in Dirk's photograph – to the surface of the timber floor, and everything lying on it – the archaeologists did something that seems, perhaps, rather odd. They chopped into the timbers and took out segments – complete with any human remains or artefacts that happened to be lying on top. They divided the remains of the Bettelbühl burial chamber as if they were slicing into a tray bake. But there was method behind this apparent madness. Once the archaeology was in manageable chunks like this, it would fit into a CT scanner. And so the archaeologists proceeded to CT scan each of these slices of the chamber. This gave them the opportunity to see the detail of artefacts and human bones before each slice was carefully manually excavated in the lab.

Dirk took me downstairs to the basement lab, where some crucial slabs of the burial chamber – the ones bearing the principal burial – had been laid out. He introduced me to his colleague, archaeologist Nicole Ebringer-Rist, who had been working on the project since its inception. There, on the table in the centre of the lab, were three large, rectangular, dark brown slabs and a smaller, slightly rounded one. The bones and artefacts were almost squashed flat against the floor timbers. Each slab lay in a tray of plaster lined with cling film, to keep it together. These sections were usually covered and stored at a carefully controlled temperature and humidity, but while uncovered and being worked on in the lab, they need to be kept moist. Nicole periodically sprayed them with water while she talked to me about the burial.

My eyes were drawn first to the central slab, which bore a wide strip of green and badly degraded bronze. But, despite the degradation, it was possible to make out a pattern of repeating concentric circles across the verdigris on its surface.

'This is the belt,' explained Nicole. 'It is wide and very long – over a metre. The part in front is a single plate, and then it is made of bronze strips supported on leather and textile, and wrapped around the body.'

Above the belt, on the same slab, I could see the remains of the spine – really nothing more than a patch of darker crumbs lying on the dark oak plank. Below the belt, the lower part of the pelvis and the head of each femur, which formed the hip joints, were better preserved. The femoral heads looked relatively small, but most of the pelvis was concealed under the wide green strip of the belt, which had sagged over the upper part of the sacrum.

I really wanted to see the anatomy of the pelvis – the best part of the skeleton for inferring the sex of an individual. A male pelvis tends to be narrower, with a characteristic notch at the back, close to the sacrum. In a female pelvis, this notch – known as the greater sciatic notch – tends to be much wider. Although I couldn't see this area from looking at the remains themselves, I could look at the CT scans of the block containing the pelvis. The greater sciatic notch described a wide arc. The small hip joints, the slender arm bones on another slab and the wide greater sciatic notch meant that this skeleton was most probably female. She was also an adult; the bones were fully formed and the degree of wear on her teeth revealed that this woman was likely to have been aged between twenty-five and thirty-five years old when she died.

I looked at one of the larger slabs, bearing the remains of this young woman's right arm and hand. The bones were as dark as ebony, slightly crushed and looked as though they would crumble at the gentlest touch. Conserving these human remains was going to be a real challenge, but the CT scans meant that important data could be captured before the conservators attempted to lift the bone away from the underlying wood.

I could see two circular indents near the wrist, and Nicole told me that this was where two jet bangles had already been lifted from the block. She pointed out a dark, almost shiny material lying on the inner side of the elbow. It was leather, probably the remains of a leather pouch that the woman had worn at her waist, and it contained a perfectly preserved hazelnut. It's very rare for organic material to be preserved so well; the archaeologists at Bettelbühl were finding grave goods that would simply rot away in most burial environments. Of course, the unusual conditions also meant that the timber planks forming the chamber itself were well preserved – and this provided the archaeologists with the opportunity to undertake dendrochronological or 'tree-ring' dating of the wood. It yielded a precise date.

Radiocarbon dating is great, but it always gives a date range. These planks of oak had stood the test of time, and could therefore tell us the exact year in which the oak tree was felled: 583 BC. As Dirk pointed out, you could argue that these might have been timbers which had been reused, and that the burial chamber dated to much later than the year the oak tree was felled. But there were also those two fir planks in its floor, and they too had yielded a dendrochronological date: 583 BC. It seems most likely, then, that both trees were felled specifically for this purpose, and that 583 BC was indeed the year in which this Iron Age woman had died and been laid to rest in her wooden chamber, covered with a burial mound.

It's more difficult to place a date on the interment of the second individual in the chamber. She was also a young female, probably around twenty years of age, and apparently buried only with a couple of bronze bangles. Her bones lay, not directly on the timber floor, as with the first burial, but on a twenty-centimetre-thick layer of mud in the corner of the chamber. It is possible that her body was washed into this position after the chamber had begun to disintegrate and fill with mud. But Dirk thinks it more probable that this was a later burial – that the tomb had been opened in one corner, perhaps some years after the primary burial, to insert the body of this deceased individual into it.

The grave of the child – the original discovery before the main burial was found – lay outside the main, wooden chamber. The child's bones were too young to be either characteristically male or female, but this was probably a little girl, given the nature of the gold jewellery buried with her. This burial, dug into the gravel outside the primary shaft containing the wooden chamber, was certainly later than the main grave, containing the two women.

Somehow, these three females were linked to each other and the nature of that connection only became more apparent when the team looked closely at the objects that had been found alongside the older of the two women.

We left the lab and Nicole opened a large vault with a massive steel door, bringing out a metal crate, which she carried into another lab, where a table stood ready, draped with a black cloth. She opened the crate and I helped her take out a series of unremarkable-looking Tupperware boxes of various sizes. We started to open them and lay out their contents on the table. By the time we'd finished, there were two gold fibulae, five large gold beads decorated with gold filigree, and a strip of gold with a fastening that would have turned it into a large hoop, with a decorated gold bead suspended from it at the bottom. All of these objects were associated with the primary burial in the chamber – the woman of around thirty years of age. But there were also two small gold fibulae and a pair of earrings. These were the finds from the child's grave – including that fibula that had made its way to the ploughed surface of the field.

The quantity of gold was astonishing. Nicole talked about how incredible it was to excavate such finds. Bronze and iron oxidize in the ground, becoming progressively more degraded until eventually there's virtually nothing left, except, respectively, a green or rust-red stain in the soil. Gold stays unchanged. So, when you dig up a piece of gold jewellery, it gleams as brightly as the day it was made. These gold objects had needed a bit of cleaning to remove the soil sticking to them, but there was no challenging conservation required, as there most certainly would be with the woman's heavily oxidized and degraded bronze belt.

Looking at the items more closely, I could see the quality of the workmanship was astounding. I had to keep reminding myself that I was looking at gold jewellery made in central Europe more than 2,500 years ago. I've done a tiny bit of silversmithing myself, enough to get a feel for what a craft it really is. The gold beads were magnificent mini-masterpieces. Each one was a sphere, about two centimetres in diameter, with a tiny ribbon of gold around its equator and filigree patterns added to it using a minutely looped gold wire. Firstly, these goldsmiths must have had extremely good eyesight, and secondly, they knew their craft – it's very difficult to stick gold to gold. These objects give us another insight into this Celtic society: whoever made them was no amateur. He or she was surely a professional, and such a profession depends on local demand for luxury goods.

The decoration on the fibulae was different – and reminiscent of the belt plaque and shoe fittings of the Hochdorf Prince. The main body of each fibula, curved and leaf shaped, was embossed with a pattern, which had been created using a stamp. Three strips bore stamped ridges, like the rungs of a ladder, and the two lozenge-shaped spaces between the strips were filled with tiny round dots of gold. The gold bead hanging from the loop of the earring was also ornate. There was a dish-like concave impression at its centre, and the edge of it was decorated with a looped ribbon of gold again, like the other gold beads from the main grave.

But, for me, the real impact of these objects came when we compared the finds from the child's grave. The small fibulae had exactly the same pattern as the large ones belonging to the woman in the burial chamber – the same strips of stamped ridges and the same lozenges with gold dots. The girl's earrings were beads, suspended from bronze rings, and very similar indeed to the bead hanging from the woman's hoop earring. Each had a similar concave impression at the centre and the same, looped-ribbon edge.

'I believe these objects were made by the same goldsmith,' said Nicole. It certainly looked like it. The little girl's brooches were, in particular, just like miniature versions of the thirty-year-old woman's. It seemed entirely reasonable to assume that these two were related: that the little girl was the woman's daughter.

Nicole said that the team had attempted to extract DNA from the skeletons of both individuals, but had failed so far.

They were trying again – and were just about to take samples from the teeth – but had no answer yet. This would provide the essential evidence needed to prove – or disprove – the connection between these two individuals. But the similarity between those earrings and brooches was already compelling.

Holding one of the larger fibulae carefully in two hands, I felt an incredible sense of connection to this woman, who had died more than 2,500 years ago. I imagined that someone who knew her and loved her had prepared her cold body for the grave, dressing her with care, wrapping the great bronze belt around her waist and fastening her fibulae to her dress at the shoulders. It's at moments like these when the years, the decades, the centuries fall away and you are simply in the presence of another human being.

I thought about her relationship with the child, buried so close to her. If the child was her daughter, did she die years after her mother had been interred in her burial mound? Dirk certainly thinks that the child's grave was dug into the mound at some later date. There was no wood to provide a dendrochronological date in that small burial, and so it's likely that we will never know precisely when the child died and was buried. Objectively, we must leave the enquiry there, and be grateful for the wealth of facts already yielded by the graves. But I couldn't help wondering – did this thirty-year-old woman die in childbirth, perhaps, with her baby surviving, but in the end only living for a few years? As a mother, I thought about that woman dying and I hoped she knew in that moment that her daughter was alive, and that she never knew the child would die so young. Life back then would have been so much more brutal than we know now, and childhood mortality may have been so common as to be half expected, but these people would have loved, and suffered loss, just as we do.

This personal story of what may have been a Celtic mother and her young daughter is only a tiny part of what this grave has revealed to us. Its location, buried so close to Heuneburg, under one of the many tumuli that encircle the hill fort, makes it likely that this woman lived up on the acropolis. The nature of the tomb and the artistry of the gold objects clearly indicate her high status: she was one of the elite of Heuneburg – a princess. She must have seen many sunrises from that vantage point – the first flicker of light making the Danube sparkle. And she would have been so familiar with that view, with the snowy Alps on the southern horizon. But, in her grave, the archaeologists found one more object that illuminated another aspect of her life, and revealed another dimension to the story of the early Celts in central Europe.

At first, the wedge-shaped object had the archaeologists well and truly foxed when they discovered it – until they put it through the CT scanner. Only then did they see the iron bit and the iron rings, which helped them to identify it as a chamfron – a bronze plate that would have been attached over the front of a horse's head. There were even small iron bells attached at the back of the chamfron, which would have jingled as the horse moved. The Bettelbühl Princess was an equestrienne, and this connection with horses, as much as the gold jewellery, was a sign of her elite status in early Celtic society.

Perhaps even more significantly, the importance of horses and horse riding reveals another connection between the

Celts of central Europe and the wider world. While the walls of Heuneburg in the sixth century and the fashion for wine drinking may have been Mediterranean imports into Celtic Europe, the interest in horses and horse riding seems to have disseminated from much further east.

In the Bronze Age, the vast Pontic steppe, to the north and east of the Black Sea, was home to nomadic people who relied on horses to move with ease across those grasslands. The 'catacomb culture' in what is now Ukraine included key characteristics: pottery that was decorated with string or 'corded' imprints, polished battleaxes and catacomb-style graves with chambers off to the side of a main shaft. Importantly, these Bronze Age people were essentially eastern European cowboys – riding on horseback, breeding cattle. Elite burials often included wagons and early chariots, and even clay death masks.

The Mycenaean Greeks may have been the descendants of these steppe cowboys. The famous gold death mask found by Heinrich Schliemann at Mycenae in 1876 – which, it was optimistically suggested, once lay on the face of Agamemnon in his tomb (but, really, it is probably too early for that) – may hark back to this cowboy culture of the Pontic steppe. It is thought that these catacomb-building cowboys could have been the Cimmerians described by Herodotus in his *Histories*. But there were other horsemen ranging over the Pontic steppe, too. Herodotus describes the Scythians in the east, flooding westwards and forcing the Cimmerians out. This is probably much too simple a story, but, archaeologically, there was a change in the Pontic steppe in the first few centuries of the first millennium BC: the catacomb culture was replaced by the timber-grave culture. The burials that give this culture its name were very characteristic: a pit was dug, a wooden cabin constructed to contain the body of the deceased together with the grave goods, and, finally, a mound was built over the grave. It all sounds very familiar.

The Scythian migration was just the latest in a whole series of migrations, as steppe people moved westwards. This repeating pattern went right back to the third millennium BC, when the Yamnaya steppe people moved into Europe, bringing the Indo-European language with them. After the Yamnaya, the Scythians, the Allans, the Sarmatians and the Huns all did the same, periodically migrating from the less fertile eastern end of the steppe to the westernmost part – the Great Hungarian Plain.

Historical sources bear witness to the upheaval in the eighth century BC, when horse-riding nomads, identified as both Cimmerians and Scythians, surged south into Asia Minor. There, the Assyrians were embroiled in a battle with the kingdom of Urartu, and the equestrian warriors easily found work as mercenaries. Then, around the middle of the first millennium BC, the distinctive Scythian culture spread from the Black Sea, westwards, into the Middle Danube region – roughly corresponding with modern Hungary and Romania. This cultural spread could reflect a migration in that direction – perhaps of elites, rather than whole populations – but it could also have resulted from strengthening trade links and a healthy flow of goods and ideas. One of the most distinctive features of this culture, evidence of which archaeologists find right across the Great Hungarian Plain by the fifth century, was its focus on horse riding.

Going back to the earliest evidence of Scythian culture on the great Eurasian steppe, perhaps the best example comes from the burial mounds, or kurgans, at Arzhan, in the Tuva Republic of southern Siberia. When the large kurgan known as Arzhan 1 was excavated in the 1970s, it was found to contain a timber structure with numerous chambers. Although the grave had been damaged by looting, the remains of at least sixteen people, including a 'royal couple', were still in evidence. And in and around the kurgan were the remains of 160 horses. The grave goods inside the mound included bronze daggers, battleaxes and arrowheads, as well as ornate bronze and gold horse trappings, decorated with images of boars, tigers and leopards. This kurgan, dating to the boundary between the ninth and eighth centuries BC, provides an insight into the very earliest Scythian culture and clearly demonstrates the importance of horses to this society, and the association between social status and horses.

Another kurgan, imaginatively named Arzhan 2, was excavated more recently, between 2001 and 2003. This burial mound is somewhat later, dating to the seventh century BC, but still an early Scythian monument. Importantly, this mound had escaped the looters' notice – it was intact, and contained over twenty graves. Among these was an elite double burial. In a carefully constructed wooden chamber with a planked floor lay the skeletons of a man, around fifty years old, and a woman of around thirty, together with spectacular grave goods.

The man had been buried with a gold torc decorated with a spiralling frieze of animal figures. His clothes had decayed away, but they had been covered with rows of inch-long gold panthers and tiny golden beads. His head-gear had been decorated with golden winged horses and a gold deer. His iron dagger was also decorated with gold panthers and his quiver of arrows bore a gold plaque with a fish-scale pattern. The woman had also worn a headdress with golden horses decorating it, and she had necklaces of gold, amber, garnet and malachite beads. She also seemed to have been wearing a cape decorated with gold panthers. Her boots had decayed away, but the tiny gold beads that had decorated them lay around the bones of her feet. In another grave in the kurgan, the archaeologists discovered the skeletons of fourteen horses, buried with their gold trappings. Once again, the importance of horses and their connection with high social status is explicit in this collection of graves. It's also notable that the woman's burial is just as rich as the man's.

A century or two later, and nearly 5,000 miles away, the Bettelbühl Princess was interred, with her golden finery and her horse's decorated bronze chamfron, in a plank-floored wooden chamber, under a mound. Her culture bears witness to Mediterranean influences, but also enshrines ideas that connect her with those horse-riding, timber-grave-building nomads of the Pontic steppe.

The Princess's grave provides us with important insights into early Celtic society in south-west Germany. Her burial shows how ideas from other cultures had been incorporated into a new cultural identity. Only a couple of centuries before, when the Urnfield culture of the late Bronze Age prevailed, it was still usual practice to cremate the dead and bury their remains in urns. Now, in the early sixth century BC, the elite

– at least – were being buried in timber chambers under great mounds of earth and stone. It was an idea from the east that may have seemed exotic when it first arrived, but which spread like wildfire.

If you were anybody who was anybody, you could expect to be buried in such a way. And you'd probably be buried with objects associated with horses, as these economically important animals were now even more emblematic of social status than they had been in the Bronze Age.

But one of the most striking messages from the grave of the Bettelbühl Princess is that the higher echelons of this society were not exclusively reserved for men. And not only was it possible for a woman to possess such high status, her children – including daughters – would inherit that status. Thinking back to the matching gold fibulae in the child's grave, it seems most likely that this small child was the respected daughter of the 'princess'.

These finds in Germany are wonderful. It's incredible to have such intimate knowledge of individuals like the Hochdorf Prince, the Bettelbühl Princess and the child that was, most likely, her daughter. And the new recognition of Heuneburg and centres like it as city states, equivalent to those in northern Italy, shakes up any preconceptions we might have had about the barbarian nature of those Iron Age populations north of the Alps. Although these stories are new, and include some challenges to conventional views of the Celts, they are still extremely traditional in one very important way. In this paradigm, an area in central Europe – including southern Germany, Switzerland and eastern France – is seen as the

Celtic 'heartland', following indications from the classical writers. And Hallstatt is taken to represent the characteristic culture of the early Celts. The Hochdorf Prince and the Bettelbühl Princess were both Celts because they lived in Iron Age central Europe. This isn't entirely unreasonable – Strabo wrote about the Celts north of the Alps, including the large tribe called the Boii, who later migrated south of the mountains into northern Italy, in the fourth century BC. But whether or not those people thought of themselves as Celts, or spoke a Celtic language, is unclear.

When we label a great swathe of territory across central and western Europe as 'Celtic', that strongly implies a common identity, material culture and language. But one of the key features of the early Iron Age in central Europe is missing in the west: the rise of the 'princely seats' or 'city states', like Heuneburg. So are the elite tombs. And the wagon burials. What one archaeologist has called 'the ridiculous problem of uniformity' is laid bare. And this makes us go back to that question of what 'Celt' actually means. We shouldn't actually expect ethnic identity, language and material culture to coincide in a neat package – anywhere, any time.

The old standard model of the origin and spread of the Celts leads us to expect an expansion of people – and their culture – from central Europe out to the western periphery. And so there's been a tendency to focus on the core zone of the Hallstatt culture, almost as though we're seeing the birth of a new cultural 'species' there, before it spreads out into new habitats, forcing other species to go extinct. But, rather than look for evidence to support this (very strange and outdated) assumption, we should try to avoid preconceptions and look at western Europe more objectively. What was happening there in the transition from the late Bronze Age to the Iron Age? And how were Britain and Ireland interacting with the continent? Did an invading wave of Celts bring the new metal, along with the new ideas, to these islands?

WARRIORS, SWORDS AND TORCS

THE EBB AND FLOW OF IDEAS
IN IRON AGE EUROPE

A New Dawn and the Corrard Torc

Eight hundred BC is the date when the Bronze Age ended and the Iron Age began, in central and western Europe. That makes it sound like an incredibly abrupt transition: a revolution, perhaps. The rounded-up nature of the figure arouses suspicion. Of course, there is no such precise date in reality. The transition happened at different times, and at different rates, in different parts of the world.

Divisions and boundaries between 'Ages' might be useful constructs at times. They help us understand changes on a continental and millennial scale, but they are abstractions. They don't actually represent the reality on the ground. Real revolutions – at least, those that might be perceived as such by people living through them – are mercifully rare. Most often, social and cultural change happens slowly, and in a piecemeal fashion.

The Iron Age in Britain and Ireland was a slow starter. While a few iron objects began to appear in the eighth century BC, it would take much longer before they became commonplace in Britain. The centuries between 800 BC and 500 BC saw a gradual phasing in of iron. The metal was hard to extract and to shape, but iron ores were much more widespread than the sources of tin needed to make bronze. Some scholars have suggested that an increasing use of iron – particularly in weaponry – could have caused the collapse of the affluent Mediterranean civilizations at the end of the Bronze Age. Iron technology could have been a democratizing force, undermining societies whose wealth and power had depended on controlling access to the metals needed to make bronze. But environmental and social factors may have already disrupted the long-distance supply of tin, before iron was adopted.

There are signs of a shake-up in western Europe, with something very strange happening to metal possessions. In the late Bronze Age, from Portugal to Scotland, people seem to have been throwing away vast quantities of bronze objects – burying them in the ground or consigning them to lakes and rivers. From buried hoards of bronze axes, to cauldrons and roasting spits, to bronze swords, it's a practice that has given us some of our most impressive archaeological finds from the Bronze Age. But it raises a host of questions about the motivations behind what appears to have been a widespread, deliberate disposal of material wealth.

Many archaeologists interpret these buried hoards and depositions of bronze objects in watery places as evidence of ritual acts. But I think we should consider more prosaic explanations before resorting to the interpretation of these hoards as ritual offerings.

Could it have been carelessness or misfortune that led to at least some of these metal objects ending up in watery places – for example, having gone adrift at fording points on rivers, lakes or lochs? While it's certainly possible that some objects may have been genuinely lost in this way, it's not a satisfying explanation for the broader phenomenon. Why should people – in Britain, Ireland and France – suddenly have become so clumsy, reckless and improvident? The amount of metal 'lost' in this way in the late Bronze Age really is extraordinary. The odd sword or cauldron ending up at the bottom of a lake could certainly be seen as carelessness, but the enormous quantities of bronze disappearing underwater or under the ground in Britain and Ireland in the ninth century BC is beyond careless. Many of these objects – like the flamboyant Battersea shield dredged up from the Thames – must have been prized possessions. It's difficult to imagine how that shield might have accidentally slipped into the water before someone had a chance to grab it.

So it seems that people must have been deliberately depositing these objects, especially the ones that are buried in the ground. But what might have driven them to do that? In the end, this probably boils down to one of two reasons. If you're a late Bronze Age person burying metal in the ground, you're either hiding it from someone, or it's a ritual act, motivated by your beliefs and superstitions. If, however, you're flinging a metal object into a river, I don't think you're planning to ever recover it – so that's almost certainly ritual. Well, either that or sheer madness (or, as we've already discussed, inordinate clumsiness).

The buried hoards might have been about concealment – a way of avoiding handing valuables over to someone else. Perhaps violent raids were becoming common. Or perhaps the chieftain who always collected the tithes was on his way out. The stability of the stratified Bronze Age society must

have depended to some extent on the willingness of produ
cers and owners of bronze objects to hand them over, as a
form of tax, to chieftains. The power of the elite flowed from
their ability to accumulate and control resources – both food
and metal. Perhaps the bronze hoards are an indication that a
trend towards concentrating power in the hands of the few
was undergoing a reversal – much like the shift from centralized to decentralized power in central Europe that occurred
centuries later and perhaps led to the abandonment of
princely seats like Heuneburg.

While it's conceivable that the motivation behind the
buried hoards might have been these kinds of social and
political changes, it's still hard to imagine how the depositions
in water fit with this idea. And hoards from Brittany add
weight to the idea that this whole phenomenon could have
been driven by ritual intent. While the practice seems to have
come to an end in Britain and Ireland by 800 BC, in Brittany,
hoards continued to be buried into the eighth and seventh
centuries BC. These caches of bronze consisted of specially
made socketed axes – too full of lead and too soft to have been
usable. And there were a lot of them. Together, the Armorican
axe hoards represent some eight tonnes of copper, seven
tonnes of lead and two tonnes of tin.

Superstitions and beliefs are ephemeral things. They do
not fossilize and they can only be traced indirectly, through
evidence of ritual behaviour in the archaeological record, in
prehistory. They also have a life of their own, seizing on minds
and spreading through populations. But it may still be possible to relate the appearance of new rituals, or a change in
rituals, to shifting social patterns or structures. This apparent

crisis, with huge amounts of metal being consigned to the ground and deposited in water, surely marks a shake-up in society during the transition from Bronze Age to Iron Age in north-western Europe. And, in turn, that shake-up may have been driven by external factors.

The archaeological evidence suggests that there was a population collapse around this time, with a reduction in both the numbers of settlements and in craft production. Pollen records from Ireland show a peak in farming activity in the eleventh century BC, followed by a decrease in the ninth and into the eighth century BC. The vigorous exchange networks of the Bronze Age also seem to have been disrupted to some extent. And, further afield, this was also the time when Scythian culture expanded – pushing into eastern Asia and westwards into Europe. Archaeologists have suggested that all these changes are linked: they were caused by a global downturn in climate, leading to the failure of crops and the loss of livestock, destabilizing society. Perhaps, then, this was the ultimate cause for the appearance of so many hoards and depositions in water at the end of the Bronze Age. Starving, angry and desperate, people sought to appease their gods with offerings of hard-won metal.

In Ireland, sections of ancient oaks dug out of peat bogs seem to attest to just such a climatic downturn, with a series of narrow tree rings – relating to years of poor growth – dateable to the twelfth century BC. Separate evidence of a disruption to climate in the middle of this century comes from fine layers of ash, again preserved in peat bogs, which appear to record the eruption of an Icelandic volcano called Hekla. But this seems too early to explain the shake-up that society was experiencing in the late Bronze Age, in the early centuries of the first millennium BC.

Recent research has thrown up another problem with this climatic hypothesis. A new analysis of the environmental evidence from Irish peat bogs shows that there was indeed a rapid shift to colder and wetter conditions – but that this occurred around 750 BC. This timing is backed up by data from other sites in north-western Europe. But this time, the change in climate is too late to explain the archaeologically-attested population crash of the late Bronze Age, which took hold at least a century before this climatic deterioration. The authors of this new piece of research believe that we need to look to other factors to explain the late Bronze Age population crash. They suggest it could simply have been due to the appearance of the new metal: that the arrival of iron technology broke the Bronze Age system.

The Bronze Age elites needed to be able to control resources and the exchange of metal assets – especially the tin and copper, which could be combined to make beautiful, hard-wearing and sharp-edged bronze objects. In stark contrast to tin, in particular, iron ores were widely available across the European landscape. Could the dawn of the Iron Age itself have been a democratizing influence that spelled the end for Bronze Age social structures, wresting power from the elites and disrupting trade?

But this hypothesis is stymied by the fact that iron technology – despite the wide availability of ore – was relatively rare in north-western Europe until the sixth century BC. In addition, the exchange networks of the early Iron Age seem to have been operating robustly and, if anything, the emerging

Mediterranean civilizations were driving an increased demand for metals such as tin. Some archaeologists argue that this was the ultimate cause of the 'bronze crisis' – that the hoards somehow represent a response to the insatiable appetite of the Mediterranean for the metal wealth of Britain, Ireland and France. As the elites demanded more and more metal to feed that demand, did the relationship between producers and their rulers break down?

It seems like we're going round in circles. When a piece of new evidence emerges, we see old theories being picked out of the dustbin of history, dusted off and re-presented. Then another new bit of evidence turns up, and one theory is overturned by another. The cycle continues. And yet we keep looking for more new evidence because we believe that, eventually, it will all come together. And it might do. But, for now, I feel safest saying that we don't yet know for sure what caused the crisis, what lit the fuse, what ultimately induced people to bury or to drown their metal wealth so spectacularly at the end of the Bronze Age. But the evidence does seem to indicate a ritual activity. 'Ritual' is so often a get-out clause for archaeologists. But, here, it seems like the best explanation.

I asked archaeologist Barry Cunliffe what he thought about these Bronze Age hoards.

'Why do I throw coins in the spring in Bath whenever I go? Why do people throw things into the fountains in Rome? It's a very interesting question. I think there's a very strong belief in the chthonic deities in prehistory. If you look at the hundred or so Celtic deities, they divide into two types – there are essentially two sets of gods: one up there and one below. The chthonic ones live in the underworld, they're associated with fertility, they're usually female and they preside over place, and they're often associated with water. So, by throwing something into water, you're making an offering to the chthonic deities.

'There's an element of trying to communicate with the other world, which is similar in some ways to Jews writing messages on pieces of paper and sticking them in the wailing wall. And the Roman curses thrown into the sacred spring in Bath – that's also people trying to communicate with the deities.'

I wondered if there could possibly be any connection between the appearance of these hoards of metal objects and the absence of burials. Archaeologists had, at one time, considered the possibility that the bronze finds in rivers were all that was left after a whole body, complete with sword and shield, perhaps, had been thrown into the water. Barry Cunliffe thought this an unlikely explanation, but agreed that the deposits could still be associated with a funerary ritual.

'If we just look at Britain; at the time we're getting offerings to the gods in rivers, bodies are being excarnated or cremated. This could reflect a divide between the gods of the sky and the gods of the earth: objects are being given to the gods of the earth, and the bodies and spirits are being given to the gods of the sky. It doesn't work for every part of Britain, but it could be part of the explanation.'

There's also a possibility that the hoards and deposits fulfilled another role associated with funerals – that of conspicuous consumption. Perhaps the burial of material wealth provided an opportunity, even without the burial of a body, to display the wealth and status of the deceased. It may also have given associates of the family of the deceased a chance to offer their own gifts, thus displaying their own wealth in public, as well as securing an ongoing relationship with the family of the dead person.

Archaeologically, the presence of metal objects deposited in watery places provides evidence of connections between the communities of Atlantic Europe. Right across Iberia, both intact and broken swords, dating from the late Bronze Age, have been found – often at the bottom of rivers, just as in Britain and Ireland.

Whatever the hoards represent, it is clear that the early Iron Age in Atlantic Europe, rather than being an abrupt transition, saw the continuation of important themes that had emerged in the Bronze Age – just as the Hallstatt period in central Europe saw the development of trends that had begun in the preceding Urnfield. Although there are signs of societal instability at the end of the Bronze Age in north-western Europe, the early Iron Age saw an intensification of farming, as more land was pressed into production – and trade with the continent continued to thrive.

Those networks of exchange allowed both materials and ideas to travel large distances. In the past, it was often assumed that innovations would only ever arrive in the west from the east, often in the hands of invaders. But archaeology is revealing a different reality. It seems that it was these exchange networks – not the arrival of invading hordes of Celts from central Europe – that brought the Iron Age to western Europe. And, while the technology of ironworking itself may have spread from the eastern Mediterranean all the way to the Atlantic coast, that wasn't the only direction of travel.

The Atlantic fringes of Europe had been interlinked since the arrival of the first farmers there, around 4000 BC. Complex maritime trade networks grew up in the Neolithic and Bronze Age, binding the communities of western Europe together, and continued to function into the early Iron Age. The items being traded were not just metal ingots, but finished objects in characteristic styles, which allow archaeologists to track just how far items moved. Calling this 'trade' perhaps creates the impression that this flow of goods was purely commercial, in the modern sense. But much of that Bronze Age trade may have been in the form of the exchange of gifts, forging and honouring ties between communities. And, of course, objects could travel with their owners – a spear with a wandering warrior; a golden torc around the neck of a princess, travelling to marry into another tribe. It's also important to realize that, between the place where it was manufactured and the location in which archaeologists would finally find it, an object might have changed hands several times.

Archaeologists have found that Bronze Age Sicilian axes made their way up to Brittany and the south coast of Britain. In the thirteenth century BC, particular objects from central Europe also found their way out to south-eastern Britain – including Urnfield-type bronze swords, cauldrons and flesh hooks. But there are other examples which show that it's wrong to see Britain and Ireland as only ever in receipt of goods and ideas from the continent – there was a healthy flow of goods in both directions. Distinctive lunate spearheads from Ireland ended up in the sea near Huelva, in south-western Spain. A particular type of bronze weapon known as a Ballintober sword was probably first manufactured in south-eastern Britain, spreading from there to Ireland (where it was first discovered and named), and also across to France. Gold bar torcs – beautiful twisted neck-rings – seem to have originated in Ireland or southern England in the fourteenth century BC, but over the following two centuries they start to appear in Wales and France.

On a recent visit to the Ulster Museum in Belfast, I was lucky enough to see – and even more fortunate to be allowed to hold – one of the most impressive Bronze Age Irish gold torcs. It was discovered in a boggy field in County Fermanagh in 2009. The Corrard torc was made by hammering a gold bar to create a square cross-section, then it had been twisted along its length – the characteristic twist that gives a torc its name. Around five centimetres at each end of the bar were left untwisted, forming a slightly conical terminal. These had been folded back against the twisted bar – a typical feature of these torcs – so that they could be used as an interlocking clasp. But, curiously, the whole torc had also been been coiled into a tight spiral – too narrow even for a hand and wrist to fit through.

One suggestion, based on a torc found in north Wales, which was coiled up and apparently stored in a pot, is that torcs may have bent in this way to make them easier to trade and transport. But perhaps the torc had been bent round in this way to 'decommission' it – as it's unusable as a neck-ring in this form – before it was deposited in water as an offering to the gods. The bent torc reminded me of the Hochdorf

Prince's gold brooches, with their pins bent back on themselves to make them unwearable. Is it possible that the Corrard torc is the only surviving, visible element of a funerary ritual? This is surely an interesting suggestion – if the body of a dead person was cremated, perhaps a prized possession of that person was being 'buried' in its stead. Could the torc be a grave good without a grave? It's a possible explanation, which could extend to some of the other mysterious bronze hoards and watery depositions of the late Bronze Age in western Europe. Perhaps they represent the possessions and the material wealth of the elite dead, whose bodies were disposed of separately.

Although we'll probably never know why exactly the Corrard torc ended up in the bog, its original owner must surely have been someone powerful – and quite obviously rich. The torc weighs 720 grams and is almost pure gold – 87 per cent gold, to be exact. An object like this makes you wonder how the Bronze Age warrior elite rose to ascendancy – just how does such an unequal system get going? Somehow, the warriors were able to grow rich and powerful, probably by offering protection in exchange for a tithe paid in food and metal. Irish law tracts from some two millennia later describe a similar arrangement between protectors and producers. However it worked on the ground, it certainly did work. The stratified society, dominated by a warrior elite, continued into the Iron Age. Whatever the true nature of the crisis that marked the end of the Bronze Age, the basic structure of society seems to have changed little. Perhaps power had changed hands – but it was still possible to be powerful. The trappings of a warrior elite – including swords and cauldrons

– were still to be found in the early Iron Age. But unlike Germany – where the bodily remains of princes and princesses have been discovered under their tumuli, surrounded by sumptuous grave goods – we've never come face to face with the elite of Britain and Ireland.

This seems to come down to a fundamental difference in funerary practices. There's nothing like the Hallstatt 'princely' graves in Britain and Ireland, at least not in the early Iron Age, between 800 BC and 400 BC. Archaeologists talk about the 'disappearing dead of the Iron Age'. The easiest way to make a body disappear is to leave it exposed, to let it become stripped of flesh, and eventually even the bones will disintegrate too. This sounds like a very disrespectful way to treat a dead body, but we have to somehow step aside from the traditions of our own culture. There are contemporary cultures where exposure and excarnation is, or has been until very recently, common practice: the Zoroastrian Towers of Silence, Tibetan sky burials on mountains and Siberian sky burials on raised platforms in the Arctic taiga. So the absence of burials or interred cremations does not imply a disregard for the deceased in any way. But it certainly makes the job of the archaeologist much harder. Any information that might have been extracted from complete skeletons is lost forever. In the early Iron Age of Britain and Ireland, from around 800 BC to 450 BC, the only bodily remains of people tend to be single bones found in settlement sites. There are no grave goods, because there are no graves. Objects are found in the landscape, divorced from their owners.

Even without burials to accompany them, the metal objects found buried under fields and thrown into rivers and lakes tell us something important about British and Irish society. Long bronze swords, designed for slashing, appear in Britain from the thirteenth century BC onwards, along with bronze spearheads and round shields. As well as weapons, archaeologists find the accoutrements of feasting, and all of these objects mark a new social phenomenon which echoes changes on the continent: the emergence of a Bronze Age warrior elite.

But in the eighth and seventh centuries BC, new objects started to appear in hoards: continental-style horse harnesses and cart fittings. So, are these traded objects or hard evidence of an invasion by a horse-riding elite from the continent at the dawn of the Iron Age? For a very long time, it was thought that another type of object – a particular type of sword – also testified to a Hallstatt invasion of Britain.

Iron Age Knights and the Invasion that Never Was

In the first half of the eighth century BC, a new style of sword appeared in Britain – and, for decades, this distinctive weapon was seen to signal the arrival of a new breed of warrior into Britain: one that hailed from the Celtic heartland of central Europe.

Back in the early eighteenth century, the antiquarian Edward Lhuyd had drawn on historical and linguistic evidence to suggest that Britain and Ireland had been settled in antiquity by two waves of invading Celts from the continent. These invaders brought the Celtic language with them, but there was a difference in the language of the second wave: the consonant *q* was replaced with *p*. Archaeologists enthusiastically embraced Lhuyd's model, and talked about invading 'Q-Kelts', or Goidels, and 'P-Kelts', or Brythons. Both branches of the language family persisted, with Goidelic as the linguistic ancestor of the Gaelic languages – Irish, Scottish Gaelic and Manx – and Brythonic (or Brittonic) as the ancestor of the Welsh, Cornish and Breton languages.

By the end of the nineteenth century, this idea of two waves of invading Celts had taken root, and archaeological discoveries in central Europe provided these invaders with a cultural identity. The first wave of Goidelic Celts was thought to have arrived in Britain in the eighth century BC, bringing their continental Hallstatt culture with them. In the early twentieth century, some archaeologists were expressing disquiet about this hypothesis, pointing out that changes in language often can happen without the migration of people themselves, that the arrival of the Celtic language in Britain and Ireland was essentially undatable, and that the absence of any pottery in a Hallstatt style in Ireland weighed strongly against the presence of Hallstatt people there.

And yet British archaeologists seemed to cling to this idea of invasion as a civilizing influence on the barbarian inhabitants of Britain and Ireland. In the mid sixties, the prehistoric archaeologist Grahame Clarke wrote that scholars had suffered from 'a form of invasion neurosis', which compelled them to ascribe every single cultural or technological development to outside influences. He argued that hypothetical invasions had somehow become more 'real' than the archaeological evidence itself. And the invasion neurosis reaches its apotheosis when it came to Iron Age Britain.

Three cultural phases were recognized and each one asso-ciated with a new invasion: a Hallstatt invasion in the eighth century BC, a Marnian invasion from France in the fifth century BC and a Belgic invasion from Belgium in the first century BC. Grahame Clark was sceptical about these inva-sions. Why would Hallstatt invaders, coming from the con-tinent, where they built rectangular houses, suddenly start building roundhouses like the natives as soon as they set foot in Britain? Why would they use weaving combs and ring-headed pins that looked just like the ones the British had made and used in the Bronze Age?

Rather than invasion, Clark suggested, it could be that we're seeing a familiar pattern: the elite were engaging in conspicuous consumption, including adopting exotic styles. And this then explains why we see all these beautiful, continental-style bronze cauldrons and buckets, horse trap-pings, jewellery and weapons appearing in Britain and Ireland in the eighth and seventh centuries BC. Ornate, foreign-look-ing objects are more likely to be a signal, not of an invading aristocracy, but of the increasing wealth of the native elite. Indeed, prestige items that seem most exotic in style are often, on closer inspection, locally made objects that combine native features with continental fashions.

And yet the invasion hypothesis did not die. The idea that Britain was invaded at the end of the Bronze Age by a horde of Hallstatt knights still gripped the popular and academic imagination. And one particular type of weapon was held up as the ultimate proof of this idea. The Gundlingen sword – a long, leaf-shaped sword, which was carried in a scabbard tipped with a very characteristic bronze chape – was typical of the early Hallstatt period in central Europe. Projecting wings on the chape might have been a useful feature for a horse-riding knight – allowing him to catch the end of the scabbard with his foot, making it easier to draw his sword. These Gundlingen swords were found in Germany and France, and, in the early eighth century BC, they started to appear in Britain too. The Hallstatt knights had clearly arrived.

But recent research turns this idea on its head. Combining a careful analysis of sword styles with, where possible, dendrochronological dates, it seems that the Gundlingen sword type actually originated in Britain. This remarkable theory suggests that the Gundlingen design was based on a sword type that was common in the Thames Valley, and known as a 'Thames sword'. These long, bronze swords had spread eastwards to the continent, evolving into the Gundlingen type, and later being made out of iron rather than bronze. In the well-connected world of Bronze and Iron Age Europe, with its complex exchange networks, we can now imagine ideas travelling and spreading without needing to invoke mass migrations of people. Influences can arrive in the absence of invaders, and innovations don't just appear and spread – *ex oriente lux* – from east to west. Indeed – as we see with the torcs and these swords – sometimes the light comes from the west.

Barry Cunliffe, Emeritus Professor of European Archaeology at the University of Oxford, has spent decades digging down into the Iron Age and trying to understand the emergence of what we recognize, archaeologically, as Celtic culture. He was always dubious about the persistent idea that the Celts and their culture had arrived in Britain and Ireland in a wave from the continent. The archaeological evidence, to his eyes, never seemed to support such a notion. Instead, he saw culture evolving where links between different places were strong, where ideas could flow easily.

Barry Cunliffe has written extensively about the strong maritime links between Ireland and Britain and the continent – particularly the parts of the continent facing our islands: northern France and the Low Countries. The archaeological evidence implies that social bonds and obligations were being created and maintained through gifts of prestigious items, including horse gear and weaponry, and it's likely that strategic marriages also helped to reinforce ties between tribes on each side of the North Sea. These connections grew out of links that had been forged in the Bronze Age, and perhaps had even deeper roots, going right back into the Neolithic.

It's a fresh view, informed by a more objective approach to the archaeology itself. We see Britain and Ireland intimately connected with the continent by bonds of kinship, flourishing networks of exchange, and shared behaviour and culture. Rather than an obsession with mass migrations, it focuses on people's mobility. We can imagine our ancestors travelling to trade, to marry, and coming together for feasting and festivals. According to this theory, the Iron Age in western Europe developed in the context of those maritime networks, which fits the evidence much better than the old idea of Celtic invasions.

Moving on into the fifth and fourth centuries BC, the close contact between the coastal communities of north-west Europe continued and was expressed through similarities in

The 'Giant's Castle' – the Heuneburg hill fort looming over the upper reaches of the Danube in southwest Germany

Artist's impression of the Celtic city of Heuneburg in 600 BC
© Kenny Arne Lang Antonsen and Jimmy Antonsen

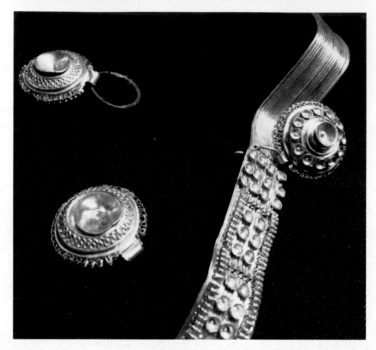

The gold jewellery found in the grave of the Bettelbühl Princess and the associated child's grave signifies the high status of these individuals in Celtic society. Above right: the earring found with the Bettelbühl Princess, consisting of a strip of gold with a dangling gold bead. Above left: gold bead earrings found in the child's grave. Below: the large gold fibula belonging to the Bettelbühl Princess and a smaller version found in the child's grave

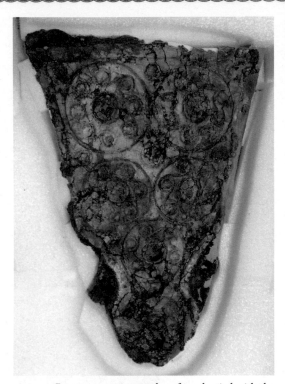

△ Bronze pony cap, or chamfron, buried with the Bettelbühl Princess, showing the importance of horses and horse-riding to the Iron Age elite

◁ La Tène sword found at Bucheres in France

▽ La Tène sword scabbard found near Lake Neuchâtel, Switzerland, showing characteristic swirling patterns and animal motifs of La Tène art

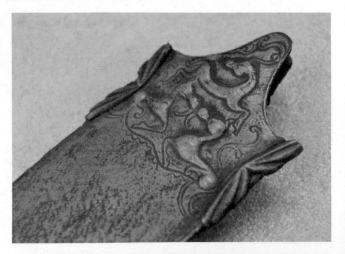

Some of the torcs and torc fragments from the Snettisham Hoard – discovered in 1948 it remains the largest collection of Celtic torcs ever found in Europe

The Great Torc of Snettisham reveals the skill and artistry of British Iron Age goldsmiths

pottery types – particularly between eastern Kent and Belgium and north-east France. These pots, including plain and painted vessels, were not prestigious objects, like the swords and horse trappings. They were the trappings of everyday existence. They epitomize the flow of objects and ideas that were relevant to the culture and identity of ordinary people, and not just to the elite that held the power in that society.

But around this time, in the middle of the first millennium BC, a new influence began to emerge. There was a significant change in the style of the prestigious items that made their way into Britain and Ireland. This new art style had its origins in central Europe, where the Hallstatt culture had morphed into something new, something different. The arrival of the new style in Britain prompted British archaeologists in the early twentieth century to invoke yet another Iron Age invasion: the 'Marnian'.

But, once again, a dispassionate approach to the archaeological evidence suggests that this new style arrived via those well-established networks of exchange. Once it reached Britain and Ireland, designs were copied and elaborated on by local artisans, producing an extraordinary flourishing of art. Although there are many different styles of art produced through the centuries, across the Celtic world, it is this particular style that is often thought of as 'Celtic art'. That designation is perhaps unhelpful, creating a narrow focus which means we miss the true variety of Iron Age art across a significant swathe of Europe. But, on the other hand, this style of art is so beautiful, complex and attractive that it's not surprising it caught on so readily across central and north-western Europe in the later Iron Age, nor that it captures our attention today. The style is named after the site where it was first identified, on the continent: La Tène.

The New Wave

In 1857, just eleven years after Ramsauer began excavating the early Iron Age cemetery near his salt mine at Hallstatt, metal objects began to turn up in the shallows near the north-eastern shore of Lake Neuchâtel, in Switzerland. A drought had led to a significant drop in the level of the lake, and antiquarians Friedrich Schwab and Edouard Desor began to pay the fishermen to dredge out objects near the shore, for their collections.

In 1879, the lake level was lowered even further as part of river management in the area, and evidence of prehistoric villages – together with two bridges – appeared. The site became known as La Tène ('the shallows' in French). Sadly, many finds disappeared into the hands of private collectors at this time, but more formal excavations were carried out in the first decade of the twentieth century.

The archaeology represented a sequence from the Neolithic, Copper Age, Bronze Age, through to the Iron Age. Eventually, more than 2,500 objects were recovered from the exposed lakebed. The waterlogged conditions of the site had preserved wooden bowls, yokes, wheels, leather, ropes, nets and baskets. But most of the objects were metal, and, of those, around sixty per cent were weapons or associated artefacts. It has been suggested that iron swords were being thrown into the water, perhaps as offerings to the gods, from the bridges of La Tène. But modern scholars are now returning to one of the original interpretations of the site: that it was a cult centre of some military significance. They suggest that the wooden piles, driven into the lakebed, represent the remains of a trophaeum, built over the water, where the weapons and possibly even the mutilated bodies of enemies were displayed – eventually falling into the river.

Dating of the site suggests that the first bridge, known as Pont Desor, after the antiquarian, Edouard Desor, was erected around 650 BC. But the Iron Age weaponry, which seems to suggest the existence of a cult site, comes later – around the middle of the third century BC. Dendro-chronological analysis carried out on a timber from the later of the La Tène bridges, known as Pont Vouga, and on a wooden shield has yielded dates of around 250 BC and 225 BC respectively. The site is right in the heart of the Swiss plateau, the territory of the Celtic Helvetii tribe, first mentioned by Posidonius at the end of the second century BC. Many of the metal objects from La Tène were decorated with characteristic swirling patterns. And it's this La Tène style, so different to the art of the preceding Hallstatt period, which has become synonymous with 'Celtic art'.

Other sites, such as the spectacular grave of the Glauberg warrior from west-central Germany, show that the La Tène culture emerged in the mid-fifth century BC, and it seems there was a distinct shift in power at this time. The Hallstatt hill forts like Heuneburg were abandoned, and the character-istic elite burials close to them, like Hochdorf and Bettelbühl, came to an end. Instead, power seems to have shifted to the north, where aristocratic high status burials started to appear in Marne, Moselle and Bohemia. These burials emphasized the elite status of the warrior – something which had not seemed so important in the Hallstatt societies of central Europe. But there is also evidence of continuity with that preceding Celtic culture: funerary carts (though now two-wheeled rather than four-wheeled) and drinking equipment were often included in elite La Tène burials.

Links with Etruria also remained important; the richly furnished fifth-century graves in the Moselle valley were stuffed full of Etruscan amphorae, flagons and bowls. And it seems that it was these Mediterranean objects that somehow provided the inspiration for the La Tène artists. Etruscan flagons often had animal-shaped handles, together with other animal decorations, and sometimes small human heads. Greek bowls and cups were decorated with plant designs – palmettes and lotus buds. The Celtic metalworkers of the fifth century took these ideas and transmuted them, giving them an almost dream-like quality. Plant forms curled into abstract tendrils while animals and human heads became stretched and abstracted, sometimes melting away into organic twirls. Human faces might have been hidden in patterns, only recognizable from one angle. It's been suggested that this art reflects the theme of shape-shifting, which appears so often in Celtic mythology.

It wasn't long before the new style started to appear in Britain and Ireland. With those well-established exchange networks linking Britain to France, it's not at all surprising that the new style taking off in Marne, one of the centres of La Tène innovation, was to spread across the sea – without the need for a 'Marnian invasion'.

The earliest La Tène artefacts from Britain are two bronze scabbards, which appear to be locally made but inspired by new continental designs. One of these, the Minster Ditch dagger, from North Hinksey, near Oxford, dates from the mid-fourth century BC and is an iron dagger with a bronze scabbard decorated with zigzags, rings and dots, and with an elaborate, lyre-shaped chape. The Wisbech scabbard, from Cambridgeshire, dates to around 300 BC, and is decorated with a symmetrical pattern of swirling, S-shaped scrolls.

South-west of Marne, there was another important La Tène centre at Bourges, connected to Armorica and Atlantic trade routes via the Loire River. In Brittany, pottery of the fifth century bears witness to the influence of La Tène – it looks very much as though potters were adopting motifs they had seen on imported metalwork to beautify their vessels with stamped designs. Over in Ireland, it seems that Iron Age metalworkers of the first and second centuries BC were getting their inspiration from British La Tène objects, such as scabbards, as well as directly from the continent, probably via the western seaways connecting Ireland directly with Armorica and the more southerly west coast of France.

But, in north-east England, there's archaeological evidence of what may have been – if not an invasion, as such – a localized influx of people coming across from the continent. The evidence takes the form of unusual graves, found in Yorkshire – elite burials accompanied by weapons and chariots. The first of these graves was discovered in the nineteenth century on a Yorkshire farm, which gave its name to this 'Arras' culture. The famous Wetwang chariot burials, found in 2001 and dating to around 300 BC, belong to the same culture.

These burials have been interpreted by some as representing an invasion of La Tène warriors. But, once again, although there are similarities with continental practices, there are also important differences. On the continent, bodies were laid out straight in the grave; in Yorkshire, the body was placed in a crouched position. On the continent, whole chariots were buried; in Yorkshire, the vehicles were dismantled before being consigned to the grave. And while the weapons in the Yorkshire graves were La Tène in style, they were British made. Some scholars have suggested that the British were simply copying a continental funerary custom. Others have proposed that a small influx of people from the continent could have been assimilated into the local population, and that this accounts for the blending of continental and British customs.

British and Irish artisans seem to have enjoyed developing the new styles arriving from the continent. Far from blindly copying them, they took the new motifs and forms and made them their own, and the style reaches its apogee on metalwork, including swords, shields, scabbards, mirrors, brooches and torcs. There is no way you can look at the British and Irish artwork as a barbaric imitation of a style emanating from a superior civilization. The La Tène artefacts from Britain and Ireland are astonishing works of art in their own right, combining consummate skill and ingenuity in metalworking with aesthetic prowess. One of the most stunning examples of British La Tène art comes from a field near Snettisham, in Norfolk, where a great mass of Celtic treasure was found buried. The whole collection is impressive, but there's one piece that really stands out: an Iron Age masterpiece known as the Great Torc. A twisted gold neck-ring ending with wonderfully ornate terminals, it's one of the most magnificent pieces of jewellery from the Celtic world.

The first pieces of the Snettisham treasure were turned up in 1948, by a farmer ploughing his field. He came across what he thought were just parts of an old brass bedstead, and he tossed them aside. Fortunately, a passer-by noticed the gold and took it to an archaeologist friend who recognized the pieces as parts of a hollow torc. Then, a couple of years later, the plough dragged up the Great Torc itself. In 1990, the British Museum decided to investigate. They excavated an area of more than two hectares, finding hoard after hoard. The amount of metalwork recovered from that field in Norfolk really is astonishing. Buried across some fourteen separate hoards were hundreds of coins, over a hundred metal ingots, several bracelets – and around 175 torcs and fragments of torcs: neck-rings made of gold, silver and bronze. The sheer number and variety of the torcs from the Snettisham hoards exceeds that found in any other Iron Age locality, not just in Britain, but in Europe.

There were very few signs of any other human activity in the vicinity of the hoards – no settlement, no burials; only what seemed to be an unprepossessing ditch. Archaeologists have tentatively suggested that this ditch marked out an enclosure, perhaps a sacred grove, in which the hoards were buried as ritual offerings. Even if this idea of a sacred grove is stretching it a bit, there certainly seems to be something weird about so many hoards – so much metal – having been buried in an otherwise unremarkable place.

Today, the Snettisham Hoard is kept at the British Museum, where I was able to look at some of it, liberated from the glass cases where the treasure is usually kept on display. On a table in front of me, deep in the basement of the museum, lay five almost complete torcs and several fragments. The colour of the torcs varied quite widely – from a bright, brassy gold, to reddish gold, to silver. In fact, none of them was actually pure gold. They were all alloys of gold, silver and copper, in various proportions. These alloys had been deliberately created to achieve certain properties – to make the metal easier to work, but also to give a particular colour. Mixing gold with copper and silver in specific proportions can create an alloy that has a melting point considerably lower than any of its three components. Pure gold melts at around 1,063 °C, copper at 1,084 °C and silver at 962 °C. Mixing them together, there's a certain balance of the metals that hits a eutectic sweet spot, bringing the melting point of the alloy down to as low as 788 °C.

The fact that the Iron Age goldsmiths mixed their metals deliberately like this, and probably melted down and recycled old metalwork as well, creates a problem for the archaeologists. It makes it impossible to track down the original source of the gold by looking for characteristic levels of impurities. But it seems likely that a lot of British Iron Age gold came from the continent. Indigenous gold mining had practically ceased during the Iron Age. Bronze Age Britons had been mining gold, but then there was a hiatus until the Roman period, when gold mining, especially in Wales, took off again.

The drop-off in demand for indigenous gold is curious. Was there simply enough coming in from the continent to remove any need to mine it locally? Perhaps the drive to accumulate gold in order to demonstrate wealth and power was less important in the British Iron Age than it had been in the Bronze Age. Perhaps powerful individuals were expressing their status more through their potential to bring together large numbers of people to create monumental hill forts. Nevertheless, there was still a need for some luxury gold items, as the Snettisham Hoard itself reveals. It's not known for certain where all the torcs from that Norfolk field were made, and there's no evidence of metalworking anywhere near Snettisham. But many of the neck-rings are distinctly British in style – including the Great Torc itself. And a couple of very similar torcs have been found else-where in East Anglia, making it more likely that they were all made locally.

I examined the torcs closely, trying to understand how they had been made. The selection in front of me ranged from a very simple gold torc to the magnificently ornate Great Torc. I could easily see how the simplest torc had been constructed: a thick rod of gold wire had been closed into a loop and twisted to form a double spiral, ending in a loop at each end, and then bent in a C-shape to fit around a neck. It's the twist along their length, rather than the overall curve of these neck-rings that gives them their name. There were a couple of torcs where the basic technique had been doubled up, with two double-helix strands twisted together. And another torc was made of three such twists, wound around each other, but leaving a hollow centre. The twisted strands of this silvery torc lay so neatly against each other that they looked like chainmail.

This technique was pushed to an extreme in the exquisite Great Torc. This incredibly ornate neck-ring is made of eight ropes of gold, twisted together, and each of those ropes consists of eight thick golden wires, spiralling round. But it was the symmetrical ends, or terminals, of this torc that really blew me away. Each of them had been cast on to the gold rope using a lost technique, with even finer details added after casting. Each terminal was, in its own right, an exquisite work of art – raised arcs of gold swept across the surface and a line of stamped dots sat behind each of these embossed arcs. Some of the spaces outlined by the arcs were filled with a hatched texture, but the goldsmith had resisted the temptation to cover every inch of the surface with pattern; other spaces had been left empty and smooth. This type of design, with flowing curves and a careful balance between dense decoration and empty space, epitomizes the British La Tène style. But, while the Great Torc is certainly British, it was clearly influenced by foreign designs. I was reminded of some of the wonderful German La Tène bronzes I'd seen – there were clear echoes of that continental style here, in this magnificent torc from Iron Age Norfolk. But this was no pastiche; the ancient British goldsmith, a master at his craft, had taken that originally continental style and given it a distinct local twist, making something truly beautiful – something that would still be marvelled at over 2,000 years later.

Looking at the Snettisham Great Torc, you do wonder if it was actually designed to be worn. It seems so big and heavy, and the gap between the two bulbous terminals is far too narrow to slide it easily on to any adult's neck. But the torc is not solid gold. The centre of each eight-stranded rope is hollow. They were probably made by wrapping the eight gold wires around something like a slender hazel twig. Fragments of charcoal have been found inside other torcs, providing a clue to this technique. There's also a hollow space between all the eight-stranded ropes as they spiral round, in the centre of the torc. So the whole thing is lighter than you'd expect – although it's still a hefty kilogram of gold – and it's flexible enough to twist the terminals apart in order to place it around a neck.

I wasn't about to try twisting the Great Torc, even less to attempt to wear it. The curators at the British Museum would, I was quite sure, take quite a dim view of that. But the Great Torc has, apparently, been tested for wearability in modern times. Soon after its discovery in 1950, it was taken to Sandringham for King George VI to take a look at. He asked to whom the treasure belonged, and was told that, as treasure trove, it was the Crown's – it effectively belonged to him. And, with that, so legend has it, the King picked up the Great Torc – and put it on.

There were several torcs in the Snettisham Hoard that had been repaired – badly repaired, it's fair to say. There was one where a terminal had clearly fallen off, and it had been crudely tied back on with gold wire. Another had broken at the back – presumably from having been twisted open too many times to place it on a neck. This one had a piece of gold foil wrapped around it, and had been fixed with gold wire too. One of the terminals must have come loose as well – it was tied on to the twisted strands of the neck-ring with some lead wire. The terminals of this repaired torc were beautiful, and contained half-hidden details, including a feature that looked like a human face, with spirals for eyes and a lozenge for a nose. Next to that face, perhaps being devoured by it, was a smaller face-like motif. If this was the only example of face-like designs in La Tène art, you might be tempted to say that the similarity was merely coincidental, and that we're just predisposed to seeing faces in patterns, whether you're looking at clouds or the terminal of a torc. But other La Tène art has more obvious faces and animals embedded in it. Art historian Paul Jacobsthal has nicknamed this sort of La Tène design 'Cheshire Cat Style' – a face peers through plant-like tendrils, or sometimes it's just part of the face that appears, like the Cheshire cat's grin.

Apart from its curious (or even curiouser) terminals, this broken torc was interesting precisely because it wasn't intact. It showed signs of use, of having been worn – in fact, worn many times. Other evidence for the wearing of torcs comes from literature and art. Warriors and gods are described or depicted wearing torcs, which are interpreted as symbols of power. On the Gundestrup cauldron – a beautiful silver vessel, dating from the third century BC, found in a bog in Jutland, in 1891 – a seated god holds a torc in one hand, but he also wears one round his neck. In 361 BC, a certain officer in the Roman army, called Titus Manlius, was involved in a battle against the Gauls. He took on a Celtic chieftain in single combat. This chieftain is described as going into battle stark naked, except for his shield, two swords, armbands and his torc. Titus Manlius killed his opponent and took the Celt's torc for himself, gaining the epithet 'Torquatus'. And, some 400 years later, Boudica, Queen of the Iceni, was described as riding into battle wearing a cloak and a gold torc.

Indeed, there is even a theory that the Snettisham torcs might represent the crown jewels of the Iceni, the Celtic tribe whose territory included modern-day Norfolk. But the metalwork is too early to be associated with Boudica herself, the famous Celtic queen who led the British rebellion against the Romans in 60 AD. A date of around 70 BC, from the Gallo-Belgic coins which form part of the Snettisham Hoard, suggests that the hoard is even too early to have been buried in response to Julius Caesar's first invasion of Britain, in 55 BC. We have to accept it's most likely that we'll never know who owned and wore the Snettisham torcs – they were found in hoards, not in graves. But they surely belonged to Celtic royalty – possibly Iceni royalty – and were probably worn by both kings and queens. When Boudica is described as wearing a torc, there's no suggestion that it was unusual for a woman to wear such a symbol of power. And torcs from graves on the continent have been found in association with both male and female human remains.

The Snettisham torcs have yet more secrets to reveal, though. Using a state-of-the-art electron microscope, metallurgists have detected evidence of mercury or fire-gilding on one of the torc fragments. The bronze rod used to make the torc would have been covered with a slurry of mercury and powdered gold, and then heated until the mercury had been driven off, leaving the rod coated in a skin of gold. This was a completely different method of gilding from the way in which the Hochdorf Prince's dagger and belt had been gilded in preparation for the grave. There, fine sheets of gold had been applied to the bronze artefacts. The technique of mercury gilding is extremely sophisticated, but it's unlikely to have been a local invention. With no source of mercury in Britain, both the metal and, presumably, the idea of using it in this way must have come from somewhere else.

Fire-gilding seems to have been invented around the middle of the first millennium BC, and was a relatively common technique in the Mediterranean world by the third century BC. It's possible that the technology and the mercury came to Britain from Spain, along those well-used Atlantic seaways. There are late Iron Age Spanish torcs, which – though very different in style from the British ones I was looking at – are gilded in the same way. There were also sources of cinnabar, the bright red mercury ore, in Iberia.

Once again, we're reminded that Britain was far from being a backwater. The Celts here were culturally and technologically linked to their neighbours on the continent, especially to other Iron Age societies in western Europe – in Belgium, France and Spain. They were part of a much wider community, linked by sea trade, on this Atlantic fringe of Europe – and had been throughout the Bronze Age, and even further back, into the Neolithic.

Hill Forts, Husbandry and Hostility

The new interpretation of the Iron Age of Britain and Ireland, describing exchange networks and the flow of ideas between these islands and the continent, seems like a much more satisfactory, mature approach to the evidence than the old invasion hypothesis. But we shouldn't imagine all these communities on the Atlantic fringe of Europe living in a Golden Age of complete harmony and never coming to blows. The prestige attached to warrior status itself suggests that life was not always peaceful and serene.

Around the third century BC, the hill forts of southern Britain were strengthened. Ditches were dug even deeper and ramparts piled higher. Some hill forts, like Maiden Castle, were surrounded with multiple lines of defence, rippling out around their peripheries. Many of these British hill forts had originally grown up in the early Iron Age, around the same time as the Hallstatt hill forts were being constructed on the continent. But the British ones are thought to have been very different in purpose, at least to begin with.

The early Iron Age in Britain saw an intensification of agriculture and a proliferation of farmsteads. At the heart of many of these were impressive roundhouses, some up to fifteen metres in diameter. And then, mainly in southern Britain, but extending up into eastern Scotland, there's evidence of hilltop enclosures, circumscribed by a bank and ditch. In fact, these appear not to be forts at all, but corrals for livestock. Barry Cunliffe suggests that these may have formed important gathering places for communities – coming together, perhaps on an annual basis, to exchange or cull animals, and to feast and celebrate. Like an early Iron Age precursor of the Bath and West Show.

But, between around 600 BC and 400 BC, the landscape changed, and more regional differences started to appear. In the west of Scotland, and in Wales and Cornwall, well-defended homesteads prevailed, suggesting that cattle raiding may have been an enduring problem for these pastoral communities. In Scotland, some of these defended homesteads took the form of stone-built wheelhouses and circular towers known as brochs. The tallest surviving one – over thirteen metres high – is the formidable Mousa Broch on Shetland.

In the east of England, there are also plenty of farmsteads – some enclosed, some not. But in a swathe from the south coast of England, through the borders of Wales and then again in eastern Scotland, hill forts dominate the landscape. Up until around 400 BC, in the early Iron Age, these don't seem to have functioned as mini-citadels like the hill forts of the Hallstatt zone. While some – like Maiden Castle – show signs of permanent occupation, others don't appear to have been lived in. Nevertheless, they were certainly impressive structures – designed to create impact, much as Heuneburg was. And yet the British hill forts are interpreted as expressions of communal effort and community cohesion, rather than representing the possibly megalomaniacal ambitions of singularly powerful individuals or families.

Recent excavations at Burrough hill fort, near Melton Mowbray, in Leicestershire, have revealed evidence of metalwork and craftwork up on the hill, as well as 200 storage pits for grain. It's clear that this hill fort was well used in times of peace. It probably acted as a hub for the community – for farmers, whose own homesteads were scattered across the landscape. At the hill fort, people could meet, trade and acquire the iron tools that had become essential for farming. Iron-tipped ards made ploughing more effective, while the rotary quern, sometimes held in place by an iron bar, made grinding grain more efficient.

Agricultural improvements in the Iron Age made it possible for communities of farmers to generate a grain surplus – a source of wealth and power, as well as the food to fuel population growth. It's estimated that, by the end of the Iron Age, the British population had reached over a million. The booming population led to growing tensions that would see the defensive role of hill forts coming to the fore. Over time, the pattern of hill forts in use changed: some hill forts were abandoned, while others grew in importance.

The archaeology reflects a political landscape in flux, with shifting centres of power. From the third century BC, many of the hill forts got facelifts. The reconstruction of their perimeter defences strongly suggests that they were being used as fortresses – easily defendable strongholds that would come into their own when hostility broke out. Archaeologists interpret this as meaning that warfare – not just cattle raiding – was becoming endemic. And there are signs that some of these forts were involved in battles, including evidence of burning, collections of sling-stones ready to fire at attackers, and human bones bearing cut-marks from weapons. One particular hill fort, Bury Hill, in Hampshire, yielded great quantities of horse trappings and chariot fittings, leading archaeologists to suggest that its occupants were specializing in chariot warfare – something that was noted by Julius Caesar two centuries later when he described the use of battle chariots by the British in his *Bellum Gallicum* ('The Gallic War').

As always, it's important not to assume that life was homogeneous – and, in this case, homogeneously violent – in all places, all of the time. In the summer of 2015, the latest phase of excavations at an Iron Age site near the village of Winterbourne Kingston in Dorset revealed a large, undefended settlement on low-lying ground. The settlement, dating to around 100 BC, includes about 200 roundhouses – making it large enough to be called a town. Sitting squarely in the territory of the Durotriges tribe, this Iron Age town has been nicknamed 'Duropolis'. The site is not only Britain's oldest town, it challenges the idea that everyone in the later Iron Age was holed up in well-defended hill forts – like the magnificent Maiden Castle in Dorset. The people living and farming around Duropolis, in such an unprotected settlement, can't possibly have been living under constant threat of raids or warfare.

The hill forts, so prominent in the landscape, have perhaps drawn more than their fair share of archaeological attention, and maybe there are many more 'Duropolises' lying, as yet undiscovered, under our fields. Nevertheless, despite that peaceful oasis in the rolling hills of Dorset, if we take the rest of the available evidence at face value, the general picture across Britain does seem to be one of increasing tension, and increasing violence, in the later Iron Age.

Archaeology, then, presents us with a picture of the later centuries of the Iron Age in Britain and Ireland, where skilled metalworkers were producing their own interpretations of continental La Tène art, where connections with the continent remained important and where there's no need to invoke invasions to explain the evolution of culture. But, while there's no evidence of an invasion, there are signs of increasing tension in Celtic society. Perhaps due to population expansion and competition for resources, it seems that tribes and regions were increasingly coming into conflict. In Britain and Ireland – as far as we know, with no historical record to enlighten us – this warfare seems to have been contained within the coasts of these islands. On the continent, though, it was a different story. The Celtic populations north of the Alps were expanding and looking to colonize new territory. At the same time, new superpowers were emerging in the south. Conflict was looming, the age of the warrior king had arrived and the Celts were about to march into the pages of Roman history.

CLASHING
WITH EMPIRE

IRON AGE GEOPOLITICS –
CELTS ON THE MOVE

The Battle of the Allia and the Migration that Probably Was

> The Romans looked out from their vantage point up on the citadel and saw Rome overrun with enemies, swarming through the streets. They couldn't keep track of what was happening, as one quarter of the city after another went up in flames. It was an assault on the eyes and ears. They could hear the battle cries of the enemy, the terrible shrieks of women and children, the roar of the flames and the crash of buildings collapsing in the inferno. They could do nothing but watch and listen. It was as though the gods had put them there – to be witnesses to the fall of Rome.
>
> Livy, *History of Rome*

In 390 BC, an army of Celts from north of the Alps defeated the Romans beside the Allia Brook, a tributary of the Tiber, close to Rome. The next day, the Celts walked into Rome itself.

The Battle of the Allia and the Celts' ransacking of Rome was described in detail by the Roman historian Titus Livius Patavinus, better known as Livy, writing in the late first

129

century BC. After defeating the Roman army, we are told, the Celts waited until the following day to enter the city. In the intervening hours, many citizens fled from their homes. Some men of military age stayed behind to defend its core, withdrawing to the Citadel and the Capitol with their wives and children. But there was limited space up on the hill, and the old men resigned themselves to staying down in the city itself, to face the Celts and their own fates. These elderly men went back to their own homes. Those among them who were high-ranking officials put on their robes of state and sat in ivory chairs in front of their houses, waiting.

The Celts walked into Rome with no opposition. They had already beaten the Roman army. They found themselves entering what seemed to be a ghost town, although there were signs that the Citadel had been prepared for war. In the neighbourhood of the Forum, they came across the elders of Rome, sitting in front of their mansions. The patricians sat waiting, in their splendid regalia, still as statues.

A Celtic warrior reached out to touch the beard of one of these old men of Rome. The Roman suddenly sprang into life – he struck the Celt on the head with his ivory staff. And he paid for this attack with his life. Then the Celts were off – slaughtering the patricians in their chairs, ransacking the city and setting it on fire. The Romans holed up in the Citadel watched helplessly as their city was reduced to ashes and ruins.

After several days dedicated to wrecking and burning the city, the Celts switched their focus to the Citadel. But the Romans at the top of the hill were ready, and had the advantage of a steep-sided stronghold. Whenever the Celts attempted to climb up, Roman defenders would charge down the hill to thwart them. And so the Celts prepared for a battle of attrition, sending some of their number into the countryside to source provisions.

And this is where the story takes a turn. We glimpse the Celts through the eyes of Romans. In Livy's *History Of Rome*, the exiled commander, Camillus, describes the imminent arrival of the Celtic army at Ardea, some twenty miles south of Rome, on the scrounge for food to support the troops laying siege to Rome. Camillus is reported as saying, 'Those who are coming here in loose and disorderly fashion are a race to whom nature has given bodies and minds distinguished by bulk rather than by resolution and endurance.' He tells the inhabitants of Ardea that the Celts have given up trying to attack the Citadel and Capitol because it's just too difficult. Faced with a formidable enemy, the Roman stereotype of the Celts, as disorderly and drunken barbarians, becomes a source of hope. Camillus says that the Celts tend to gorge on food and wine and then go to sleep anywhere, with no real thought about protecting themselves at night. And so Camillus ends up leading a small army from Ardea, and they creep out of the city in the dead of night, find the Celts' camp, unprotected, just as Camillus has predicted, and they slaughter the warriors where they lie.

Meanwhile, in Rome, the Celts were attempting another attack on the Citadel and Capitol. One night, a group of warriors managed to scale the steep sides of the hill, but frightened a flock of geese at the top and the clamour roused the Romans in their garrison. One Roman soldier, Manlius, barged a Celt with his shield, sending him down the slope, then set to slaying other Celts who were clinging to the rocky precipice.

After that, the siege dragged on. Both sides were suffering from famine, and disease spread through the ranks of the Celts camped out in the ruins of Rome. The Celtic dead were piled in great heaps and burned. But the army of the Capitol was facing starvation. Eventually, a Roman tribune from the Capitol came down to meet the Celtic chieftain, whom Livy names as Brennus, and a settlement was reached: the Romans would pay the Celts a ransom of 1,000 pounds of gold for the release of their city.

But at that moment, Camillus – now recognized as the leader, the 'Dictator', of the Romans in this 'state of emergency' – marched on Rome and demanded the return of the gold and the withdrawal of the Celts. A battle ensued in which the Celts were routed. Camillus was lauded as a hero and saviour of Rome. He ordered the temples of the city to be restored and purified, and he celebrated the victory by establishing the Capitoline Games. But Camillus also became aware that Roman officials were encouraging the citizens to leave their burned and ruined city, to go and settle in Veii, ten miles to the north of Rome. This wealthy Etruscan city, right on the southern border of Etruria, had been at war with Rome for some 300 years, but the Romans had finally captured it in 396 BC – just six years before fighting the Celts at the Battle of the Allia. And the general leading that victory for the Romans had been Camillus himself. It's easy to see how it would have been very tempting for Roman citizens to go and settle in this now safely Roman and nearby city, rather than staying in Rome for what would be a mammoth rebuilding project. But Camillus, who had delivered Veii into Roman hands, was firmly opposed to his compatriots upping sticks and moving north.

He addressed the citizens of Rome and entreated them not to abandon their burned and ruined city – not to abandon the Capitol, the seat of Jupiter Optimus Maximus, indeed, which had been preserved throughout the Celts' siege. Camillus appealed to his fellow Romans' religious convictions and argued that the sacred rites associated with Jupiter and Vesta could not be properly performed anywhere else. But it's clear that he was also very concerned about the message that deserting the city would send to the wider world. Having been soundly beaten by the Celts on the banks of the Allia, abandoning the city would signal a more complete defeat: the end of mighty Rome. Camillus even warned that, if the Romans were to abandon their city, there would be nothing to stop the Celts coming back and taking it for themselves. 'Are you prepared to allow this crime and endure this disgrace because of the trouble of building?' he asked his fellow citizens.

Camillus' speech had an impact, but it needed something more for the senators and people of Rome to finally decide to stay put. While the senators were discussing the proposed migration, a cohort of soldiers returning from guard duty marched into the Forum. The centurion called a halt, and ordered the standard bearer to plant his flag. The senators rushed out and pronounced this to be a good omen, and the work of rebuilding Rome finally began.

The Celts seem to have returned home after the Battle of the Allia, 1,000 pounds of gold richer. The whole enterprise appears to have been more of a raid than an attempt to capture new territory, and, indeed, Celtic raids into Italy continued sporadically over the ensuing decades. Carrying out such raids may have been important to the status of Celtic warriors: the spoils of war included prestige as well as gold.

By this point in time, it seems that the homeland of the Celts was no longer restricted to the barbarian hinterland north of the Alps. The Celts who walked into Rome hailed from the Po Valley in northern Italy, framed by the Alps to the north and by the Apennines to the south. So how did the Celts end up south of the Alps? Several classical historians wrote about a Celtic migration into the Po Valley, but they disagree over when it took place. The Greek historian, Polybius, writing in the second century BC, places this folk movement at around 400 BC; Livy believed that it happened earlier – around 600 BC. It may be that it was difficult to pin a precise date on the migration – any settlement of the area is likely to have been preceded by a period of trading and raiding.

The archaeological evidence suggests that there might have been an initial incursion of Celts south of the Alps in the fifth century BC. But that evidence is difficult to read. The culture of the Golasecca region, south of the Alps, is very similar to that of the Celts to the north of the mountains. In the seventh to the fifth centuries BC, the Golaseccans were using similar weapons, carrying out similar funerary rituals – including vehicle burials – and speaking a similar language to their neighbours in the north. That language was Lepontic, and stone inscriptions allow it to be traced back to the sixth century BC. It's an Indo-European language – indeed, it seems to be an early Celtic language.

So how can you spot, archaeologically, when actual Celts turned up south of the Alps, where the indigenous culture is already so 'Celticized'? There are some useful clues from even further south, in Etruria. Stone grave markers, or stelae, from Bologna, dating to the fifth century BC, depict Etruscan soldiers fighting Celtic warriors. The historical sources suggest that, by 400 BC, there was a strong Celtic presence in the Po Valley, with the Celtic tribes – including the Libicii, Insubres, Cenomani, Boii, Lingones and Senones – occupying a broad swathe of territory, flanked by the indigenous cultures of the Ligures in the west and the Veneti in the east, and by the Etruscans in the south. But we need to be cautious about differentiating between 'indigenous' and 'Celtic' communities, as indigenous people may have been becoming Celticized. We also need to be careful about taking the historical sources, which imply a mass migration of Celts, at face value. It's clear that what we recognize as La Tène culture was spreading, but was this a movement of people or ideas? That's a tricky question to answer, looking at the evidence from material culture alone, but it's now possible to apply a range of modern scientific techniques to archaeological evidence, and to human remains in particular, allowing us to begin to tackle such questions. Analysis of strontium and oxygen isotopes in teeth, which act as a fingerprint for a particular geological area, can indicate where an individual grew up. Applying these techniques to a range of skeletons from German, Swiss and Italian cemeteries dating to the early La Tène period – just when those migrations were said to have happened – researchers obtained some surprising results. They found that the majority of individuals in a cemetery came from nearby: they were locals. Incomers made up only a small fraction of the population sampled in those cemeteries. So it looks like La Tène culture may have rippled out, borne by the movement of just a few people, rather than riding on the crest of a wave of mass migration.

Perhaps the classical historians saw that spread of culture and interpreted it as evidence of a migration. It seems they were in no doubt that the Celts had moved *en masse* into the Po Valley, and they suggested two main reasons for this. One was the lure of Mediterranean luxuries – figs, grapes, oil and wine. After centuries of trade with the Etruscans and the Greeks, the Celts simply wanted a little more of the good life. On their doorstep. But another (on the face of it, more likely) reason given for the supposed folk movement was overpopulation in the Celtic homeland.

Livy tells the tale of Ambigatus, who was king of the Bituriges tribe, in the centre of what is now France, but also king of all the Celts. Ambigatus, 'wishing to relieve his kingdom of a burdensome throng', sends his two sons off – each leading a horde of Celts – to find and settle new territories. One son, Segovesus, makes for the Hercynian highlands: the Black Forest and Bohemia. The other son, Bellovesus, crosses the Alps and heads south, to Italy. There, having fought with and defeated the Etruscans, the Celts create new settlements, including Mediolanum (Milan), Como and Verona. Whatever the truth of the migrations into northern Italy, the Celts of the Po Valley – even if they were Celticized indigenes – seemed a belligerent lot.

The Celts' war with Rome, which brought them to the banks of the Allia brook in 390 BC, started in the Po Valley, with the Etruscans. Livy describes an attack on the Etruscan city of Clusium, by the Celtic tribe called the Senones, who were already settled in north-east Italy. The Clusines appealed to Rome for assistance, and the Romans sent ambassadors to help with negotiations. The Celts were apparently amenable to a diplomatic solution, if the Clusines were willing to cede some territory to them. But the Romans (and presumably the Clusines too) thought this was an outrageous request. Diplomacy broke down, and violence ensued. The Roman envoys should have remained neutral, but they took up arms with the Etruscans, against the Celts – and one of the Roman ambassadors slew a Celtic chieftain. The Celts retreated, but they were incensed that the Roman envoys had joined the battle, against the law of nations, and they in turn sent ambassadors to Rome, demanding that these men be punished. But the belligerent ambassadors weren't punished at all; instead, they were elected to high offices. The Celts saw this as an act of hostility, gathered their army together and marched on Rome – covering the ground so quickly that, when the hastily assembled Roman army met the enemy, they were a mere eleven miles from Rome, close to the point where the Allia flows into the Tiber. The Celts directed their initial attack on the reserves, and panic began to spread through the ranks of the Roman army. The fleeing troops were slaughtered by the Celts, who couldn't quite believe that they had scored so easy a victory.

The terrible defeat at the Allia and the sacking of Rome would not be forgotten by the Romans. In fact, the Celts didn't allow the Romans to grow complacent. During the third century BC, Celtic raids into Italy continued, while Romans moved into Celtic territory north of the Apennines. As the power of Rome grew, it became clear that the only way to eliminate the threat from the north was to bring the Po Valley under Roman control. By the end of the third century, the Romans had wrested more land from Celtic tribes, further staking their claim and marking their territory by founding colonies in the Po Valley.

While Roman historians inevitably focused on Celtic migrations that affected Italy, they also recorded an eastward expansion of the Celtic 'empire'. Livy's tale of the sons of Ambigatus has Segovesus and his followers heading off for Bohemia, and, by the middle of the fourth century BC, there are historical accounts of Celts in the Balkans, and intimations that they had got as far as Romania.

Archaeology reveals an increasing Celtic cultural influence in Bohemia in the fourth century BC, while there's evidence of a corresponding depopulation in the Rhineland. But, just as in western Europe and northern Italy, we shouldn't be too quick to assume that a change of culture necessarily signals a massive population replacement. As archaeologist Barry Cunliffe is careful to point out, changing styles of burial, brooches and blades may reflect exchanges that are both complex and various, including large-scale migrations, movement of wives and warriors, and the 'Celticization' of indigenous communities. Nevertheless, the fourth to second centuries BC saw a widespread dissemination of La Tène culture, with evidence of the characteristic warrior burials found from

This eighteenth-century artwork, *The Gauls in Rome* (1883) by Alphonse de Neuville, depicts the moment the victorious Celts entered the city and confronted the elders of Rome

Arc de triomphe d'Orange, in Orange, southeast France, probably built during the reign of Emperor Augustus, to celebrate Rome's victory in the Gallic wars

Statue of Vercingetorix, who led the Gallic rebellion against the Romans, which ended in defeat at the Battle of Alesia in 52 BC

Recreation of the fort of Mont Auxois, near the village of Alise-Sainte-Reine, France, thought to be the site of ancient Alesia, the location of Vercingetorix's last stand

The Dying Gaul. Roman copy of a third-century BC statue commissioned by Attalus I of Pergamon to celebrate his victory over the Galatians

The Vachères Warrior – a statue from the first century BC, now in the Musée Calvet in Avignon, France. Many scholars believe the warrior's mix of Gallic and Roman clothing, weaponry and jewellery show him to be a high status Gaul who has adopted elements of Roman dress, perhaps even serving in a Roman unit

△ The site of Gordion in the Anatolian Plains, where Celtic migrants from Europe are thought to have settled as Galatians. ©Stipich Béla

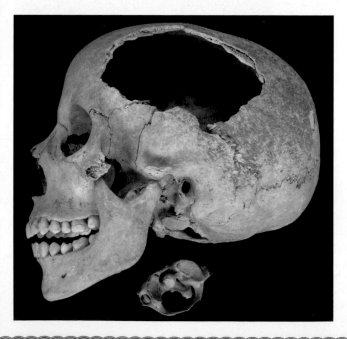

Isolated skull and vertebrae from the excavations at Gordion have been interpreted as evidence of Celtic headhunting – but with no cut-marks on the bones

Marne and Mosel in the west, to Bohemia and Wroclaw in the north-east, and to Transylvania in the east. But, just as the Celts pushed southwards into Etruria and threatened the Romans, they were also poised to penetrate further south into the Balkans.

In 334 BC, the Romans had negotiated a peace treaty with the Senones in north-east Italy – a treaty that turned out to be worth not much more than the paper or vellum it was written on, as Celtic raiding continued until the Romans crushed the Senones and colonized their territory. Over in the Balkans, it was the Celts who were concerned about the expansionist policies of their neighbour – Macedonia. In 335 BC, the Celts had approached the leader of the expanding Macedonian empire, Alexander the Great, to secure a friendly alliance. Strabo recorded this meeting in his *Geography* and described Alexander receiving the Celtic envoys and asking them what they most feared. Strabo thought that this was probably a loaded question – Alexander would have liked to have heard that the Celts were in awe of the mighty Macedonians. But the Celtic emissaries revealed both courage and humour in their reply, a line which fans of Asterix might be familiar with: 'We fear nothing except that the sky might fall on us.'

And so the Celts and Macedonians seem to have amiably rubbed shoulders with one another – until the death of Alexander and the collapse of his empire, that is, when the Celts in Illyria spotted an opportunity. In 280 BC, they joined forces with the Thracians and attacked the Macedonians. The head of the Macedonian leader ended up on the tip of a Celtic spear. It's possible that these events in the Balkans were linked to the unrest in northern Italy. The Senones had finally been defeated by the Romans in 283 BC, and displaced Celts may well have spilled eastwards, along the Adriatic coast, into Illyria.

Having triumphed in Macedonia, the Celts surged southwards. And then some continued south, into Greece, while others headed east, across the Hellespont, into Asia Minor. The southbound group, probably consisting of a large band of warriors, fought their way towards Delphi – where the history becomes a little confused. There seems to be no doubt that the Celts suffered a resounding defeat. But whereas the Greek sources record that the Temple of Apollo was protected by the gods, with thunderstorms and earthquakes deterring the Celts, other accounts describe the pillaging of the sanctuary. In this latter version, the Greek treasure gets carried off by the retreating Celts, eventually ending up at Tolosa (Toulouse).

The eastbound Celts – 20,000 of them, half of whom were not warriors but women, children and merchants – seem to have been looking for new territory to settle. It is this group of Celts, finding a home in Asia Minor, that became known as the Galatians. According to Livy, they included three tribes – the Tolistobagii, the Trocmi and the Tectosages – and they seem to have been encouraged to settle in Anatolia by King Nichomedes I, in 278 BC. Nichomedes ruled the kingdom of Bithynia, on the coast of the Black Sea. He was keen to employ the Celtic warriors as mercenaries, offering them land to settle in return. But once they had rooted themselves in Asia Minor, the Galatians made a nuisance of themselves, raiding the rich cities of the Hellespont, the Aeolian coast and inland Asia Minor. In 233 BC, King Attalus I of Pergamum defeated the Galatians, an event which he commemorated by commissioning the now famous statue of the *Dying Gaul*. Originally included in a monument on the Pergamene capitol, this statue is now known to us through a Roman copy.

We're provided with various visions of the Celts, and in particular the Celtic warrior, by the classical writers. Greek mythology embraced the Celts, giving these people a divine or semi-divine origin, as the descendants of the Titaness Galatea, or perhaps of the Giant Keltos, or of Heracles and Keltine, the daughter of King Bretannos. In the fourth and third centuries BC, the Roman and Greek image of the Gallic warrior was informed by their contact – by their bloody battles – with the Celts who were spilling south, through the Alps and down through the Balkans, towards the Mediterranean. This was the image then painted for us by the later classical writers, who portray the Celts as barbarians: brave, certainly, but savage with it. They go into battle naked. They paint their bodies. They are prone to drunkenness, and they probably indulge in human sacrifice and even cannibalism. These Celts are not civilized, Mediterranean types. They are quite clearly 'Other'.

And yet the *Dying Gaul* from Pergamum portrays a somewhat different image. On the one hand, he is clearly a barbarian – with long, tousled hair and a moustache – and he has gone naked into battle. But he wears a torc around his neck, a symbol of his elite-warrior status, and his body is lean and well muscled, like a Greek god. This man is noble in defeat, facing his inevitable death. He sits on his shield, his discarded sword beside him. His right leg is bent in front of him, with his left leg stretched out to the side. He leans on his right arm, while his left hand presses down on his left thigh. Blood drips from a mortal wound in the right side of his chest. He hangs his head, his eyes downcast and a slight frown knitting his brows. It is clear that the Pergamenes respected the enemy they had defeated. Of course, this also says something about the victors, too, and their need to portray the Celt as a worthy enemy. He is a noble savage, a formidable warrior, and he is brave in the face of death – he is clearly an enemy worth beating. It's such an interesting statue, because this Gaul appears in some ways heroic. Except, that is, for his dishevelled hair. He might appear noble in defeat, even godlike, but we're reminded that he is an uncivilized barbarian. And this image must have resonated with the Romans who copied it. The *Dying Gaul* presents an antithesis to the orderly, civilizing force of the Roman Empire.

But the Galatians, as a group, survived in Asia Minor, and were drawn into fighting other people's wars, as mercenaries. It seems that it was important to Celtic warriors, and probably to their status and identity, to have something warlike to do, and this need appears to have been satisfied by raiding or by fighting as mercenaries. Various Celts, originating from different tribes, ended up on both sides, fighting with Pergamum and against it. By the second century BC, the Romans were moving into Asia Minor and they attempted to subjugate the Galatians. Although Celtic raids in Asia Minor continued, the Galatians became subsumed into the Roman world. Today, they are probably best known, not for their prowess as warriors and their involvement in the wars in Asia Minor in the third and second centuries BC, but as recipients of an epistle from the Christian apostle, Paul, in the first century BC.

While the migrations of the Celts from the Balkans into Macedonia and Asia Minor are well attested in the classical histories, finding archaeological evidence of these mass population movements is surprisingly hard. Using material culture to track the movement of a particular group of people is fraught with difficulty; it is in the nature of human culture that it is transmissable, and not just vertically, like genes, but horizontally too. As we have seen, the biggest problem with those old invasion hypotheses in Iron Age Britain is that culture can spread without the mass movement of people themselves. Correspondingly, a large movement of people could be masked, in terms of their material culture, if they quickly adopt the customs and styles of their new home. Put succinctly, a localized change in culture doesn't necessarily indicate an invasion, and an invasion may not lead to a localized change in culture. And yet, archaeologists excavating the iconic site of Gordion in Turkey claim to have found something that indicates a clear Celtic identity and heritage. This time, it's not torcs, shields and swords. It's human sacrifice and headhunting.

Gordion and the Galatians

In the first century BC, our old friend, Strabo, wrote:

There is also among [the Celts] the barbaric and highly unusual custom (practised most of all by the northern tribes) of hanging the heads of their enemies from the necks of their horses when departing from battle and nailing the spectacle to the doorways of their homes upon returning . . . The heads of those enemies that were held in high esteem they would embalm in cedar oil and display them to their guests.

The Greek historian Diodorus Siculus wrote a passage which is almost identical, and it's thought that both Strabo and Diodorus are quoting the earlier Greek writer, Posidonius, who visited the south-east corner of Gaul in the early first century BC.

This description of headhunting is shocking to us today, and would have been no less shocking to civilized Greeks and Romans. In fact, there are plenty of passages in the works of classical scholars describing the warlike nature of the Celts, and several which specifically describe human sacrifice, including the killing of prisoners of war in order to honour the gods. Lucan described hanging as a particular mode of death carried out in order to propitiate the god Esus. He also wrote about a sacred grove, in southern Gaul, where 'gods were worshipped . . . with savage rites, the altars were heaped hideous offerings and every tree was sprinkled with human gore'.

I visited Anatolia to meet with archaeologists at Gordion who had reportedly stumbled upon evidence of similarly horrific practices among the Galatians, the distant cousins of the Gauls whose practices were so graphically described by Posidonius and Lucan.

Gordion is famous for its mythical knot. In 333 BC, Alexander the Great was passing through Anatolia and stopped off at Gordion, promptly writing himself into legend by parting the Gordian knot. The knot seems to have signified kingship. In the palace at Gordion, an ox cart stood tied to a post with an extremely complicated knot. The ox cart itself was legendary; in ancient times, it had been the cart of a peasant who had driven it into the city, unaware that an oracle had decreed that this would make him the rightful king of Gordion. Alexander tried to untie the knot and failed, so he cut it with his sword. The meaning of this myth may be that, by severing the knot, Alexander ended the rule of the existing dynasty in Gordion, and thus became, himself, a legitimate ruler in Anatolia. The arrival of the Galatians in Anatolia, some sixty years later, was intrinsically linked to events following Alexander the Great's death, as his generals carved up his empire among themselves.

Located on the Anatolian Plain, Gordion had been an important place since the beginning of the first millennium BC. It had been the capital of ancient Phrygia, and the home of the legendary King Midas, long before the Galatians arrived to settle there at the invitation of King Nichomedes of Bithynia, probably around 270 BC. By the second century BC, Livy tells us that Gordion had developed into an 'oppidum' and 'emporium': a fortified town and trading centre. Excavations at Gordion in the twentieth century found evidence that accorded with this description of a wealthy merchant town, with houses containing stone sculptures and gold coins. And while the classical texts describe the arrival and settlement of the Galatians in Anatolia, the excavations at Gordion provide an opportunity to look at the material culture of these eastern Celts. I was particularly intrigued by reports of odd burial practices – including human remains intermingled with animal remains and possible decapitations – which might provide a crucial cultural link to burial rituals elsewhere, and perhaps reveal how values and beliefs were shared right across the Celtic world.

The archaeological site of Gordion was discovered in the late nineteenth century. The Germans were building a new railway through Anatolia in 1892, looking for the path of least resistance through valleys and between hills. A German archaeologist recognized the abandoned site, from descriptions in ancient sources, as the lost city of Gordion. The landscape around was punctuated with manmade lumps and bumps, including around 150 burial mounds. The citadel hill itself was flanked by two smaller mounds – the remains of ramps built by the Persians in the mid-sixth century BC in order to deploy siege engines against the perimeter defences of the lower town, beneath the citadel. Around that lower town, there had been an exterior settlement. The current village of Yassihoyuk occupies just a small area of what would have been the outskirts of Gordion.

So Gordion presented a familiar plan – this citadel / lower town / exterior settlement design. All over Iron Age Europe, then, from the Mediterranean to north of the Alps – just as I'd seen at Heuneburg – this type of settlement had sprung up. It was their function that drove their design. These early castles provided imposing seats of power for increasingly powerful elites, as well as giving the populace a place to retreat to in times of strife.

The citadel mound at Gordion was largely flat topped, but even from a distance I could make out undulations at the eastern end of it – the evidence of archaeologists carving out the hilltop in search of its secrets. American archaeologists from Penn State University had started a long-running investigation of the site in 1950, but focusing on the Phrygian phases of Gordion, which predated the Persian phase, hoping to track down King Midas. They had undertaken extensive excavations on the eastern side of the mound, finding the entrance to the citadel and uncovering Phrygian buildings inside it. This was all extremely ancient history compared with the time frame I was most inter- ested in – starting with the arrival of the Galatians in the third century BC.

A significant clue to a Galatian presence at Gordion had emerged some distance from the citadel itself – from a burial mound known as 'Tumulus O'. When archaeologists discov- ered this tomb, it was practically empty – it had been robbed long ago, in antiquity. It contained just the broken remains of a terracotta sarcophagus. But the stone tomb itself was inter- esting; it bore a marked resemblance to other tombs, near Ankara. And one of those tombs bore an inscription, telling us who was buried in it. It was the resting place of Deiotarus the Younger, who died in 40 BC, and who was a member of a high-ranking Galatian family, mentioned in historical texts. The stone tomb under Tumulus O was so similar to these other aristocratic tombs that, for archaeologists, this strongly suggested that the individual buried in it was also likely to have been a Galatian leader, and that the importance of Gordion itself as an elite centre had continued into the first century BC. But tombs such as this were not uniquely Galatian. In fact, this tomb at Gordion and the ones like it near Ankara were similar to elite tombs in Bithynia, in the north-west of Turkey. In their tomb building, at least, then, the Anatolian Celts didn't seem to be marking themselves out as members of a distinct ethnic group, but rather adopting the practices and styles of the local elite. This type of tomb, in this region, was part of how you demonstrated your elevated status. In the end, it was only the historical texts – identifying Deiotarus as a Galatian – that allowed these tombs to be labelled 'Galatian'.

In recent excavations, archaeologists have been focusing on 'Galatian' archaeology up on the citadel mound itself. You still feel a sense of awe as you approach the citadel. The archaeological excavations of the mid-twentieth century had revealed the great towers flanking the gate of ancient Gordion. They were huge, built of massive blocks, reminiscent of the Cyclopean architecture of Mycenae. The towers stood some ten metres high on either side of the entrance into the citadel. They would have stood even taller in antiquity – the tops of them had been levelled off for subsequent phases of building. But these towers were from the early Phrygian days of Gordion, dating back to the ninth century BC – earlier than Midas, even, and much earlier than the Galatian phase of settlement. The first archaeological forays at Gordion, in the fifties, had concentrated on this Phrygian period, digging down through the overlying later layers to reach it. But over on the north-western side of the citadel mound were trenches from the excavations of archaeologist Mary Voigt, in the 1980s and 90s, where she had also looked at later phases of the site, including archaeology from the third and second centuries BC, when the Galatians were settled here.

I made my way up and out of the excavated Phrygian town, on to the top of the mound, and walked over to Mary Voigt's trenches. From this position, I was also looking down on the Sakarya River. This river had changed course over the millennia, moving from the eastern to the western side of the citadel. But it had always run close by, and this – just like Heuneburg and the Danube – helps to explain why Gordion became such an important place. Standing up on the citadel mound, I could see for miles in every direction. Gordion lay at the junction of two wide valleys, as well as being situated close to the Sakarya River. It was in a commanding position in the landscape and in a perfect place to control trade routes.

Mary Voigt's trench, overgrown with grass and weeds, still had some easily recognizable features. A two-metre-wide wall, built of massive stone blocks, ran through the trench. This dated to the time of the Galatians, and had been constructed using stone from the earlier, Phrygian buildings of Gordion. The Galatians had no need to hew out new stone when the city they had inherited was essentially already a quarry of ready-made blocks. Near this impressive wall was the corner of a stone building, which, unusually, had been roofed with tiles. It must have been something important – a high-status house or perhaps even a temple. But, unfortunately, the only find from inside it was a small piece of carved ivory, leaving us guessing about its function. Between the large wall and this building – in fact, abutting the wall – was a more basic building, with walls made of wattle and daub. There were features here that may have been small kilns, and fragments of pottery inside and outside the building, suggesting that this could have been a potter's workshop. From the broken pots and scattered loom weights on its floor, it looked as though this building had been abandoned very suddenly. Over time, this building had fallen into ruin and was later rebuilt. Once again, part of it seemed to have been used as a workshop, this time for making stone figurines. And then, sometime around the end of the third century BC or the beginning of the second century BC, the building is abandoned again.

Livy records an attack on Gordion, led by the general Manlius Vurso, in 189 BC. In fact, when this Roman army arrived at Gordion, they found it already abandoned – but they pursued the fleeing refugees into the mountains and fought them there. It seems that the archaeological sequence uncovered by Voigt may record that event. But Voigt's excavations also showed that Gordion wasn't abandoned for good at this time. Once again, in the second century BC, there's evidence of rebuilding and craft activity in the area where the big stone house and the old wattle-and-daub workshop once stood. And then, in the first century BC, the Romans finally arrived in force and took control of Gordion, levelling the ground and turning Gordion into a military fort.

So there's some evidence for a change in building techniques corresponding with the time when the Galatians are thought to have arrived in Gordion, and for episodes of abandonment and rebuilding, which may relate to Roman attacks on the unruly Galatians, but this is all based on some very small-scale excavations on the mound. Voigt acknowledges that, in order to understand how things really changed in the citadel, you would need to look at occupation over a relevant slice of time, across a much wider area. There are a handful of finds that, it has been suggested, provide evidence of a new Celtic population at Gordion: an iron fibula in the La Tène style, a button and a pair of sheep shears. But these 'exotic' items could easily have arrived through exchange. The vast majority of finds look Hellenistic.

So, despite some subtle changes in building techniques and pottery use around the time when the Galatians are thought to have started living in Gordion, there's really not much evidence of a new group of people, or a new culture, arriving on the scene. Perhaps the incomers had readily adopted local styles and artefacts, quickly forgetting their own cultural heritage.

But it's down in the lower town, beneath the citadel mound, where archaeologists believe they've uncovered some evidence that reveals a distinct underlying vein of Celticness pervading the practices of the Galatians. Despite the outwardly Hellenistic appearance of their culture, the Galatians appear to have been carrying out rituals which were also practiced by the European Celts – at least, according to the classical sources – including headhunting and human sacrifices.

By the third century BC, part of the lower town was no longer being lived in, and was being used instead as a cemetery. Some small-scale excavations carried out in this area in the 1990s have revealed a range of different, and somewhat bizarre, burial practices. Although the human remains haven't been radiocarbon dated, there seem to be two distinct phases in the cemetery, corresponding with the later Hellenistic period (the time of the Galatians) and the subsequent Roman period. During Roman times, this area looked like a formal cemetery; the archaeologists found twenty-four burials, where the bodies had been laid out with straight limbs, many of them in wooden or mud-brick coffins, and two cremations. But the earlier, apparently Galatian, period in the cemetery was very different. There was just one formal burial in a coffin. Other burials involved bodies lying in strange positions, the remains of partial skeletons, and even human bones mixed up with animal bones.

One of the odder burials from the cemetery included the remains of at least two individuals. Neither skeleton was complete, and there was only one skull between them. One partial body seemed to have ended up on top of another partial body, and there were some animal bones found with these remains as well. The extremities – the hands and feet – of both skeletons were missing. Both appeared to be female, one aged around her mid-teens at the time of death, and the other aged slightly older – perhaps in her late teens or early twenties. The position of the remains in the ground, and the partial nature of the skeletons suggests that the bodies may have already started to decompose by the time they were buried. There was no way of telling how these women had died, and we're also left guessing about why their bodies were left out in the open. Were they both victims of a violent death, and no one had cared enough to bury their bodies until much later? Did they die from a disease that made people too scared to approach their bodies? Or was the exposure of the bodies, and subsequent burial of the partial bodies along with animal bones, a ritual act? It's impossible to tell.

Another collection of bones, which archaeologists have suggested represents evidence of ritual – and, specifically, decapitation – consisted of a human skull with its mandible in place, together with the uppermost two vertebrae of the spine: the atlas and the axis. These bones had belonged to someone who was around fifteen years old when they died, and it's impossible to know if this was a young man or woman. Alongside this skull there was a fragment of a pelvis from an older man, and the skull, hip bone and thigh bone of a dog. The close association of the skull, mandible and the vertebrae suggests that the head was still partially fleshed when it was buried. Perhaps these were remains from another body that had been left out, unburied. Indeed, the skull showed some sign of weathering, suggesting that it had been exposed. The piece of human pelvis was even more heavily weathered. The lower of the two vertebrae associated with the human skull was damaged, but it was the type of damage that could easily have happened post-mortem. There were no signs of cut-marks on the vertebrae or on the skull itself – so nothing to suggest that a sharp blade had been used to decapitate this person. It's possible to imagine that the neck was cut through until the bones could be broken, in order to separate the head from the body, leaving no mark on the bones themselves. So the remains neither confirm nor rule out the possibility of decapitation – either as the cause of death or as part of a headhunting ritual carried out soon after death. As for the association of this skull with animal bones, it's impossible to know for sure if this was a deliberate arrangement, carried out as a ritual, or just incidental. A larger bone cluster from the same trench as this skull contained a great mass of mainly animal bone, with a few human bones mixed in. Whether this represents ritual or a much more mundane disposal of animal and human remains, which are deliberately or naturally buried after having been left exposed for some time, is open to interpretation.

One skull from Gordion did show evidence of having been used as a symbolic object after death. While cleaning the skull of a young male, the archaeologists discovered what appeared to have been wood inside the large hole, the foramen magnum, under the skull. But where the archaeologists again see this as evidence of decapitation, this is conjecture. From the evidence itself, it seems that a human skull was mounted on a wooden stake. But we don't know how the skull became separated from its body. Did someone clean up a decapitated head, removing the vertebrae from under the skull so that a stake could be pushed up into the hole where the spinal cord exits the head? Or did someone pick up an old skull, which was already devoid of flesh, and place it on the stake?

Among the other bones I had a chance to look at were two skeletons that had been found buried in a pit. One was the skeleton of a young woman, around twenty years old, who was laid in her grave in a crouched position, lying on her right side. Two large, lozenge-shaped quern stones had been placed in the grave with her, lying over her upper body. Another body, that of an older woman, aged between thirty and forty-five years, had been placed in the grave on top of the younger woman. Some bones from two children were also found in this grave, around the feet of the older woman. The older woman's skull showed evidence of trauma, with a large depressed fracture on the right side, towards the back of her skull. This is a typical injury from a blow using a blunt object. It is very likely to have been the cause of death.

Whereas some of the other human remains from the site suggested that bodies had been left out for some period of time, these bodies – or at least, those of the two adults – had clearly been buried soon after death, and carefully arranged in the grave. The quern stones were very unusual inclusions with a burial. They were clearly placed deliberately in the grave – this is evidence of ritual, even if we don't know its meaning. The older woman died a violent death, but again it's impossible to know the circumstances of that death. Warfare was endemic in this part of the world in the Iron Age – after all, that's reputedly what brought the Galatians to Anatolia in the first place. So we can't say whether that older woman was the victim of interpersonal violence, warfare, or something more heavy with ritual meaning, such as human sacrifice.

From the position of skeletal remains in the ground, archaeologists have suggested that some skeletons represent individuals whose necks have been broken. But the bones are undamaged, and so it seems more likely that the odd angles of these necks just relate to the way the bodies have been positioned and then settled in the ground as the flesh rotted away. Some of the skeletons were certainly positioned in odd ways, which looked as though the bodies had been uncere-moniously dumped on the ground, or in shallow pits, rather than being laid out with any care.

So, while there's some evidence of violence and of bodies being disposed of in what seems like a peremptory fashion at

Gordion, I could see no really convincing trace of sacrifice, headhunting, or, indeed, a deliberate, ritual association of animal and human bones.

In fact, uncontested archaeological evidence of human sacrifice in the Iron Age is very rare. There does seem to be some evidence for ritual killing from a few Iron Age bog bodies from England and Ireland. Bodies thrown into empty corn storage pits at Danebury in Hampshire have been compared with the remains at Gordion. But again, it's very hard to know if the Danebury dead were sacrificed. The bodies have certainly been deliberately placed in the pits, but were these individuals the victims of human sacrifice or of – probably much more common – less ritualistic violence? Some of them may even have died natural deaths. While the placing of the bodies in the pits is undoubtedly a ritual act, the death of those individuals may not have been.

Perhaps I am being too cautious, and further work at Gordion may reveal more evidence of heads separated from bodies, and perhaps actual neck fractures. But it's very easy to get into circular arguments, and to start looking for practices we read about in the classical literature, rather than approaching the evidence objectively. It's also important to remember that the classical historians may not have been entirely objective when they described the practices of the barbarians living beyond the frontiers of their civilized world. They had a vested interest in portraying the Celts as uncivilized. In addition to that, the classical reports of headhunting relate to the Gauls, in what is now France – a long way from Turkey. Should we really expect such practices to be replicated right across the Celtic world? If Celtic archaeology teaches us anything, it's that the 'Celts', through time and from the Atlantic to Anatolia, were culturally diverse. There is no one package of Celtic material culture and behaviour.

For the sake of argument, even if we were to accept that headhunting and human sacrifice were cultural norms for Celts, right across the Celtic world (and I don't think we should), there's nothing about those human remains from Gordion which looks diagnostically 'Celtic'.

In fact, we're left with very little convincing trace of the Galatians in Anatolia when we turn to the archaeology. The theme emerging from the archaeology at Gordion is largely one of continuity. History tells us the Galatians arrived in Anatolia in the early third century BC, but there was little or no change in the material culture of the region. The incoming Galatians seem to have quickly picked up local customs and styles, making it particularly difficult to spot them as a distinct ethnic group in the archaeological record. Most of the artefacts from the 'Galatian' period in Gordion are distinctly Hellenistic in style, just as they had been in the decades before the arrival of the Galatians. Greek-style figurines found in Gordion suggest that the Galatians had even adopted some elements of Greek religion. But, on the other hand, these Greek-style objects and Greek inscriptions fit well with Roman descriptions of the Anatolian Celts as 'Gallograeci'.

I asked Gareth Derbyshire, one of the archaeologists working at Gordion, about this: 'Just supposing you didn't have those historical sources, and all you had was the archaeological evidence, would you know that the Galatians were in Anatolia?'

Gareth smiled wryly. 'Probably not.'

While it might feel frustrating that archaeology is failing to reveal an immigrant culture in Anatolia that could match up with the historical records of the Galatian migration, the findings are still illuminating. There are enough different historical sources, from different times, detailing different events, to be sure that Celts did end up in Anatolia, living in a territory called Galatia. But this great, straggling mass of migrants would have looked very different when it ended up in Anatolia, to when it started off in the Middle Danube Valley, in what is now Hungary. Some people would have been shed, others – presumably all sorts of dissidents – would have joined the flow. And, when they reached Anatolia, these immigrants became Hellenized, they became 'Gallograeci'.

Focusing on this historically attested migration of the Celts exposes the Celtic package for the illusion that it is. The Celts are different depending on how you define them – archaeologically, historically, artistically, linguistically. You can see why some archaeologists advise against using the C-word at all. And yet, if we're interested in the spread of ideas, and how culture evolves, it's still useful to try to track all those fluctuating aspects of 'Celticity'.

Barry Cunliffe argues that there is legitimacy in trying to create a composite picture, as long as we are clear about how it is constructed. It's acceptable, and indeed worthwhile, to lump together Gauls, Galatians and Celts, because there are broad similarities between them all. And it's the historical accounts that provide us with evidence of some similarities in Celtic behaviour and society between widely separated regions. Barry sees similarities between Livy's descriptions of battles in Anatolia, including the picture he paints of battle behaviour and the power of women, and the picture painted by Posidonius of the Celts in north-west Europe.

There's one source, in particular, which tells us that the Galatians – despite becoming Hellenized and, later, Romanized – still hung on to one crucial part of their Celtic culture. As late as the fourth century AD, St Jerome wrote that the Galatians spoke a language that was very similar indeed to that spoken by the Treveri tribe, of Trier, in Germany. In other words, the Galatians – hundreds of years after their arrival in Asia Minor – were still speaking a Celtic language. Again, it is language that provides us with some telling insight.

It's impossible to know if the Celts who migrated into Greece and then into Anatolia perceived any shared ethnic identity with the Celts who still lived in the Danube Valley. Did the Galatians see themselves as Celts? We don't know. But, perhaps, as Barry has cautiously suggested, the retention of the name 'Galatian', coming from the same root as the word 'Gaul', might suggest a 'folk memory' of ethnicity.

Ultimately, the diaspora of the Celts as far as Anatolia was intimately related to the break-up of the Macedonian empire. And the turmoil following the death of Alexander the Great also drew the Celts to Egypt – arriving in North Africa as mercenaries, just as they had done in Asia Minor. After Alexander's death, with no clear successor identified, the Macedonian empire split up into warring states, with half-brothers and cousins fighting each other to carve up the territory. In what is now north-west Turkey, King Nichomedes of Bithynia, embroiled in battles with his half-brother Antiochus I, invited the Celts into Anatolia to fight for him. In Egypt,

Ptolemy II also enlisted Celts in his army – to help him fight against Antiochus in the east, and Magas in the west. When these Celts started to carry out raids in Egypt itself, Ptolemy drove thousands of them on to an island in a branch of the Nile, where they were left to starve (though other sources suggest they ended up murdering each other). But other Celts settled in the Fayum area of Egypt, acting as a 'sleeper cell' of warriors who could be called upon to fight for the Ptolemaic dynasty when needed.

While there's a real lack of any material culture that could be interpreted as recognizably Celtic in Anatolia, we do see signs of a Celtic identity persisting among the migrant populations in Egypt. A complete wooden Celtic shield was discovered at the Fayum oasis, preserved in the desert sand. In Alexandria, there are also funerary stelae inscribed with Celtic names, and depicting Celtic shields.

But just as that empire which Alexander the Great had fought so hard to create was breaking up, another empire was rising and expanding to dominate Europe. The Galatians had already felt the sharp edge of the Roman sword, and eventually became subsumed into the Roman Empire in the first century BC. Right over the other side of Europe, on its western edge, the Romans were encroaching on Celtic territory as the empire set its sights on Gaul – and Britain.

Under the Yoke

The expansionist ambitions of the Romans led to inevitable clashes with the Carthaginian empire. The Phoenician city of Carthage had been orphaned when the other

Phoenician cities in the eastern Mediterranean were swal-
lowed up into the Babylonian empire. But, in the centuries
that followed, Carthage had developed into an important
power in the Mediterranean in its own right.

In the later years of the third century BC, and into the
second, the Romans were embroiled in a series of battles
against Hannibal and his Carthaginian army – the Second
Punic War. After that war, the Romans launched into a
concerted effort to expand their empire – to the north, east
and west. The reasons for this expansion undoubtedly
included military security – Rome had learned, to its cost, the
danger of allowing potentially quarrelsome tribes to occupy
the Po Valley, for example. But, in some ways, the highly
civilized Romans were extremely similar to their Celtic neighbours. Young men could gain kudos and power in Roman
society by fighting in foreign campaigns, just as their counter-
parts among the Celts could secure their social status as
warriors – in raids or full-blown battles, or even as mercenaries. But there was surely also an important economic
imperative behind Rome's imperial expansion. Bringing new
territory under the yoke of Rome meant more food, more
mineral resources and more manpower, including soldiers
and slaves, and a greatly expanded market for the empire.

In every direction – in northern Italy, in the Balkans and
Asia Minor, and in western Europe – the Romans were
encroaching into Celtic territory. In the early decades of the
second century BC, the Romans took control of the Po Valley,
forcing many Celts to migrate back, north of the Alps. In 206
BC, the Romans captured the Carthaginian colony of Cadiz,
in southern Spain. After nearly a century and a half of Romans

fighting with the native Lusitanians and Celtiberians, western Iberia was taken by Julius Caesar in 61 BC. Southern Gaul – the modern French Riviera – provided an important overland connection between Italy and Iberia. The busy riverine trade routes providing a connection to the north along the Garonne – flowing to the Atlantic, and the Rhone – grew even busier. The Roman hunger for metals and other raw materials was virtually insatiable, while the estates of Rome kept a steady stream of wine flowing into thirsty Gaul.

Over the century or so before Caesar's conquest of Gaul, the region took delivery of tens of thousands of wine amphorae from Italy. The Celts really loved wine, as the Roman writers were so fond of reminding us. Here's Diodorus Siculus, quoting Posidonius on the subject:

> They are extremely partial to wine and glut themselves with the unmixed wine brought in by merchants. Their desire makes them guzzle it and when they get drunk they either fall into a stupor or become manic. For this reason, Italian merchants, with their usual love of money, regard the Celtic passion for wine as a source of treasure.

Energized trade networks also saw an increased flow of goods into and out of Britain – much of this trade taking place through Hengistbury Head on the south coast. Strabo mentions the valuable commodities that Britain offered to the empire. Curiously, he omits metals, but lists hides and hunting dogs, corn and slaves.

Increasingly intimate contacts and, particularly, trade with the Roman Empire seemed to catalyse the development of new political and trading centres, which the Romans called 'oppida', right across the Celtic world. Most of these oppida had some form of earthwork defence, probably supplemented with walls or at least timber palisades. Some, like Bibracte in central France, occupied elevated positions in the landscape, like the older hill forts. Some, like Manching in southern Germany, were well-defended settlements on level ground, while others were situated on clifftop promontories.

Contact with the empire also had another important impact on Celtic society. As Celtic lands became Romanized, leaders could gain power and prestige by becoming an ally of Rome, while young warriors could prove themselves by fighting as auxiliaries in the Roman army. But the basic structure of Celtic society seems to have remained intact. In his record of his military exploits in Gaul, *The Gallic Wars*, Caesar wrote that ordinary Celts were no better than slaves, and that the high-ranking orders in Celtic society were their priests and warriors: the Druids and the knights. By the first century BC, some Celtic tribes close to the Roman provinces seem to have been electing themselves governments, but warrior kings still ruled in the more distant Celtic lands.

Beyond the area that Caesar recognized as Gaul – corresponding with modern France, Switzerland and Belgium – lived even more barbarous and troublesome tribes. In the late second century BC, the Cimbri and Teutones, hailing from Germania, north-east of the Rhine, came rampaging down into Gaul and the Danube Valley. While the Romans tended to draw a clear line between Germans and Celts, the ethnic division was in fact much less clear, and some Celtic-speaking tribes certainly lived in southern Germania.

In the mid-first century BC, Julius Caesar was worried about the incursion of militant Germanic tribes into largely Romophile Gaul, but he may also have decided that the region would be relatively easy to conquer, and would bring him much-needed respect back in Rome. Much of southern Gaul was already under Roman control. Throughout the late second into the first century BC, Rome had extended its tentacles further into Gaul. By the beginning of the first century BC, the Rhone Valley had been brought under Roman control, and Tolosa (modern-day Toulouse) – on that important Garonne River trade route – had been absorbed into the provinces of the empire.

In 57 BC, Caesar fought his way successfully into the Belgic region of northern Gaul, roughly corresponding with modern Belgium. But tribes in Brittany and south-west France started a revolt. Archaeologist Barry Cunliffe suggests that this might have been because they anticipated the takeover of the lucrative Atlantic trade routes by the Romans. The rebellion was squashed. In Brittany, the Veneti – who may have led the revolt – were treated particularly brutally. Old men were executed while young men were sold as slaves.

Caesar had also set his sights on Britain, not least because the Britons seemed to be supporting the Gaulish uprisings against Rome. In 55 BC, Julius Caesar sailed for Britain. As his first squadron of ships approached the English coast, he saw the native armies assembled on the cliffs, ready to meet the Romans, and not looking very friendly at all. The Romans sailed on to another, more suitable, landing place, but the British also moved quickly, and made sure that there was a greeting party of warriors on horseback and in chariots, ready to meet the Romans. Caesar's troops still made their landing, and fought back the Celts, who surrendered to Caesar. But then, when a storm destroyed many of the Roman ships, the British planned to fight back. While the Roman ships were being repaired, and as supplies were running dangerously low, one legion was sent off into the countryside to bring back corn. This troop was ambushed by British warriors, and Caesar recorded their tactics – which included the use of war chariots:

> First, they drive in all directions hurling spears. Generally they succeed in throwing the ranks of their opponents into confusion, just with the terror of the galloping horses and the din of the wheels. They make their way through the squadrons of their own cavalry, then jump down from their chariots and fight on foot. Meanwhile, the chariot drivers withdraw a little way from the fighting and position the chariots in such a way that if their masters are hard pressed by the enemy's number, they have an easy means of retreat to their own lines. When they fight, they have the mobility of cavalry and the staying power of infantry.

While these chariot-riding British warriors were clearly the enemy, Caesar was obviously impressed by their military capability. Chariots had been used in Gaul in the fourth to second centuries BC, but seem to have become obsolete by the time Caesar was campaigning there. And, although the Romans were well used to the idea of chariot racing, they didn't use these vehicles in warfare. Chariots were useful if you only had small horses, but larger breeds of horse made cavalry possible. So this skirmish in Britain was his first real experience of the Celtic war chariot in action.

Archaeological evidence of such chariots comes from burials – where often just the metal fittings and, sometimes, impressions of the wooden structure, survive. But there's also a very well preserved part of a wooden wheel from water-logged deposits at Glastonbury Lake Village. And there are depictions of these chariots on coins and funeral stelae. All of this information can be used to help us understand how an Iron Age war chariot would have looked and functioned, and even to reconstruct these ancient vehicles. I was lucky enough to ride in a recent reconstruction of just such a chariot, on the long sandy beach at Berrow, in Somerset. I was surprised at just how fast, light and manoeuvrable the chariot was.

Caesar may have been impressed by the fighting prowess of the British charioteers, but his troops were taken aback by this unfamiliar style of fighting. Caesar brought reinforce-ments, and the British fell back. After another battle, the Britons were beaten, and sent ambassadors to Caesar to sue for peace. Caesar returned to Gaul with a haul of British hostages and a plan to come back and finish the job the follow-ing year.

When Julius Caesar returned to Britain in 54 BC, the British tribes had laid aside their quarrels with each other and had united under Cassivellaunus, their supreme war leader. Once again, the British warriors assembled on the coast, but, seeing the huge fleet that Caesar brought with him, they retreated to the hills. After the Romans landed, the British engaged them in guerilla warfare, launching attacks against their soldiers on the march and in their camps, but eventually the Romans prevailed, and Cassivellaunus surrendered. Caesar took British hostages, arranged the annual payment of tribute to Rome and extracted a promise from Cassivellaunus not to hassle the Romophile Trinovantes, but allow them to carry on business as usual with the Romans.

Caesar hurried back to Gaul that autumn, where several tribes were already in open rebellion. Over the winter, the revolt gathered momentum. The Arverni tribe had lost faith in their democratically elected leaders, and the old social order resurfaced as they instated a warrior king to lead them: Vercingetorix. He formed alliances with other tribes and became the supreme war leader of Gaul. Through this piece of history, recorded in Caesar's *Gallic Wars*, we get an insight into how Celtic tribal politics worked. When the Romans took on the Celts, they were not fighting another European empire. But individual tribes could come together to form larger groups or confederations – sometimes for trade and exchange, sometimes in warfare, to fight a common enemy. There's a loose analogy here with the way in which the city states of Ancient Greece organized themselves, coming together under the leadership of Athens, for example, to fight the Persians.

Faced with this confederation of Celtic tribes, led by their charismatic warrior king, Caesar threw his troops into crushing the rebellion. But the Romans were overstretched and eventually called on German tribes to help them quell the uprising. The oppida of the rebellious Gauls fell, one after another, and the rebel cavalry was routed until Vercingetorix was left holding the hilltop fort of Alesia. The Romans blockaded the fort, digging a defensive ditch around it, with wooden

167

stakes projecting from the bottom. A long and bloody battle ensued, but eventually the Gauls knew that they had lost. They surrendered, and among the thousands of captives taken by the Romans was Vercingetorix himself, who would eventually be put to death after spending six years as a prisoner in Rome itself.

Julius Caesar returned to Rome having secured Gaul, as well as bringing part of Britain into the fold. And, for a while, this north-western corner of the empire would be left alone. The eastern threat to the Roman Empire from the Dacians, based in modern-day Romania, the assassination of Caesar in 44 BC and the civil war meant that attention was focused well away from Gaul and Britain. Commerce flourished, despite heavy taxation by the empire, and once again the social elite were symbolizing their status in burials furnished with wine-drinking equipment – this time, in the form of Italian bronze vessels and amphorae. But other aspects of Mediterranean culture were also being adopted. Some of the Gaulish oppida were abandoned, as new, Roman-style towns sprang up, and prominent Celts assumed Roman names. But alongside all this Romanization, resentment towards the empire continued to simmer in Gaul, and occasionally erupted into rebellions.

The south-east of Britain, with its long-standing trade links with the continent, became even more continental in the first century AD, with oppida-like settlements appearing. Some of the British kings received support from Rome, and this now fed into the tensions between tribes, which seemed to have been endemic in Celtic societies even before the Romans stuck their oar in. Britain had been living on borrowed time ever since Julius Caesar made his first incursion into the territory in 55 BC. With the explicit aim of restoring an ousted Romophile Celtic king to power, the Roman invasion of Britain in 43 AD would also bring economic gains for the empire, as well as personal kudos for the Emperor Claudius.

The initial invasion, led by Claudius, met with British resistance but ended up securing the territories of the Catuvellauni and Atrebates tribes in south-east England. Follow-up campaigns by later emperors, right up until the last decade of the first century AD, led to the subjugation of the rest of England, Wales, and – somewhat briefly – Scotland. Many of the Celts fought against this assault on their freedom and independence. Right in the middle of this gradual and incremental conquest of Britain, in 60 to 61 AD, the most serious uprising against Roman hegemony took off, within what had been the most Rome-friendly part of Britain: the south-east. When the Iceni client king Prasutagus died, his kingdom was annexed by Rome – just as if it had been conquered – and his daughters were robbed of their inheritance. Tacitus records the sleight on the royal family going much further: Prasutagus' queen, Boudica, was publicly flogged, and her daughters raped. The incident was enough for the long simmering resentment against the Romans to translate into direct action. The yoke of Roman occupation did not sit well on the shoulders of these Celtic tribes.

The rebelling Iceni and Trinovantes, led by the warrior queen, laid waste to Camulodunum (modern Colchester), the first capital of the Roman province of Britannia. Meanwhile, Gaius Suetonius Paulinus, the Roman governor of Britain, was campaigning in Anglesey, targeting the Druids, who were perhaps even more powerful and influential than Celtic kings. Boudica's army moved on to Londinium, burning the town and slaughtering any Romans who had not already fled. Suetonius had returned from North Wales, but he didn't rush in to fight the rebels. He waited until the British had moved on to Verulamium (St Albans), and, somewhere along the Watling Street, he engaged them in battle.

Tacitus imagined Boudica driving along her troops, addressing them from her war chariot. As well as troop transport, the initial attack with spears and as a way of cycling warriors on to the frontline, this was another use of the British war chariot. These fast, light vehicles would allow a leader to travel quickly among their troops, to communicate plans and tactics, and to deliver rousing speeches just before a battle ensued.

So, with a little inspiration from Tacitus, this is how I imagine Boudica might have addressed the Britons she was leading into battle that day:

This is not the first time that Britons have been led into battle by a woman. But I am not just here as a queen of glorious ancestry, fighting to win back my kingdom and my riches. I am here as a woman fighting for freedom. And for my honour. The Romans' arrogance is beyond belief. Nothing is sacred to them. They trample over anyone who stands in their way. They whipped me until my back bled. They raped my daughters. And I want revenge.

The ancient gods are on our side. One legion has already faced up to us, and paid for it with their blood and their lives. We watched the survivors flee in terror. And now they quake in fear when they hear our battle cries. They are right to fear

I get my chance to ride on a reconstruction of a Celtic war-chariot, made by Robert Hurford

▷ Found in a peat bog in Denmark, the Gunderstrup Cauldron is decorated with Celtic iconography and is thought to date to around the third century BC, but may date to as late as 300 AD

◁ Glauberg Warrior – a life-size sandstone statue dating to the fifth century BC, found near a burial mound in Hesse, Germany

In the burial mound, which may have been 'guarded' by the Glauberg Warrior statue, archaeologists uncovered the skeleton of a man accompanied by grave goods including this torc with three bullet-shaped pendants – similar to the one depicted on the statue

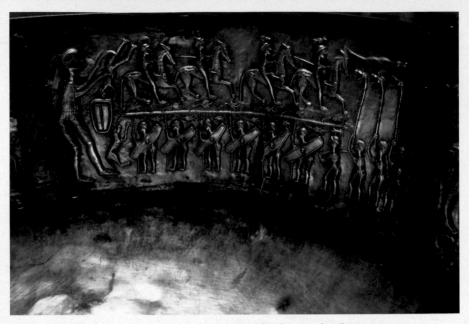

The Gunderstrup Cauldron is made of silver plates and is decorated with images thought to depict Celtic myths and deities. Here, on the left, a man is being dunked, head-first, into a cauldron

Created around the sixth century BC, the Warrior of Hirschlanden is the oldest known life-size sculpture of a human north of the Alps and belongs to the Hallstatt culture. The warrior is not only naked, he also sports an erection. This lifesize replica stands on the spot where it was found, near Stuttgart. Image courtesy of Harke

us! Look around, warriors, and see our might. And know that this is a just and noble cause we fight for.

We will fight these oppressors. This is our land that they try to take from us. We will prevail or we will die here. This is the choice we have made – not to live our lives out in bondage and disgrace – but to fight for our freedom. Celts – fight with me today!

Did Boudica think of herself as a Celt, call herself a Celt? History doesn't provide an answer to that question. The Greeks and Romans never referred to the inhabitants of Britain as Celts. Some archaeologists and historians insist that we should not use the word 'Celt' to refer to the ancient, Iron Age British. But the ancient name for Britain, Brettanike, first appearing in the snippets of Pytheas' work quoted by Strabo, certainly looks like a Celtic name. And Tacitus noted the similarity of the southern British to the Gauls in their physical characteristics, religion and language. He wrote: '*Eorum sacra deprehendas ac superstitionum persuasiones; sermo haud multum diversus*', which translates as, '[The Gauls'] religion is discernible in the strong beliefs [of the British]; their speech is not much different'. So Boudica most probably spoke a Celtic language. Perhaps that's enough. We'll never truly know if she thought of herself as 'a Celt'.

In the end, she would not prevail against the might of the empire, which had already seized her lands and her freedom. The Battle of Watling Street was swift and decisive. The Romans were no longer disarmed by the British mode of warfare and they mowed down the rebelling Celts. The only histories we have are written by the victors, so, of course, we must suspect exaggeration, but Tacitus records 80,000 Britons dying in the Battle of Watling Street, to just 400 Romans. As for Boudica herself, the historians are remarkably inconsistent. We are told that the revolt melted away; that Boudica fell ill and died; that she poisoned herself. In the end, we simply can't be sure of the fate of the last warrior queen of the Celts.

Suetonius' reprisals were brutal. So brutal, in fact, that he was replaced in case the atrocities sparked another rebellion. But, although Nero almost gave up on Britain at this point, this remote island would continue as a province of the empire until the empire itself disintegrated. The impact of being 'Roman' was far from uniform across Britain. The south-east, always the most closely connected part of Britain with the empire, even before invasion, was the most Romanized. But Roman systems of administration were largely fitted to the pre-existing indigenous political landscape. Native elites could retain positions of power within the Roman system. Native settlements developed into civitas capitals and villas sprung up in the countryside. But in the south-west, Wales and the north, Celtic life continued much as before. And while Ireland traded with Roman Britain, it remained a free, Celtic, country.

Throughout the Roman period in Britain, Latin was the language of power, spoken by the elite, but the native, Celtic language – Brittonic – continued to be spoken. It would survive and evolve into Welsh, Cornish and Breton.

After the end of the Roman Empire, there are still 1,700 years of history until the present day. And yet, despite invasions, migrations and the import of a dominant new religion from the Middle East, and the spread of a new language in

England with the arrival of the Anglo-Saxon settlers, some aspects of Celtic culture have survived. The most enduring elements of that Iron Age heritage are the language, which clung on in the Atlantic fringe, and the folk tales, myths and legends, which allow us to glimpse the complexity, strangeness and power of Celtic beliefs.

MYTHS FROM THE MISTS OF TIME

LIFE ON THE FRINGES – THE FLOURISHING OF CELTIC CULTURE IN NON-ROMAN EUROPE

The Celtic Priesthood

Thoughts and beliefs do not fossilize. Our species has existed on this planet for some 200,000 years, but for the vast majority of that time, we have no idea what people thought, or what stories they told each other. We simply don't know what they believed about their own origins or the world in which they lived, nor do we know what sort of natural and supernatural explanations they came up with for their experience of the world – of birth, death and everything in between. But we know that humans have a tendency to want to explain the world around them, and that we love telling stories. It's hard to believe that our earliest ancestors weren't doing these things, even if those myths are lost forever in the mists of time.

We can pick up some traces of behaviour in the archaeological record that would be hard to explain as purely utilitarian. Burial of a dead body may have been carried out simply to dispose of those human remains, but if the body was arranged in a certain way, or accompanied by grave goods, this suggests that the body was considered to be more than just an inanimate object. It suggests that it still contained something of the person who had once lived in it, that, perhaps, that person still existed somewhere, and needed to take certain things with them into an afterlife.

Our hunter-gatherer ancestors left very little trace in the landscape of their beliefs, but as soon as people started to settle down, in the Neolithic or just before, we see not only traces of dwellings but also of structures which are clearly not just designed to provide shelter, warmth and a place to sleep for the night. Ancient Megalithic constructions like Gobekli Tepe in Turkey or Stonehenge in Wiltshire defy prosaic explanations. They are surely temples, although we'll never know the details of the religion and ritual practices that inspired their building. In the European Iron Age, the archaeological evidence for Celtic religious beliefs and rituals includes iconography in the form of art and sculpture, burial practices, votive offerings and a few sites interpreted as shrines or temples.

As we move from prehistory to history, myths and legends start to crystallize into written form, and we suddenly have access to the beliefs of ancient people. We learn the names of their gods and goddesses, their tales of heroes and their origin myths. We can glean clues from the literature to help explain some of the more enigmatic practices that we find evidence of in the archaeological record.

The Iron Age people of west and central Europe lived right on the edge of history. The first written records of these people and their beliefs were not written by them, but by their neighbours to the south – the literate civilizations of the Phoenicians, ancient Greece and Rome. It's the Roman literature in particular which perhaps gives us the best insight into Celtic beliefs and practices – although we must always remember that these come from an outsider's perspective and telling a good tale about barbarians and their bizarre beliefs might have been more important to the writer than objectivity.

Although those Roman accounts are contemporary or near contemporary, there is another very important body of literature that provides us with a unique insight into Celtic mythology. Long after the Iron Age, in the Middle Ages, the Celtic tales themselves were committed to paper (or, possibly, to vellum) in the form of the Irish and Welsh myths. An oral tradition became preserved in written form. The earliest manuscripts of the *Ulster Cycle* and the *Mabinogion* date to between the eighth and fourteenth century AD, and were written down by Christian monks. Nevertheless, they are clearly pagan tales, and there are connections between these myths and the Iron Age archaeology of Celtic Europe.

Assembling and interpreting all of this evidence – the archaeological traces of ritual practice and beliefs, the stories embodied in art, the classical travellers' tales and the Welsh and Irish myths – is fraught with difficulty. It is all too easy to plunge into circular arguments, where archaeological evidence in one place and time is explained by accounts or myths extracted from literature written far away, perhaps even in a different century. And then, to complete the circularity, physical manifestations of religious practice or features of myths are searched for and recognized in the archaeological record. And yet, avoiding trying to make any connections between the literature and archaeology surely leaves both areas impoverished. I think it's possible to develop interpretations with caution and to be honest about the reliability of these explanations. In this field of study, it's worth generating hypotheses, even if those hypotheses remain, ultimately, untestable. As long as we're clear about where the evidence stops and speculation begins, we can allow ourselves to imagine the religious lives of our Celtic ancestors.

Like most societies, the Celts had their priests – people who mediated between the material and the spiritual worlds. They were, of course, the Druids. Julius Caesar, getting up close and personal with the Celts in the first century BC, described the role and power of the Druids in Celtic Society. He said that the social elite in Gaulish society consisted of Druids and knights. According to Caesar, the Druids presided over all of the religious aspects of Celtic life, including performing sacrifices. But they were also consulted more widely, acting as magistrates in disputes and criminal cases. There was organization within the Druid order – with one arch-Druid presiding over the rest. In Gaul, the Druids would meet annually in a central, sacred place, in the territory of the Carnutes tribe, who lived in central Gaul. The city of Chartres, a fortified town back in the Iron Age, gets its name from this tribe. According to Caesar, the annual gathering of Druids was both an occasion for a high court to assemble to settle disputes, as well as a religious gathering.

The Druids enjoyed various privileges – they were exempt from military service and from paying taxes. Caesar reports that many chose the profession of their own accord, while others were encouraged into it by their families. So it seems that being a Druid wasn't necessarily an inherited role in society, but a career that anyone of sufficient rank could aspire to. The Druids had to learn many verses and, although they apparently used Greek to write down more mundane accounts, it was unlawful to write down any of the Druidic lore; this meant that the fundamentals of their religion could only be learned by an initiate, directly from another Druid. The Druids believed in the persistence of the human soul after death, and in reincarnation. They also possessed knowledge of astronomy, geography, the natural world and the gods.

Caesar wrote that those wishing to learn more about Druidic lore went to Britain to study – and that the whole tradition had, in fact, originated in Britain. This could be true, but it could also be that the religion had become somewhat diluted by the first century BC in Gaul, and that a more powerful form of it still pertained in Britain. It's frustrating that we know so little about the Druids before Julius Caesar paints us his picture in the mid-first century BC. The first mentions of the Druids go back only to 200 BC, in two Greek books, which, though lost, were quoted by Diogenes Laertius in his *Lives of the Philosophers*, penned some 500 years later. But these are just mentions – Diogenes says that the holy men of the Keltoi and the Galatai are the 'Druidas'. Frustratingly, there is no more detail. So, as the historian Ronald Hutton so delicately puts it, 'we can be fairly (though not absolutely) sure that there were Druids by around 200 BC, but not of where they were or what they were doing.' We have to wait for, and to trust, Julius Caesar for that.

For the Romans, then, the Druids seem to have repre-sented a strange class of extremely powerful people, whose influence over the Celts seemed to transcend tribal bound-aries and who had the potential to bring disparate tribes together to fight against a common cause. In some passages in

Caesar's *Gallic Wars*, the Druids come across as respectable, almost civilized – acting as judges and guardians of knowledge in Celtic society. However, several historians have urged caution in approaching Caesar's account at face value – he may have been projecting a Roman system on to Celtic society, and he may also have emphasized the degree of organization in Celtic society, perhaps because it suggested that the Celts would take to being part of the empire more easily.

But Caesar also described another, far less civilized side to the Druids – they performed human sacrifices. Caesar described one particularly horrifying method of dispatch that involved the creation of a huge wicker man, which was filled with living people and set on fire. Caesar wrote that sacrifices of criminals were considered to be most pleasing to the Celtic gods, but that innocent people would be put to death if the supply of felons was running low.

Other Roman writers also painted the Druids in a macabre light, focusing on human sacrifice. Strabo and Diodorus both provided descriptions of the savage rituals of the Druids, which included taking home the severed heads of their enemies from battles and nailing them up to the doorways of their houses. It was gruesome customs like this that the archaeologists were trying so hard to find at Gordion. Strabo also mentioned a 'huge figure of straw and wood', which was filled with animals and humans before being set alight, as well as people being shot dead with arrows, impaled in temples, or stuck in the back with a sword.

The poet, Lucan, lived in the first century AD, in the Roman province of Baetica, in southern Spain, and he wrote a long poem, *Pharsalia*, about events which happened around a century before he was born. It focuses on the struggle between Julius Caesar and Pompey, the Battle of Pharsalus (in Greece) being a decisive victory for Caesar in the civil war. But when Lucan describes the recall of troops from Gaul, he allows himself a diversion to mention Celtic gods and the 'accursed blood' spilt in order to propitiate them: 'Savage Teutates, Esus' horrid shrines, / And Taranis' altars cruel . . .'

The Celtic names of these gods appear to be descriptive. 'Teutates' probably means 'the god of the tribe', while 'Taranis' means 'god of thunder' and is therefore equivalent to Jupiter in the Roman pantheon. 'Esus' means 'good' or 'all competent' and may equate to Mercury, the god of all arts, and to Lugh in the Irish myths.

Lucan also mentions the Druids. With the Romans out of the way, for a while at least, the Celtic priests are free to go back to their usual, ghastly practices:

> While you, ye Druids, when the war was done,
> To mysteries strange and hateful rites returned:
> To you alone 'tis given the gods and stars
> To know or not to know; secluded groves
> Your dwelling-place, and forests far remote . . .

Although there were plenty of Roman writers describing the 'hateful rites' of the Druids, it's doubtful that any of them saw these practices first hand. Historians suggest that all these descriptions, particularly those of human sacrifices, may go back to one original source – the Greek historian and polymath, Posidonius. And he probably didn't witness such rites himself. Several historians have expressed their doubts about the reliability of the testimony of Posidonius. He's been accused, on the one hand, of exaggerating the intellectual accomplishments of the Druids, while, on the other, of emphasizing the barbaric nature of the Celts. So it seems that one of the most memorable features of Celtic religious practice may be a myth itself – perhaps even something dreamed up by the Roman writers as a piece of anti-Celtic propaganda. If the mission of Rome was to civilize the known world, they needed some uncivilized tribes who were obviously in dire need of being conquered and educated.

In the light of such doubts, which make us question whether any Celts indulged in human sacrifice, it seems foolish indeed to suggest that evidence of such practices could be a mark of 'Celticity' – as at Gordion. I remain unconvinced by the evidence for anything as sinister as sacrifice or headhunting at that site, and sceptical about how much we should trust the Roman accounts of such barbarity, anyway. But there's a site in France, in the heart of Iron Age Gaul, which really does appear to represent something very macabre indeed, suggesting, perhaps, that Posidonius may not have been so wide of the mark after all.

In the 1960s, French archaeologists began to investigate what they thought might be a Roman villa site in Ribemont-sur-Ancre, in Picardie, northern France. But they discovered they'd found a temple dating to the Roman period, and, beneath that, they began to unearth Celtic remains. By the 1980s, the archaeologists were focusing on these Celtic layers, and they uncovered evidence of a bizarre and complex funerary ritual. The site at Ribemont included two enclosures. One was a circular enclosure, some forty metres in diameter. It had been partly destroyed by later activity on the site, but still contained some weathered human remains, and has been interpreted as an area where bodies were exposed and excarnated. But this wasn't the real surprise.

To the north-west of the circular enclosure was a square feature, again some forty metres across. This enclosure, marked out with a post at each corner and surrounded by a ditch, contained thousands of bones. Analysis of the skeletal remains has revealed that they represent at least 500 individuals. Most of the bones appear to have been from young men, and several bear evidence of violent injury. These appear to be the remains of men killed in battle – probably several battles. There are blade marks on some of the bones, cutting into thighs and knees. One pelvis shows at least four stab wounds on the inner surface, which must have been caused by a penetrating injury from a spear or sharp sword, passing through the belly before hitting the bone at the back. But most chilling of all are blade wounds to cervical vertebrae. Some upper neck vertebrae have been sliced into from the back of the neck, high up, just below the skull. Other vertebrae from lower in the neck are cut into from the front. This is clear evidence of decapitation. It's impossible to know if these injuries were the cause of death, or whether heads were being cut off dead bodies. But there are no skulls within the whole of the square enclosure.

The arrangement of the bones within the enclosure seemed very important. Some of the bones are isolated, scattered over the ground, but in other places it's clear that the bones represent entire limbs or torsos – parts of dismembered bodies. One arm still bore two bronze bracelets. But, far from being left to decompose and fall apart naturally, it seems there was systematic manipulation of these dead bodies.

While there's evidence of violent injury on some bones, there are no cut marks suggesting that fresh bodies were being dismembered. It seems, instead, that bodies were being manipulated as the flesh rotted away. Finding a tibia with a fibula alongside, or indeed all the bones of a leg or arm, lying in place, suggests that the bones were at least partly fleshed – still joined by ligaments – when placed in the positions in which they became buried. There's very little evidence of weathering or animal gnaw-marks on the bones, which suggests that the bodies are unlikely to have been left completely exposed to the elements, and were perhaps buried for a while before being uncovered and moved around. The French archaeologists also believe that the square enclosure may have been covered, protecting the bones from weathering. But, as the bodies decomposed and bones became easy to separate from each other, it seems that they were collected up and taken into the corners of the sanctuary.

In the northern corner of the square enclosure, the archaeologists uncovered an extraordinary arrangement of bones. Long bones – predominantly femora (thigh bones) and tibiae (shin bones) – were piled up in a very particular way, forming a criss-crossing, solid, square stack, 1.6 metres across. Along with the human bones, which represented the remains of at least 200 people, the stack contained the bones of around forty horses. There were a few human hip bones near the centre of the stack, around a small central pit into which cremated bones were placed. Among the bones were metal objects, including weapons and jewellery, of a style that places them in the late third century BC.

Later disturbance to the site, which included levelling and the construction of a temple during the Roman period, means that the other corners of the square enclosure have survived much less well. There was a scatter of bones, and the corner of what may have been a similar pile of neatly arranged bones, in the east corner, but the south and west corners were virtually empty. But with evidence of a carefully stacked tower of bones in one corner, and the remains of another in a second corner, it seems reasonable to assume that, back in the Iron Age, there would have been a square stack of bones in each of the four corners of the grove.

The site is incredibly difficult to interpret. Although there's evidence of some manipulation of human bodies and deliberate association of human and animal bones, elsewhere in France and Britain, there's nothing from this time that's quite like the site at Ribemont, with its strange, stacked bones. Archaeologists have suggested that the bodies and bones could be the remains of the dead of a vanquished tribe, brought back to this sanctuary as offerings to the gods of victory, while the heads were taken off as trophies, as described by Strabo and Diodorus. There is certainly incontrovertible evidence of decapitation at Ribemont. It may be impossible to know where the heads of the precise individuals represented in the square sanctuary eventually ended up, but archaeologists excavating an aristocratic Celtic dwelling, just fifteen kilometres from Ribemont, discovered a single, isolated skull in it.

So was Posidonius right, after all? We mustn't let our imaginations run wild. The most gory interpretation of this site

– with stacks of bones made from the enemy dead or from human sacrifices – might seem the most enticing, in a macabre way. But we can't reject the possibility that those bones could represent the dead relatives of the people who built this sanctuary – that this is just a very odd-looking (to us) cemetery. Who knows what strange ritual might have led them to treat their dead in this manner? Decapitating the bodies of the dead might have been part of a funerary ritual. Or they may have retrieved the headless bodies of their slain warriors from the battlefield, bringing them back to the sanctuary and honouring them in this bizarre way. Perhaps this is a sort of war grave. Decapitation, dismemberment of bodies and stacking of bones may have been a perfectly respectful way to treat the dead – however strange, unsettling and gruesome it seems to us today.

It is perhaps when we look at death rites which are so different to our own that we struggle most to understand other cultures, ancient and modern. We can fall into the trap of interpreting practices as sinister and macabre all too easily. The monks of the Tashi Lhunpo Monastery in Tibet still make music using trumpets made from human leg bones and drums made from skulls; whereas, in Britain, we regularly consign our dead to ovens and heat them to around 1,000 degrees centigrade, using fossil fuels. This leaves fragments of bone, which are then pulverized to produce a fine bone powder that we call 'ashes'. That's surely as weird a funerary ritual as any in antiquity – even that at Ribemont. And yet we look at those stacks of bones in the corners of the sanctuary and find them quite gruesome.

The reports of the classical writers – if they are to be believed – suggest that the Greeks and Romans found the

Celtic rituals just as alien, barbaric and abhorrent. The reports of Strabo and Diodorus, apparently based on that original observation by Posidonius, may exaggerate and embellish, but the headless dead of Ribemont, stacked into their own towers of silence, speak to us from the grave. Ribemont provides sure evidence of some form of headhunting, or at least decapitation, in a way that Gordion does not. The marks of blades on cervical vertebrae are a clear indication. But even when you know that a person's head was removed, or indeed are able to identify a cause of death, it's much more difficult – even impossible – to know why that person was killed. Ribemont also provides unequivocal evidence of the manipulation of dismembered human bodies after death – the stacking of long bones into those strange piles. But even with all that physical evidence – of decapitation, of deliberate arrangement of bones – we are still left guessing at the intent. Were these 'hateful rites' in 'horrid shrines' or a respectful death ritual, which the Greeks and Romans struggled – just as we might – to understand?

Apart from human sacrifices, other stereotypical features of the Druids – wearing long white robes, climbing up oak trees to cut mistletoe with golden sickles in the moonlight – all seem to derive from a single passage in Pliny's *Natural History* (XVI. 249–51):

The Druids – for that is what they call their priests – hold nothing more sacred than the mistletoe and the tree on which it grows, provided that tree is an oak. They choose forests of oaks, and perform no sacred rites without oak leaves, so that one might imagine that this is the root of their name, turning the word into Greek to give 'Druids'. Whatever grows upon these trees, they consider it sent from heaven, and a sign that the god has chosen this tree. Mistletoe is rare, and when found, it is gathered in a solemn ritual, on the sixth day of the moon . . . when the moon is bright enough but not yet a half-moon. Hailing the moon in their language, with a name which means 'healer of all', they prepare for a sacrifice and a feast under the oak, bringing in two white bulls whose horns have been bound for the first time. A priest in a white robe climbs the oak and with a golden sickle cuts the mistletoe, which is caught in a white cloak. Then they sacrifice the victims, begging the god, who gave them [the mistletoe] as a gift, to make it propitious for them. They believe that, by drinking [a potion prepared from] it, barren animals will be made fertile, and that the plant is an antidote against all poisons.

Pliny doesn't cite the source of this fascinating and detailed information, but it may well have come from Posidonius again. And Pliny is hardly a trustworthy source when it comes to descriptions of remote tribes. Let's remember, he told us that the Blemmyis, who lived in the Sahara, had eyes and mouths in their chests. And that there were dog-headed people living in North Africa. It's Pliny, too, who provides us with another enduring image of the Celts: women painted from head to toe in woad (although it was probably black dye, rather than blue). There could be a grain of truth in this one, though. The ancient name for Britain, Brettanike, may mean 'painted', and the Roman name for the northern people of Britain, the Picts, has the same meaning.

Still, Pliny had a habit of coming up with fanciful facts about exotic tribes, so when we focus on the Druids, we're left wondering if everything we think we know about them is actually fictitious. Even if some of it is rooted in reality, all the classical allusions may have been based on the account of just one Roman historian and philosopher, who may have had the opportunity to observe Druids in one small corner of Gaul, but who was inevitably viewing them through his own cultural lens.

Nevertheless, whatever the reality of the Druids and their rites, the Romans seemed to think that they were dangerous. And that's why Suetonius was away, leading a campaign against the Druids in Anglesey, when Boudica whipped up the tribes of eastern Britain into rebellion. Indeed, the two events may have been connected. Some historians have suggested that the Roman attack on the Druids was the trigger for the rebellion. Druids may have been more directly involved with the inception of the Celtic rebellion in Gaul, in 53 BC, which began among the Carnutes, in the central territory where the Druids held their annual meeting.

Tacitus described the Druids' last stand in his *Annals* (XIV. 29–30), adding some gory details about Druidic sacrifices, just to make sure it was clear that the Romans were doing the right thing by wiping out these abominable people:

Now Britain was in the hands of Suetonius Paulinus, who . . . aspired to equal the glory of the recovery of Armenia by the subjugation of Rome's enemies. He therefore prepared to attack the island of Mona [Anglesey] which had a powerful population and was a refuge for fugitives. He built flat-bottomed vessels to cope with the shallows, and uncertain depths of the sea. Thus the infantry crossed, while the cavalry followed by fording, or, where the water was deep, swam by the side of their horses.

On the shore stood the opposing army with its dense array of armed warriors, while between the ranks dashed women, in black attire like the Furies, with hair dishevelled, waving brands. All around, the Druids, lifting up their hands to heaven, and pouring forth dreadful imprecations, scared our soldiers by the unfamiliar sight, so that, as if their limbs were paralysed, they stood motionless, and exposed to wounds. Then urged by their general's appeals and mutual encourage-ments not to quail before a troop of frenzied women, they bore the standards onwards, smote down all resistance, and wrapped the foe in the flames of his own brands. A force was next set over the conquered, and their groves, devoted to inhuman superstitions, were destroyed. They deemed it indeed a duty to cover their altars with the blood of captives and to consult their deities through human entrails.

Tacitus doesn't suggest a link between the attack on Anglesey and the Boudican revolt, but his next chapter launches straight into an account of the rebellion:

Suetonius while thus occupied received tidings of the sudden revolt of the province . . . [The kingdom of Prasutagas] was plundered by centurions, his house by slaves, as if they were the spoils of war. First, his wife Boudica was scourged, and his daughters outraged. All the chief men of the Iceni, as if Rome had received the whole country as a gift, were stript of their ancestral possessions, and the king's relatives were made slaves. Roused by these insults and the dread of worse, reduced as they now were into the condition of a province, they flew to arms . . .

And the rest is history.

But the Druids seemed to live on – or, at least, their lore did, to some extent. I wonder if the situation in Gaul and Britain was much like that in Siberia, under Soviet rule, when the shamans effectively disappeared, ready to appear again under a less oppressive regime. Even during the Soviet era, shamanic rituals like the sky burials of people and wild reindeer continued, deep in the taiga. Whether or not, hidden in the ancient oak forests, there were still Druids cutting mistletoe in the light of the six-day moon (if that ever really happened), some of that body of esoteric knowledge, which was so jealously guarded by the Celtic priests, learned by heart and never written down, eventually appeared in literature. It's in that body of literature, and in their Iron Age art, that we find self-portraits of the Celts, and learn their beliefs and mythologies.

Heroes, Cauldrons, and Shape-shifting

The quest to get closer to the Celts, to see them more clearly and understand them more deeply, draws on many different sources. The Greek and Roman portraits of the Celts provide us with vivid and enduring images of these Iron Age people: the white-robed Druid harvesting mistletoe in the light of the moon; the accomplished charioteers riding into battle; the naked, painted warrior carrying home the head of his enemy; the warlike, rebel queen with fierce eyes and long (blonde) hair down to her hips. But were these real people or just imaginative fictions?

Barry Cunliffe – who has probably spent more time actively researching and writing about the Celts than anyone else – believes that we can trust those portraits, to some extent. The Greeks and Romans needed to present the Celts as 'Other', so, rather like drawing a caricature, they chose certain aspects and accentuated them. 'They chose wearing a torc, they chose hairiness, they chose going naked into battle. These are probably all perfectly true – they've just emphasized those features.' The cartoon-like depiction of the Celts, accentuating their 'Otherness', extended to their behaviour too. 'My favourite one,' Barry told me, 'is that the Celt doesn't dilute his wine; he drinks it neat – what a barbarian!'

But what about individual characters? Again, how far can we trust the classical accounts? Some authors have even suggested that Boudica – this vision of a powerful woman who threatened Caesar – was a Roman invention, a bit of propaganda. But most scholars accept that she did exist.

'I believe she was real,' Barry Cunliffe told me. 'It just wasn't the sort of thing the Romans did – to invent characters. It doesn't fit at all with what we know about Roman historical writing.'

And the Romans probably found her a surprising character. They were used to powerful women – the wives and mothers of the emperors held great power – but the potential for a woman to become a war leader represented a stark difference between Celtic and Roman society. Boudica wasn't the only warrior queen that the Romans would have been aware of. In the north of Britain, in the mid-first century BC, Queen Cartimandua led a confederation of Celtic tribes which were loyal to Rome – until she was ousted by her ex-husband, Venutius. This ambivalence towards gender, providing the possibility for women to become leaders of men and to achieve the highest status in Celtic society, also seems to be reflected in the chariot burials of Yorkshire: women as well as men were treated to such elite funerary rites. So there seems no reason to doubt the existence of a powerful female Celtic hero. Boudica may have been embellished, with various attributes added to her, but this tends to be the case for any war leader – the stories of Che Guevara walking on water providing a more recent example. The picture we get is a 'constructed Boudica', but the nucleus is real.

As long as we recognize that we're being presented with caricatures, that certain features are being exaggerated in these portraits, we can trust the images they give us. There's more than a grain of truth in them – they're as good as a good cartoon. And yet they are created by outsiders. How did the Celts represent themselves?

Most of the surviving Celtic artwork is on metal – in the form of decoration on jewellery, swords and shields – and consists of geometric or abstract designs. Although we glimpse stylized faces peering from the tendrils of La Tène artwork, it's very rarely that we glimpse a Celtic portrait of a Celtic person. But there are a couple of stone statues which provide us with this view, and present an interesting contrast with the famous Pergamene sculpture of the *Dying Gaul*.

The *Warrior of Hirschlanden* is a life-size sandstone statue of a man, found in 1963, in south-west Germany, near Stuttgart. It is thought to date to the sixth century BC – placing it in the Hallstatt period. The statue was discovered in the ground, close to a tumulus, and archaeologists have suggested that it may originally have stood on top of this burial mound. The style of this figure is completely different to the *Dying Gaul*. The Pergamene representation of the defeated Celt presents a naturalistic image of a human body, in the Hellenistic style characteristic of Greek art at the time, in the third century BC. The pose is heroic but natural, and the anatomy of the male human body is carefully represented. The *Warrior of Hirschlanden*, on the other hand, is highly stylized. In some ways, this isn't surprising – he comes from a different time and place. Indeed, contemporary Greek statues, of the Archaic period – typified by standing or striding kouros – were also very mannered compared with the later Hellenistic style.

The *Warrior of Hirschlanden* has a disproportionately small head, with a face almost weathered away, high shoulders, skinny arms, and legs that can only be described as hefty. But, like the *Dying Gaul*, he is practically naked; he wears a conical hat, a neck-ring and a belt. And the dagger stuck diagonally in the front of his belt does nothing to distract from his large, erect penis. (I think we also get an interesting insight into modern culture from the fact that many descriptions of this statue in scholarly works barely mention the genitalia of the *Warrior of Hirschlanden*. And if they do, they are delicate about it, using the rather obscure term 'ithyphallic' for his erection.)

So here are the Celts producing a self-portrait; perhaps their warriors really did go naked into battle. But this Celt is undefeated, even in death – if he does indeed mark the grave of a warrior. He stands solidly, a monumental figure, un-embarrassed by his nakedness. In fact, he is quite shameless; he surely intends to impress us with his raw virility. In this self-portrait, the Celt shows himself as a naked savage – and proud of it.

In the 1990s, archaeologists investigating a burial mound close to the promontory fort of Glauberg, near Frankfurt, in central Germany, found not only a princely grave, but the remains of sandstone statues. These included fragments of three large warrior statues – and one that had, miraculously, survived two and a half millennia, virtually intact.

The life-size Glauberg Prince stands nearly six feet tall, missing only his feet. He wears an extraordinary cap, which projects to the sides rather like two enormous ears. His upper lip bears the suggestion of a moustache and he wears a well-kept beard. He carries a small shield on his left arm and a sword hangs at his right side, and he wears a bracelet and a torc. But, unlike the *Dying Gaul* and the *Warrior of Hirschlanden*, this Celtic prince is clothed – he appears to be wearing an armoured, leather tunic. His torc is unusual; three bullet-shaped pendants hang from the neck-ring. And, remarkably, the grave within the mound contained the skel-eton of a young man who was wearing a very similar gold torc – quite ornate, but with three bullet-shaped projections, just like the statues that once guarded the grave. It's very tempt-ing to see this statue, not just as an impersonal or archetypal image of 'a warrior', but as a portrait of the actual individual buried under the mound. The burial and its accompanying warrior stelae date to the fifth century BC, the start of the La Tène period, when the warrior aristocracy was becoming more powerful. There is little to read in the weathered face of the *Warrior of Hirschlanden*, but the Glauberg Prince fixes us with a serious, wide-eyed stare, daring us to look away first.

In many ways, these sandstone self-portraits of the Celts, whether naked or clothed, support that classical image of the fierce and brave warrior. But these, too, are stereotypes – carefully designed to project certain aspects of themselves. And we are left only with an image of the male elite – ordinary men, women and children are left out of the picture. We are offered glimpses of those other lives through the archaeological record, piecing together the clues from grave goods buried with the elite, and finding evidence of less glamorous but no less important lives scattered underneath today's landscape in the remains of roundhouses, villages and towns. Among the ancient Celts were consummate artisans, well-travelled traders, learned men, skilled fighters and warrior queens. But the Celts were also road builders, homemakers and, perhaps above all, farmers.

Archaeology reveals the types of ploughs and querns used by our Iron Age ancestors, the sort of pits, pots and cauldrons they used to store and cook their food, as well as showing us what they ate on a regular basis – which boils down to a few staples: bread, porridge, stews and beer. Meat, while clearly important in the feasts hosted by the elite, with their roasting spits and flesh hooks, was a less common feature of the ordinary Iron Age diet. But, when it was eaten, it tended to be the meat of domestic animals – beef, pork and mutton, as well as horse and dog. Beans, cabbage and cheese also featured in the Iron Age diet, as evidenced by the analysis of residues still stuck to the insides of badly-washed-up Celtic pots.

But what did those Iron Age people believe about the world around them? What deities did they worship, and what stories did they tell each other around the fire? These seem like impossible, ephemeral ideas to grasp hold of, especially when talking about a society that was pre-literate for so much of its existence. But we know that the Celtic language was, above all, what tied this culture together, right across Europe – despite the differences in material culture through time and space. And that language, in spoken form, continued to be the vehicle for the transmission of myths through the generations, until at last the stories were written down – in the west, where the ancient languages resisted replacement – in mediaeval Wales and Ireland.

Why should we believe that these myths go back, through all those centuries, to the Iron Age Celts? Scholars argue that the ancient language itself provides the strongest link. And then there are common themes in the myths that suggest a deep ancestry. Finally, despite all the pitfalls inherent in trying to make connections between mediaeval literature and archaeology, there are some astonishing correspondences between the images in the Welsh and Irish myths and the symbolism in the material culture of north-western Iron Age Europe.

The myths are full of triple deities, shape-shifters and cauldrons. Perhaps counterintuitively, the Roman period in Britain and Gaul provides us with some of the best archaeological evidence of Celtic religion, in the form of sculptures of gods and goddesses, and inscriptions telling us their names. For instance, Miranda Aldhouse-Green, an archaeologist who has studied Celtic iconography in depth, sees parallels between the Gallo-Roman horse goddess, Epona, widely worshipped across Europe, and a heroine in the Welsh tales, Rhiannon. The more local, named water-goddesses – Sulis at Bath, Coventina in Northumberland, Sequana in Burgundy – speak of the sacred nature of springs and rivers, which is well attested in the Celtic myths.

The Irish myths are contained in three cycles of prose stories: the *Ulster Cycle*, the *Mythological Cycle* and the *Fenian Cycle*. The earliest version of the *Ulster Cycle* appears in the *Book of the Dun Cow*, written in the eleventh century AD, but the language and the content seem to hark back to a much earlier origin. This Cycle focuses on a story called '*Tain Bo Cuailnge*' ('The Cattle Raid of Cooley'), which describes a war between Ulster and Connacht. The power of Ulster had largely faded by the end of the fifth century AD, suggesting that this tale dates from an earlier period – when Ulster was still great. The *Mythological Cycle*, containing descriptions of the Celtic gods, and the *Fenian Cycle*, about the adventures of the hero Finn, are known from twelfth-century copies.

The Welsh myths come down to us in two main collections: the *White Book of Rhydderch* and the *Red Book of Hergest*, both dating to around the fourteenth century AD. These books contain several mythological tales, like 'Peredur' and 'Culhwch and Olwen', as well as the '*Pedeir Ceinc y Mabinogi*' (the 'Four Branches of the Mabinogion').

These tales are the remnants of the Celtic version of a phenomenon that seems to have existed everywhere in the ancient world – the tradition of storytelling. History and myths were preserved and passed on from one generation to the next in the form of spoken narrative. It's easy to imagine how these stories would change over time, as the storyteller or bard adapted the tale for a particular place and audience, or added embellishments of their own. And, rather like the Druids, storytellers would have been powerful cultural figures, curators of knowledge, wisdom and history. At the other end of Europe, this storytelling tradition is also reflected in the epic poems of Homer, the *Iliad* and the *Odyssey*, which are thought to date back to at least the ninth century BC.

In a couple of passages in the fourth branch or section of the *Mabinogion*, we get a rare glimpse of the storyteller – the *cyfarwydd*. In fact, in this story, one of the principal characters – the magician, Gwydion – pretends to be a *cyfarwydd* in order to gain access to royal courts:

He went, with Gilfaethwy and ten men with them, to Ceredigion – to the place that is nowadays called Rhuddlan Teifi. There was a court of Pryderi's there, and they went in, in the guise of bards. There was joy at their arrival . . .

Gwydion himself was the best *cyfarwydd* in the world. And that night he delighted the court with entertaining recitals and storytelling, until he was feted by the whole court, and it was with pleasure that Pryderi conversed with him.

Gwydion, the magician and storyteller, also uses poetry to call his nephew – who has taken the form of an eagle – down from an oak tree. Storytelling, poetry and magic are all intertwined.

We still describe people captivated by a great raconteur as being 'spellbound'.

The *Mabinogion* is full of magical tales and bewitching images: a woman made entirely from flowers, a shining white boar, the spectral hounds of Annwn. But the second branch also contains a recurring theme in Celtic myths: the enchanted cauldron. In this story, the King of Ireland, Matholwch, marries Branwen, sister of the King of Britain, Bendigeidfran. But Branwen's half-brother, Efnisien, is unhappy with this arrangement and attacks Matholwch's horses. Bendigeidfran tries to make amends by giving Matholwch more horses, treasure, and a magic cauldron. Later on, when the British go to war with the Irish, the cauldron is used to resurrect the Irish dead, until Efnisien gets in it and smashes it apart. In another Welsh myth, Ceridwen's magical cauldron is used to brew up a potion that imparts wisdom. Enchanted cauldrons also appear in the Irish myths: the King of Ulster had to bathe in one at his inauguration, and the god Daghdha had a cauldron that provided an inexhaustible supply of food.

In both the Welsh and Irish myths, cauldrons seem to be important cultural objects, with magical associations. And, of course, they also appear, as symbolically significant objects, in the archaeological record. The cauldron was important in feasting – it epitomized conspicuous consumption. The feast was an important feature of Celtic society, allowing the elite to demonstrate their wealth, to secure the loyalty of noblemen and to bond with allies. And, as the Hochdorf Prince's grave distinctly demonstrates, feasting was expected to continue into the afterlife. Both the Irish and Welsh myths describe feasts in the Otherworld, where meat, especially pork, and alcohol are consumed in prodigious quantities. In the Irish tales, this excessive consumption often depends on a magical source of the food or drink: a regenerating pig, for example, or a self-replenishing cauldron. Back in this world, real cauldrons also ended up at the bottoms of lakes and rivers, as votive offerings.

Some Iron Age cauldrons are quite plain; others, highly decorated. The most ornate of all is the Gundestrup cauldron, discovered in a bog in Jutland towards the end of the nineteenth century. It's both a stunning work of art and a real puzzle. It's not as big as the Hochdorf Prince's cauldron, but its sides are covered with fabulous images, in relief, inside and outside, of humans, animals and gods. It's made of gilded plates of silver, which had been taken apart and stacked before being left in that Danish bog, where the peat grew over it. Based on the metalwork and iconography of the cauldron, it has been judged to date to the third century BC, using Thracian-style metalworking techniques but involving Celtic imagery. Jutland itself has never been considered to be Celtic, even under the broadest definition, so experts have looked further south for its origin, suggesting the lower Danube Valley, where Celtic and Thracian tribes came into contact. But recent radiocarbon dating of beeswax residues on the cauldron, and of the metal itself, suggest a different – much later – origin. The cauldron may come from central or western Europe, and may date to as late as 300 AD. This would certainly complicate the story. It would mean that we are looking at an object from the Roman period in Europe, displaying iconography that seems to be rooted in the Iron Age.

The cauldron is constructed from silver plates: separate internal and external plates. One of the internal plates of the cauldron shows a god with antlers, perhaps the 'horned god' Cernunnos, or Hern the Hunter. He sits cross-legged, and wears a torc around his neck while holding another in his right hand, and gripping a snake in his left hand. He is accompanied by a stag and a smaller deer, and by two other creatures, which appear to be a dog and a lion. Other images on the inner surface include the bust of a woman, surrounded by wheels, elephants and griffins; the bust of a bearded man holding a broken wheel; and a bull-fighting scene. It has been suggested that each of these inner plates represents a story or myth. The outer plates are quite different; each one bears a large head-and-shoulders portrait, perhaps of a god or goddess. The bottom of the cauldron bears an embossed image of a dying bull, accompanied by a tiny man waving his sword, and a dog.

The images on the Gundestrup cauldron have a magical quality to them. It's not unreasonable to suggest that the stories represented here, on the inside, are mythological rather than historical, and that the faces staring out from its sides might represent gods rather than mere men. As we have seen, in other examples of Celtic art, particularly of the La Tène period, abstract shapes predominate, occasionally with animals and human faces well hidden among tendrils and spirals. But the Gundestrup cauldron is an unusual – and, as we now suspect, probably a very late – piece of Celtic art, where the elements of the stories, if not the stories them-selves, are easy to discern. The Greeks used to illustrate their pottery with images and stories of men and gods; this could be a Celtic version of the same thing.

While we may never be able to interpret these images fully, or to know exactly what myths and deities are depicted, there's one scene on the inside that seems to link to the story of the cauldron in the *Mabinogion*. On this inner plate, a line of marching warriors is shown, accompanied by three carnyx players. The carnyx was a strange, upright trumpet, with an animal's head forming the bell at the top, and it is known from actual archaeological finds, as well as from images like that on the Gundestrup cauldron. But this scene, on a cauldron, also contains a cauldron. A giant or a god is dunking a man, head first into the vessel depicted on the inner plate. Is this dangling man a dead warrior, about to be reborn from the magical cauldron?

Warriors and heroes are conspicuous in Celtic art. The warriors marching in relief around the inner surface of the Gundestrup cauldron are just one example. The *Warrior of Hirschlanden* and the Glauberg Prince are two of the most striking examples, life-size and sculpted in the round. The graves of the elite on the continent, and the watery offerings of exquisite swords and shields in Britain and Ireland, proclaim the wealth and power of the warrior aristocracy.

The warrior-as-hero is a common figure in myth – and not just in Celtic mythology. The warriors of myth are often superhuman, sometimes even demigods. The Welsh hero Pryderi, in the *Mabinogion*, is the son of Pwyll, lord of Llys Arbeth, and Rhiannon, a horse-goddess. Pryderi's parentage is at once noble, divine and intimately connected with that animal so beloved by the Celts: the horse. His connection with horses is emphasized again when he is abducted as a newborn baby and then turns up lying on the threshold of a stable – where Lord Terynon of Gwent-Iscoed happens to have just snatched a newborn foal back from the claws of a monster. Pryderi is happily reunited with his parents a few years later.

The archetypal hero of Irish mythology is Cú Chulainn, the formidable champion of Ulster. He appears in '*Tain Bo Cuailnge*', 'The Cattle Raid of Cooley', the story of a clash between the states of Ulster and Connacht. Cú Chulainn's parentage isn't made clear, but scholars believe that there's a strong implication that he's the son of the god of light, Lugh. He's a naturally gifted warrior, possessing super-human strength. His incredible might is evident even while he's just a child, when he shatters one set of weapons after another. His real name is Setanta, but he gets his nickname after killing the dog of Culann the smith. The warrior is penitent, and offers his services as a replacement for the beast, saying to the smith, 'I will be your hound, and guard yourself and your beasts'. Setanta's new name, Cú Chulainn, means 'Hound of Culann', and it was a mark of respect. The hound, especially the hunting dog, was a noble beast whose character was admired – loyal, brave and tenacious. A stone carving from Southwark in London shows a hunter, inter-preted as a Celtic god, standing between two hounds. And a shrine at Nettleton Shrub in Wiltshire was dedicated to Apollo Cunomaglus – Apollo the 'Hound-Lord'. Like Pryderi in Wales, Cú Chulainn is also strongly associated with horses. Two foals were born at precisely the same time as Cú Chulainn himself, and they grew up to pull his chariot. Just before Cú Chulainn's last battle, one of the horses wept tears of blood.

The descriptions of Cú Chulainn in battle are terrifying. He was trained by a wise woman, who seemed to unlock in him the potential to unleash a fury in battle that made him invincible and deadly. He is described as going into spasm, with his limbs twisted, his muscles bulging and his lips curling back to his throat as he utters a dreadful howl. He slaughters his enemies, and his own men are in danger of being cut down if they get in the way. Sometimes the only way they can rescue him from these berserk attacks is by plunging him into a cauldron of icy water to cool him down.

The transformation of Cú Chulainn when he is gripped by these war spasms, as well as his close connections with dogs and horses, suggests an element of shamanism in Celtic religion and mythology. Miranda Aldhouse-Green interprets several recurring themes in the myths – such as the importance of watery places, close connections between humans and animals, and shape-shifting – as all essentially shamanic.

As well as Cú Chulainn's own body-twisting spasms, he is stalked by a shape-shifting battle goddess – the Morrigan. Disguising herself as a noblewoman, she propositions Cú Chulainn, but he rejects her advances. A prodigious shape-shifter, she becomes his nemesis, attacking him in the form of different animals: an eel, a she-wolf and a heifer. When he is about to die, she appears at the ford to wash his armour, and when he finally dies, she perches on his shoulder in the form of a crow. Elsewhere in Irish mythology, the Morrigan appears as a whole flock of carrion crows on a field after battle. Shape-shifting also takes place in the Welsh tales; in the *Mabinogion*, the troublemaking brothers Gwydion and Gilfaethwy are punished by being transformed into a series of different animals. For a year at a time, they exist as a pair of deer, as wild boar and as wolves.

The shape-shifting in the myths is echoed in the art and archaeology of the Iron Age, and continues into the Roman period. The beautiful bronze flagon that accompanied the Glauberg warrior to the grave is decorated with small figurines at its rim; a seated god sits between two sphinx-like creatures, each with the body of a lion, but with a human face attached to the back of the neck, looking straight back at the seated deity. Other strange, mixed-up creatures appear in Celtic artwork: horses with human faces, snakes with rams' horns. The antlered god shown on the inner surface of the Gunderstrup cauldron sits next to a stag with identical antlers, almost as though, as Miranda Aldhouse-Green points out, the man is about to turn into the stag, or the stag into the man.

Some collections of skeletal material contain both human and animal bones – often looking more convincingly deliberate rather than accidental, as may have been the case at Gordion. Particular combinations of articulated animal bones also suggest some form of ritual deposition. For instance, at Danebury in Hampshire, archaeologists discovered a whole dog skeleton together with the articulated bones of a horse's leg. It's hard to put this down to the mere disposal of carcasses and, in this case, I have to admit that it looks like there may have been some ritual intent. And there are other cases of associated dog and horse remains – both powerful animals for the Celts.

Excavations of the Iron Age site of Duropolis in Dorset have uncovered more than fifty storage pits, dug down into the chalk and probably originally used to store grain. But many of the pits seem to have been decommissioned in a very particular way once they were no longer used for storage, by placing particular animal and human remains in the bottom, and filling them with earth. Some contain complete human skeletons; others contain animal limbs; a few hold combinations of body parts from different animals. One contained the skeletal remains of a headless sheep, with a cow skull placed carefully at its tail. There seems to be a deliberate intent to create a hybrid animal: a chimera.

It's also important to realize that the skeletons of these animals at the Duropolis site would have been fully fleshed when placed in the pits. They are not leftovers – not the waste after a feast. These would have been whole dead animals, or parts of animals, representing a substantial amount of meat. Archaeologists have suggested that such deposits, often in disused storage pits on Celtic sites, may represent acts of thanksgiving to the gods. One of the lead archaeologists at the Duropolis site, Dr Miles Russell of Bournemouth University, certainly thinks that's a reasonable explanation for these odd burials: 'The original inhabitants seem to have been dismembering the bodies of cow and horse, only to reassemble the body parts at the bottom of the disused pits. This seems bizarre to a modern audience, but to the original inhabitants it would have made perfect sense: offerings to the gods to ensure the increased success of the tribe and fertility of both crops and animal herds.'

Strange combinations of different animals, or animals and humans, may hint at shamanic practices and beliefs, where animal spirits could help humans to enter the spirit world. But sometimes the shape-shifting is about replication rather than a transformation into a completely different animal. It's very striking that, in both the Welsh and Irish myths, things often come in threes. In the *Mabinogion*, Branwen is one of three principal maidens of Britain; Rhiannon has three magical birds; Gwydion curses his brother three times. In Irish mythology, both the Morrigan and the Babdh, goddesses of war and death, sometimes appear in triplicate, rather like the witches in *Macbeth*. There are also three deities representing crafts, and three different goddesses of Ireland. And there are stories of kings and warriors being killed in three ways. This is one piece of Celtic lore that some archaeologists have claimed to be more than just a myth. They say there is hard, physical evidence for the triple death of kings.

Murder on the Mire

One Irish story, in the *Cycle of Kings*, describes the events leading up to the convoluted death of King Diarmuid. The king slays the man his wife has been having an affair with, and a Druid, or prophet, named Bec Mac De, foretells that he will suffer a three-fold death as a result – at the hands of one of the adulterer's relatives, Aedh. The prophecy was very precise: Diarmuid would be killed by wounding, burning, drowning and a ridge pole falling on his head (a fourfold death, in fact). Eventually the prophecy is fulfilled. Black Aedh, in the doorway of the house where the king is feasting, pierces Diarmuid through the chest with his spear and breaks his spine; Diarmuid flees back into the house, but Aedh's men set it on fire; Diarmuid immerses himself in a vat of ale to escape the flames; finally, the roof beam of the burning house falls on his head and finishes him off.

The triple deaths of kings and warriors described in the Irish myths, very often prophesied in advance, involve accidental fatal injuries as well as intentional assaults, but they may mythologize an actual practice: a ritual form of threefold killing. Perhaps this is a rare and valuable clue, from Celtic – rather than Roman – literature, that the Celts did indeed carry out human sacrifices.

The Roman accounts of gruesome practices among their barbarian neighbours north of the Alps may well have been deliberate anti-Celtic propaganda. They could also have stemmed from a misreading of funerary rites that seemed alien to them, perhaps inspired by ossuaries like Ribemont. The accounts of human sacrifices, in particular, could be malicious fictions, but there's another interesting possibility. If sacrifices did take place, could they have been a form of ritualized capital punishment? Caesar described the Celts undertaking human sacrifices to appease the gods, to secure protection or a victory in battle, but he also said that the Celts preferred to sacrifice thieves and criminals where possible. (It is interesting, of course, that the Romans appeared to consider the killing of people for religious purposes as barbaric, whereas gladiatorial contests and throwing people to the lions – killing for fun – were perfectly acceptable.)

The Irish tales suggest that the threefold death may have been associated with the sacrifice of kings – a very particular punishment reserved for failed rulers. This, argues Irish archaeologist Ned Kelly, is precisely what we are seeing in several recently discovered bog bodies from western Ireland.

I visited the National Museum of Ireland in Dublin to see two of these bog bodies. Crouching down beside a large glass case, I looked straight into the strangely crushed and twisted face of a bog body known as Clonycavan Man.

He was discovered in 2003, during peat cutting in County Meath. His body – or, at least, half of it – was found in the peat extraction machine. The body was the same colour as the peat itself – a deep orange-brown. The machine had cut straight through the body, at the waist. The human remains consisted of the upper body, the left upper arm down to the elbow, the right arm down to wrist, the head and the neck. While crushed and contorted, this half-body was well preserved, with soft tissues, including skin and hair, intact. Radiocarbon dating revealed the body to be between 2,200 and 2,400 years old – a Bronze Age predecessor of the Iron Age Celts. Although the lower half of his body has been lost, there was enough there to determine that this was a man, probably around the age of thirty when he died.

I looked closely at this half-body. His face was crushed fairly flat, but I could clearly see his blackened lips, his twisted nose and his eyelids. The skin had sagged over the bones, which had themselves softened and collapsed long ago in the acidic, watery grave of the bog. There was a tear in the skin at the bridge of his nose. He still had hair: long hair piled up on his head and also a few strands still clinging to his chin and upper lip – the remains of a goatee beard and moustache. Across the side of his jaw and in front of his crumpled ear, the skin was clean shaven.

The skin was so well preserved that it retained its texture – I could see its pores. But, at the same time, it had been stained brown and essentially turned into leather by the peat bog. It's odd to see human leather. We're quite used to leather made from animal skin, but human leather, even when it's the result of natural mummification like this, seems strange and a little unsettling.

The strangeness doesn't stop there. Human remains in the ground are usually fairly swiftly reduced to just hard tissues. It's the bones and teeth that persist the longest. But a peat bog does something quite different to a body. The soft tissues become tanned – naturally embalmed. The bone mineral dissolves in the acidic water of the bog; the bones soften and the three dimensional structure of the body collapses. I looked at this body dispassionately, objectively, interested to learn what I could about this individual and his death. But a bog body is also a very weird thing. The transformation of this body was extraordinary – its colour and shape had been changed in death. His dark brown skin now lay in folds and creases. His hair was reddish – stained by the peat. The head, lying on its right side, was flattened so that it was only a few inches wide. His neck was oddly contorted. The bog had transformed this dead human body into an other-worldly creature, like a twisted Cú Chulainn, frozen in his war spasm. Perhaps I'd been reading too many Celtic myths.

It was also clear that this man had not died a natural death. Pathologists have examined the body and found evidence of several injuries. A blow to the face had broken his nose, and the back of his head appears to have been struck several times with an axe. He clearly suffered a violent death. Other bog bodies also provide evidence of extremely violent deaths, suggesting that there may be something strange – and system-atic – going on here; something more interesting than simply the disposal of the bodies of murder victims in the bogs.

Just a few months before Clonycavan Man was found, another Irish bog body came to light – one which showed even more extreme evidence of violence. This body turned up in May 2003, during the digging of a drainage ditch in Old Croghan Bog. The remains of this bog body are also on display in the same gallery in the National Museum of Ireland, Dublin.

The remains of Old Croghan Man consist of a man's torso with arms and hands attached. The head and the lower half of the body are missing. He was an adult man, over twenty-five years of age, and powerfully built. He was probably quite tall – his height has been estimated at around six feet three inches. The body was naked when it was found, apart from a plaited leather cord around his left arm. I looked carefully at his hands. They were so amazingly well preserved that I could see his fingerprints. They were smooth, uncalloused. The nails were neatly trimmed. Archaeologists have suggested that these smooth and manicured hands indicate that this man wasn't used to manual work – that he was someone of very high social standing.

The dismemberment of this body seems to have happened, not in the steel teeth of an industrial peat-cutting machine, but at around the time of death. And, as well as being decapitated and sliced, quite cleanly, in half, this man suffered a stab wound to the left side of his chest. I could see the slightly gaping leaf-shaped incision. Any one of those violent injuries could have caused death – this is an example of what archaeologists call 'overkill'. The violence is much more than is needed to simply end someone's life. From the insults visible on this half-body, this man does look as though he's been killed in at least three ways: stabbing, beheading and being cut in half.

There were other, less severe, but even more peculiar injuries on the half-body of Old Croghan Man. His arms had been cut and hazel withies inserted through them. And his nipples appeared to have been partially cut. It's hard to know what to make of these other injuries, especially as there's no real way of knowing whether these insults to the body happened before or after death. The withies through the arms and the nipple slashing could be evidence of torture. But archaeologist Ned Kelly, the former Keeper of Irish Antiquities at the National Museum of Ireland, believes that there is something more strange going on – and that these injuries were part of the rites that accompanied the killing of a king.

I met up with Ned Kelly and we drove off to another site, to the museum labs at the old Collins Barracks. Ned had promised me that I was going to see a much more recent discovery there, and one which seemed to offer some other evidence of a ritual dimension in the killing of these individuals whose bodies were then consigned to their watery graves.

Discovered in Rossan Bog in 2012, the body that has become known as Moydrum Man had once again been found during industrial peat cutting. It had been badly damaged by this process, and wasn't noticed immediately, so it suffered further deterioration as it dried out – until eventually someone noticed that something other than peat had been pulled up out of the bog. What makes Moydrum Man so interesting is not so much the cause of his death, but the contents of his guts. In the lab, I was able to examine the remains of this body, which consisted of a flattened torso with some lower neck vertebrae still attached, but the head missing. The preserved intestines of this man were full of oval fruit stones. Moydrum Man had been X-rayed, and I could see the stones clearly on the radiograph – small, radiolucent ovals in the abdomen of the bog body – hundreds of them. Around 300, in fact.

Sloes are unpalatable fruits (unless used to flavour gin), and yet Moydrum Man had eaten hundreds of them. The sloe stones had reached his large intestine, so pathologists have estimated that he ate this odd meal some eight hours before he died. Ned believed that this formed a ritual meal. Sloes are important in Irish mythology and tradition. They're the fruit of the hawthorn, which itself has ritual significance as a marker of boundaries. And they ripen in late October, early November, around the time of the Celtic festival of Samhain – which we also know now as Halloween.

For Ned, Moydrum Man's last meal of sloes spoke strongly of ritual, and he believed that both Clonycavan Man and Old Croghan Man, with that clear evidence for violent assault on their bodies, were also the victims of ritual killings. He speculated that they met with this peculiar fate of triple killing, specifically reserved for a king who has failed – perhaps because the crops had been blighted by drought, or livestock decimated by disease. But Ned also believed that the triple death was about more than just punishment. There seemed to be 'overkill' – the infliction of several 'mortal' wounds, when just one of those injuries would have been enough to kill a man. Ned suggested that these 'three deaths' may have been designed to each assuage a different manifestation of the sovereignty goddess Sadhbh, who appeared in three guises: as maid, nymph and hag. The position of these bodies in the landscape was also important; they were deposited in ritually significant places, near hills where kings were inaugurated, or near boundaries between ancient kingdoms.

The problem with such interpretations of the bog bodies is that the physical evidence may cast light on how someone was killed, but, as I have mentioned before, it can never tell us why that person was killed. Was Ned just looking for ways to explain the archaeological finds through mythology? Could he justify the links he was making between accounts of history and mythology, written in the early Middle Ages, and prehistoric cultures dating to centuries, if not millennia earlier? Ned argued that there was a striking correspondence between the details described in the tales and the evidence presented by the bog bodies. But I was concerned that we risked entering into a circular argument again, using the Celtic myths to make inferences about the meaning of these deaths, interpreting them as ritualistic, and then using the bodies to support an ancient reality behind the myths.

The stories Ned told, about hills where kings were crowned, right back into the Iron Age and even earlier, about traditional boundaries having a similarly ancient origin, and about kings being ritually sacrificed to the sovereignty goddess when their luck ran out, were wonderful. I wanted to buy it. I wanted to believe in these ancient rituals and believe that the bog bodies were sacrificed kings. I wanted to believe that we could understand these ancient cultures in this much detail. But the stories only seemed to run around in circles, justifying themselves.

I wasn't convinced that the bog bodies constituted evidence of ritual death, let alone the triple death of kings. After all, Ned's story was just one among a number of possible hypotheses. There could be other reasons for very obviously violent deaths – that people were being made an example of, for instance, like being hanged, drawn and quartered. Even the withies through the arms and the cut nipples of Old Croghan Man could have been plain torture, rather than a complicated ritual associated with human sacrifice. And leaving the bodies in bogs could have been a much less thoughtful method of disposal than Ned was suggesting. And I didn't see any clear reason to infer that these deaths and depositions, sporadically appearing over the course of two millennia, should be linked by anything more than coincidence and accident. The role of chance is often underplayed, especially in archaeology. We like to spot patterns and, above all, we like to believe there are reasons for those patterns.

But what about Moydrum Man and his meal of sloes? If indeed these sloes were eaten raw, and not cooked or sweetened into something more palatable – and perhaps further chemical analyses may provide insight into that question – then they are difficult to explain away. It's hard to think of any mundane, ordinary, non-ritual reason for such an odd thing. On current evidence, I had to agree with Ned; the most probable explanation for the sloes seems to be that they were part of a ritual last meal.

But there was something about that body that didn't quite fit with Ned's more general theory of ritually sacrificed kings. Moydrum Man was very slightly built. While his head and key parts of the pelvis appeared to be missing, the bones that I could see on the radiograph were slender. The right clavicle in particular was short and slim. It was clear that this was an adult skeleton. There are further analyses to be carried out, and careful assessment of the CT scans of the body may provide useful information. But, for now, I'm prepared to stick my neck out and say that I think it's quite likely that Moydrum 'Man' was, in fact, a woman.

Murdered, Forgotten, Nameless, Terrible

The bog bodies remind us, once again, how difficult it is to reach back into the ancient depths of time, to peer through the centuries and see our Iron Age ancestors. Myths weave themselves into our imaginations, tempting us to believe we have achieved a meeting of minds with these people. But the reality is lost in translation, and in more than just the literal sense. Even the physical remains of people leave us struggling to understand them. They snatch their hands away and leave us, floating in dark water.

The day after my visit to the museum and its labs, I headed west to Old Croghan Bog, which lay darkly at the feet of Croghan Hill. Long, deep channels had been cut into the peat by industrial peat-cutting machines, and the blocks of peat lay piled up like metre-high bastions, defending nothing. Deeper ditches, filled with dark water, drained the soon-to-be-harvested peat. This peat, this not-quite-fossil-fuel mined from the ancient bogs, was largely destined to fire power stations. I kicked at the dry, dusty, denuded peat as I walked along. Fragments of half-rotted roots and branches looked like bits of a corpse, pieces of hair. But they were only the cadavers of trees and shrubs. I found a piece of a sheep's rib. Nothing more interesting.

Some distance away from the active peat extraction site on the bog was an area where this year's cutting had yet to start in earnest. I walked beside a long pile of peat, swathed in black plastic. At the end of this peat rampart, I could see a pair of wooden posts, stuck into the ground on the far side of a drainage ditch. I leaped over the ditch and made my way through the heather and bog cotton on this bank of peat, which had last been cut twelve years ago, until I reached the posts. They marked the spot where, in June 2003, peat cutting had revealed the half-body of Old Croghan Man. Given the scale of peat extraction and the mechanized nature of the mining, it was extraordinary that the body had been noticed at all. I wondered how many bodies ended up in pieces, in bags in garden centres, or in the furnaces of power stations – and how many human bodies still lay concealed under this vast blanket bog.

I sat down on a pile of peat and wondered how different the landscape would have been in the third or fourth century BC, when Old Croghan Man had been brought here to die. There would probably have been some signs of agriculture around, though perhaps not as widespread as today. There were likely to have been patches of woodland and swathes of bog then, just as there are now. The place did seem a little eerie – but was that just because I knew a man had been killed here, suffering a terrible death, all those years ago?

Had he been a king? I let myself picture that – the king of a small Celtic kingdom, who had failed his people in some way, and who had been brought out on the bogs to be sacrificed to the sovereign goddess, Sadhbh. Was that how it happened? In truth, we'll never know. But let's let our imaginations run loose a little, with the myths of old Ireland to inspire us.

It is a dismal, grey day – the last day of October. The king stands tall in the landscape; even as we see him bowed under the weight of the knowledge of his imminent fate, he is a striking figure. He is accompanied on to the bog by just a few Druids. They are clothed, but the king has been stripped naked, except for a plaited leather thong around his upper right arm. He came into the world naked; he will leave it naked.

He is a young man. He has seen twenty-six summers come and go. He looks up at Croghan Hill, rising out of the bog. Seven summers ago, at the solstice, he was made king up on the top of that hill, the fairy mound where the ancestors are buried. The same Druids who are now leading him out on to the bog had been there on the hill, anointing him and initiating him into the sacred role of kingship. Those holy men have been his friends, mentors and advisors. But he always knew his death would come at their hands. Out here in the bog, where dark pools of still water reflect the scudding clouds, the Otherworld is near. As darkness falls, the king senses the presence of the Aos Si, the shadowy people of the mounds. They are waiting for him to join them.

In this liminal place, the trappings of status and royalty have no meaning. The only power that a man may have over another man in this place is the power to take his life.

He'd woken this morning knowing how this day would end. In the pale grey light of dawn, he'd ridden off, alone, to the river. There, he drew his sword, tested in battle, and hurled it into the water, then rode back home.

The children were up when he got back to the roundhouse, but he didn't go inside. He knelt down at the door, and his twin sons came to him. He held them tight for a moment, silently wishing them strength and luck and happiness. His wife, his queen, was standing on the threshold and he stood up to embrace her. Her face was red with crying, but she did not weep now. They kissed goodbye – one last, long kiss. Leaving her, he walked to the gate of the enclosure, where the Druids were waiting for him.

His wife held the two-year-old boys close against her skirt, and watched him walk away. She was angry and resigned at the same time. She'd always feared this day would come. And when the summer rains had lasted for days, then weeks, then months, and the crops rotted in the fields, she knew that he would have to pay for the inevitable famine with his life. She knew it, but she resented it.

She believed in the small spirits of the woods and the streams and the hills. She didn't buy into the nonsense that the Druids promulgated: the sacred rites, the stupid rituals and the dogma that kept them powerful – too powerful to trust. She resented them forcing their lies on to children. But she knew that fighting the system was futile. She may have been a queen – and she would always be a queen – but the Druids were so much more powerful than mere kings and queens. She took the twins inside and pulled the heavy curtain across the door. She had no idea what rituals would be performed this day, but she knew how the day would end, and she couldn't bear the waiting.

Towards nightfall, the Druids lead the king further out on to the bog, to the edge of a wide pool. They do not speak to him. He is already a ghost in this world. A hand on his shoulder induces him to kneel. He closes his eyes and listens to the faint murmur of the wind on the water, an owl, distant, distant wailing.

And then it comes. A searing pain in his upper chest as the dagger tears through skin, muscle, lung and blood vessels. He falls forward, coughing up blood, and the sword comes down smoothly on his neck, severing it in one clean blow. He's gone. He doesn't know the rest – the cuts made to his nipples; the incisions on his arms and the withies; his body divided in two, straight through the waist. His upper body is left in that peat-dark pool. The other pieces of him are carried through the bog and left in other pools along the way, before the Druids walk in darkness up on to the top of Croghan Hill and light the fire.

She pulls back the curtain and looks out. The clouds have blown over and the stars are bright. She sees the light burning orange on Croghan Hill. It is over.

Somehow, we can still mourn the death of an individual who died centuries ago. We can read mythology and feel connected with our ancestors through ancient places in the landscape. We can take the evidence out of the ground and from ancient texts and use it to reconstruct the lives of people long gone, nameless and forgotten. We can give them new names, new stories.

Scientific techniques enable us to be more sure of some facts than we were in the past – of the precise dates of certain objects and events, of the provenance of raw materials, of the detailed manufacture of some articles, of the age, sex and cause of death of a particular person. History provides us with a fragmentary and distorted record of this ancient past. Historians caution us to approach written evidence with a critical mind, to consider how much we may trust each 'fact'.

But all these facts can seem quite stark and somehow inhuman on their own. In order to make sense of it all, to find some meaning, we must synthesize and hypothesize. The hypotheses we generate are themselves stories, or parts of stories. We must test them against the evidence, and some will prove more robust than others. Storytelling is enticing, especially when we have such inspiring material to start with. But we must try to be clear where reasonable inference ends and where real storytelling starts.

When it comes to Old Croghan Man, nobody actually knows why he was killed; nobody knows what motivated his assailant or assailants to attack him so brutally; nobody knows how his body ended up in that bog. All I really know for a fact is that he was a young man who suffered some terrible injuries, that one of the potentially fatal wounds killed him, and that his body was finally left in that bog where he was discovered. Everything else is Celtic storytelling.

IDENTITY
AND LEGACY

A NEW VIEW OF AN
ANCIENT PEOPLE

The Glittering Prizes

The Celts have inspired stories of all sorts, from archaeological and historical hypotheses to novels. Some focus
on individual lives – we can make reasonable but limited
inferences from the archaeological remains found at sites like
Hochdorf or Old Croghan Bog, and from the historical
accounts of someone like Boudica – and those satisfy our
desire to know about these ancestors, to some extent. Of
course, we can embellish the hypotheses and turn them into
half-fictional accounts to satisfy our need for meaning and
storytelling.

But a different sort of meaning is discovered when we take
a wider view, away from the focus on specific individuals,
looking at the broader landscape, as we try to comprehend
changes through time.

I started out by saying I wanted to get closer to the Celts,
to find out who they were and how they lived. Having tried to
track down the Celts – travelling from the bogs of Ireland in
the west to the plains of Anatolia in the east – I'm now more
familiar with at least a few people who lived and died in the
first millennium BC: the Hochdorf Prince, the Bettelbühl
Princess, the Glauberg warrior and, to some extent, Boudica

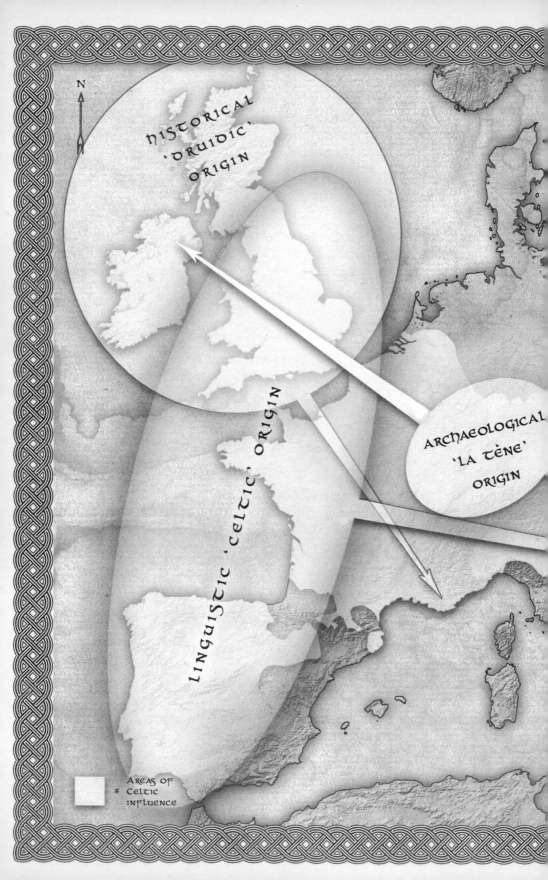

N

HISTORICAL
'DRUIDIC'
ORIGIN

ARCHAEOLOGICAL
'LA TÈNE'
ORIGIN

LINGUISTIC 'CELTIC' ORIGIN

= AREAS OF
CELTIC
INFLUENCE

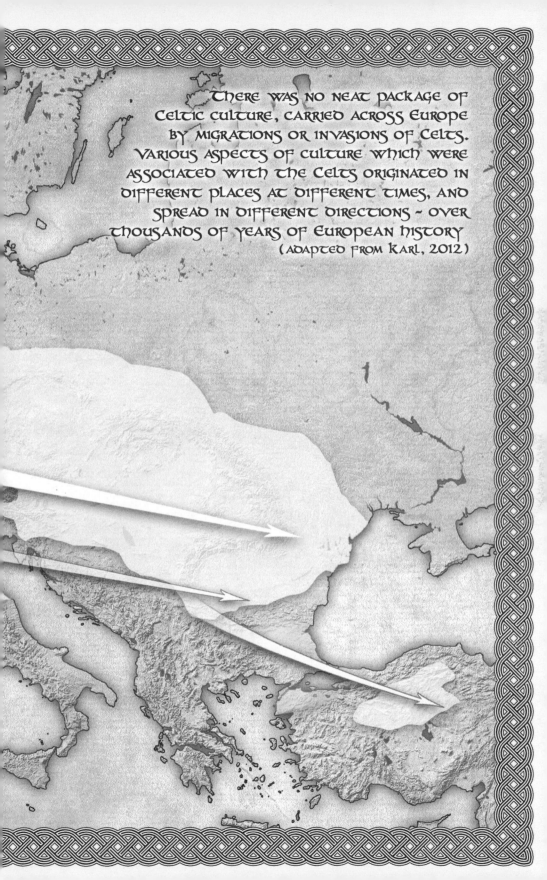

There was no neat package of Celtic culture, carried across Europe by migrations or invasions of Celts. Various aspects of culture which were associated with the Celts originated in different places at different times, and spread in different directions ~ over thousands of years of European history

(ADAPTED FROM KARL, 2012)

and Vercingetorix, as well as the people who met with violent deaths at Gordion and in the Irish bogs. The biography of each of these people is incomplete and fragmentary – sometimes drawn from classical sources; sometimes pieced together from the archaeological, material evidence. Nevertheless, they offer us intimate glimpses into the detail of life in Celtic Europe – life in what the ancient Greeks referred to, at least in part, as Celtica – at different times and in different places.

Apart from the individuals at Gordion, who may very well have been 'ordinary' people, the others are all drawn from the social elite. This is always a problem: history often tends to focus on kings and queens, princes and princesses, leaving us to guess about the lives of ordinary folk. And the problem is compounded by the near invisibility of the common woman and man in the archaeological record. Sometimes it's a question of focus – like magpies, our eyes are drawn to the golden and glittering treasures in the tombs of the elite. Walking through a museum, we might glance briefly at the less shiny pottery of the humbler home, while heading for that case where we can see the beautiful torcs shimmering.

It's hard not to be drawn to that element: the untarnished, astonishing brilliance that made the metal so attractive to our Bronze Age and Iron Age ancestors still works its magic on us today. And the permanence of metal, even heavily oxidized iron and bronze, provides us with wonderful insights into the technological knowledge and skill of those societies where this expertise was only passed on face to face – shown and spoken, but never written down. Probed with our latest technology, those metal artefacts reveal the secrets of their fabrication, but of course what they also do is show the artistic flair and appreciation that these prehistoric people possessed.

It's clear that art was important to them, just as it is to us, and yet so much of their art is, of course, lost forever – made using materials that have not withstood the test of time – designs woven into fabrics and baskets, or carved in wood. The salt mines of Hallstatt, even though they preserve objects that are more functional than beautiful, remind us just how much is missing from conventional archaeological sites. So much beauty has rotted away. Looking at the beautiful objects that have survived, then, connects us back to those ancestors in a way which makes the centuries fall away. And so I think we can forgive ourselves, a little, when our gaze settles on their most splendid and prestigious creations. Nevertheless, we must remember that, partly because of the nature of the evidence, and partly because of our predilections, we tend to focus on high art and high politics. And perhaps that concentration means we see patterns of change that would have been less acute for the commoner. Even at the level of the social elite, continuity may have been more important a theme than archaeologists have often presumed in the past.

But what do all these separate lives, these disparate collections of cultural objects, these places have in common with each other? Some might say not much, that all I've done is to blindly follow tradition, labelling the Iron Age people of Europe, north of the Mediterranean civilizations, as Celtic – a name that doesn't represent any real connection between these people and places. People might argue that 'Celtic' is a construct – a way of referring to a ragbag group of non-Greek and non-Roman barbarians who really had very little in common, that there are areas of the Celtic world where enclaves of particular types and styles of artefacts predominate, but there is not a consistent stamp of Celtic identity across Europe and throughout the first millennium BC. At least, there's nothing consistent in material culture.

But there is something that does connect all these people through time and space, and that is language. If we must choose one aspect of their culture to define the Celts – even if some warn against this – it must surely be language.

In northern Italy and Switzerland, ancient inscriptions written in Lepontic, using an Etruscan alphabet, have long been thought to represent the earliest written Celtic. They date back to as early as the sixth century BC. The Gaulish language, first written using the Greek alphabet, appears in inscriptions dating to the third century BC. And then we have St Jerome, in the fourth century AD, telling us that the language of the Galatians was similar to that spoken by the Treveri of the Moselle valley. Right across the Celtic world, then, people spoke Celtic languages. Today's Celtic languages – Welsh, Scottish and Irish Gaelic, and Breton – represent the descendants or the relics of that ancient language, which was once so much more widely spoken.

Modern Celtic identity really depends on the persistence of those languages in Scotland, Ireland, Wales, Brittany and, until very recently, Cornwall. And, since Edward Lhuyd recognized the connections between those languages back in the early eighteenth century, they have been considered to be badges of a very ancient Celtic identity. But just how far back does that identity extend?

Our understanding of the Celts has changed considerably over the centuries since Lhuyd wrote about Celtic languages. Simple themes of invasion and replacement have given way to more complex ideas and models, where culture is dynamic and multifaceted, and ideas – including language itself – are carried through networks of communication.

The evolution of the Celtic language was undoubtedly complex – it didn't suddenly spring into being, fully formed. But it must have emerged somewhere. Where and when did people start speaking a recognizably Celtic language? And did it come from central Europe, perhaps a branch of Lepontic or something similar? The old theories pointed to the traditional Celtic homeland in central Europe. But new research, bringing together exciting new discoveries in linguistics with archaeology, has recently led to a radical new theory that changes everything we thought we knew about the origin of the Celts.

And so there's one last place to visit – somewhere I didn't really expect to be heading when I started this journey. But it will perhaps provide the answer to the biggest question of all about the origin of the Celts, helping to bring together all the strands of my journey across Europe.

Tartessian and the Earliest Celts

In order to track down the earliest Celts – by which I mean the earliest people to have been using anything that looks like a Celtic language – I headed a long way south, to somewhere we don't consider to be particularly 'Celtic' today: the Algarve, in south-western Portugal. Nobody there speaks a

Celtic language any more, but new analysis of very old evidence suggests that, in the very, very distant past, they did. It was when this discovery in linguistics collided with a re-interpretation of the archaeology that the astonishing new theory of Celtic origins was born.

Barry Cunliffe is an archaeologist who, it's fair to say, is obsessed with the Iron Age. In the late nineties, he began to doubt the standard model of Celtic origins and spread. The archaeology, to his eye, just didn't fit. Based largely on archaeological evidence, he began to construct another hypothesis about the origins of the Celts, focusing not on central Europe, but on the Atlantic-facing western fringe of Europe. This emerging new 'Atlantic Fringe' hypothesis caused some consternation among Celtic scholars. But further support for it emerged from the analysis of some very ancient inscriptions in Portugal – inscriptions that are even older than Lepontic.

In 2007, the Celtic linguist John Koch met up with Barry Cunliffe, and told him that some scholars were describing some inscriptions on ancient stone stelae from southwestern Portugal as 'Celtic'. This seemed like an important lead, and John started to reanalyze the inscriptions, to test the heretical idea that they could possibly represent the earliest written evidence of a Celtic language. What John learned, from his careful deciphering of the rune-like inscriptions, convinced him that he was indeed reading the language of the ancient Celts.

John met me in Portugal and we drove to the picturesque town of Almodôvar, where the Alentejo plain grades into the hills of the Serra do Caldeirão. That evening, we tracked down what appeared to be the only restaurant in town, and

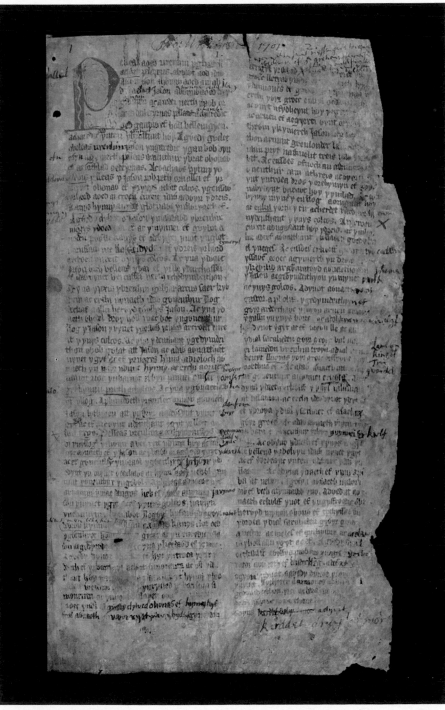

Written in the 'Middle Welsh' language and dating from around the fourteenth century, *The Red Book of Hergest* is one of the sources of the *Mabinogion*. Reproduced by kind permission of Jesus College, Oxford

Peat cutting in Ireland – to provide fuel – has been practiced for millennia

Clonycavan Man, discovered in 2003 and dating to the second or third century BC. This man is thought to have been around thirty years old when he was killed, by several blows to the head

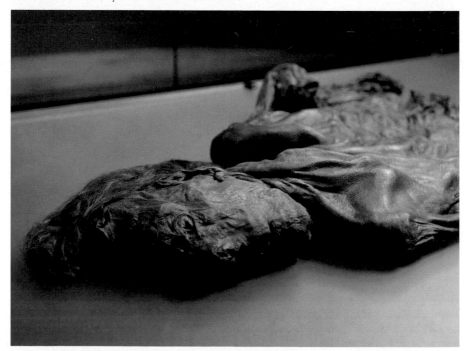

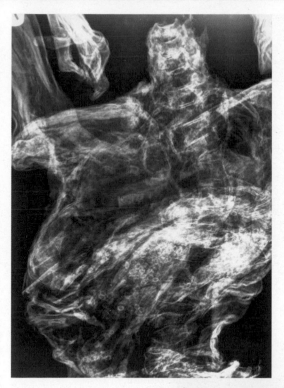

Radiograph (X-ray image) of Moydrum Man showing his last meal of sloes which Ned Kelly believes was part of a ritual leading up to this man's sacrifice or execution

Many stelae have been found in southwest Portugal bearing inscriptions in a Tartessian script – which could be the oldest attested Celtic language. This reproduction of a stela is in the Museu da Escrita do Sudoeste, Almodôvar, Portugal

Archaeologists have discovered over a hundred Tartessian inscriptions dating back to the early Iron Age, and suggesting that Celtic languages may have developed in western – not central – Europe. This one includes an engraving of a warrior, as well as an inscription

Neil Oliver and I meet up on the west coast of Ireland at the end of our Europe-wide search for the Celts

started to talk about ancient Celtic inscriptions and the origin of the Celts. Then we drove to our lodgings, up in the hills, near Almodôvar. On the way, a startled, sleek, brown mustelid dashed across the road, lit up in my headlights, but safely reached the other side. Ah, the Tartessian weasel, I thought. I'd read something about the Tartessian weasel, and I made a mental note to ask John about it. But, for now, the glimpse of such a famous beast could only be a good omen in my search for the earliest Celts.

I was rudely awoken the next morning by a particularly raucous donkey braying. Opening the shutters, I looked out over gently rolling hills dotted with olive and cork trees. It was late spring; the butterfly lavender was in flower and the gum cistus bushes were full of wide-open white blooms. Apart from a few telegraph poles and overhead lines, there was little sign of the twenty-first century here. I could be looking out over an Iron Age landscape, I thought to myself, lost in the romance of the place.

On the way to Almodôvar, to the small museum that has been created specially to house the stones bearing the ancient inscriptions, I asked John what he thought about the traditional model of Celtic origins – that old story about the source of 'Celticness' being in central Europe, with the Hallstatt and La Tène Iron Age cultures emerging around the Alps and spreading to the south, east and west.

'Well, it's essentially a nineteenth-century model of Celtic origins, based on those impressive finds from central Europe. But it ignores more recent discoveries from Iberia. Since the 1970s, there's been more evidence emerging of Celtic languages in Iberia, and that just hasn't been incorporated into the standard model. It's almost been relegated to being a footnote or an afterthought.'

'And you think that the Celts were definitely here in Iberia?'

'Yes, I think they most certainly were. We've tended to focus on what Herodotus said about the Celts living close to the source of the Danube, but he also wrote that the Celts lived beyond the Pillars of Hercules – the Strait of Gibraltar – and next to people called the Kunetes.'

'Who were the Kunetes?'

'Well, I think that they were probably Celts too. Despite the fact that Herodotus makes a distinction between the Keltoi and the Kunetes, this name certainly appears to be a Celtic one. It involves the stem "kun", which means "dog" or "hound", and is also used to describe Celtic warriors. It sounds derogatory, but the Celts saw hounds or wolves as having admirable qualities, so the epithet comes to mean a brave, fearless warrior.'

Like Cú Chulainn, in the Irish myths, then; but here was a whole population, a tribe, who seem to have been known as 'the Hounds'. I asked John if there were any archaeological traces of these people.

'We're finding more and more evidence of these people and their culture, but we've also got archaeological evidence of something else that Herodotus mentions. He talks about the Celts and the Kunetes living here, in the far west, and it's clear that he's writing about a contemporary situation. But he also mentions a civilization that has really ended by the time he is writing, in the mid-fifth century BC. This civilization was centred on a town called Tartessos. And archaeologists have found evidence of this place – we're now sure that it is modern-day Huelva, just over the border, in Spain, to the east of us.'

I was intrigued by Tartessos. It's first mentioned in ancient accounts from Greece and the Near East, and it sounds almost mythical: a rich civilization near the western edge of the known world, ruled over by an incredibly long-lived king, where the rivers ran rich with tin and silver, and dangerous weasels or ferrets roamed the countryside. These Tartessian weasels clearly made an impression on classical writers, being mentioned several times. Aelian, writing some time around the end of the third century BC, records the death of Aristides of Locris following a lethal bite from a Tartessian ferret. On his deathbed, Aristides bemoaned the fact that he had been fatally wounded by such a lowly beast; he would rather have been mauled by something more formidable, like a lion or leopard. Herodotus also mentions the Tartessian ferret as being similar to ferrets living in northern Africa. In the fifth century, Hesychius wrote a sort of dictionary, where, under the letter *T*, he includes, 'Tartessos: a city near the pillars of Hercules' and, 'Tartessians: ferrets'.

The classical writers allude to other odd beasts inhabiting the seas near ancient Tartessos. Aristophanes, in *The Frogs*, mentions a terrifying Tartessian sea-eel, which was likely to attack your lungs (although others write about Tartessian eels simply as delicious edible fish), and a later Roman writer mentions a 'monstrous sea-tiger of Tartessus'.

The Greek and Roman writers seem to be stressing how exotic Tartessos was, lying at the edge of the known world, with strange and terrifying beasts both on land and in the sea.

It was like writing *Here be Dragons* at the edge of a map. But John thought that there could have been another reason for the tales of frightening creatures. The accounts probably drew on the stories of seafarers, but, while these may have been embellished simply to make them better in the telling, this could also have been a deliberate ruse by the Phoenicians to scare off potential competitors. If they could maintain control over trade in the western Mediterranean, they were clearly on to a good thing. The wealth of Tartessos was legend-ary, and flowed from its metal resources. Tin and silver were sought-after commodities in the Bronze Age, and the city became a trading partner of the Phoenicians. Ephorus, in the fourth century BC, wrote this: '. . . a very prosperous market called Tartessos, a famous city, with much tin carried by river, as well as gold and copper from Celtic lands.'

Aristotle wrote that the first Phoenicians reaching Tartessos traded olive oil for so much silver that 'no one could keep it or accept it'. Other accounts, including several passages in the Old Testament, refer to 'ships of Tarshish', in the time of King Solomon, coming back laden with silver, gold, ivory, apes and peacocks.

Tartessos was ruled by a famous king, called Arganthonios, whose name seems to come from the Celtic word for silver, and who was said to have enjoyed an impressively long life. Herodotus writes about the Phocaeans, 'the first Greeks to make long sea voyages', visiting Tartessos and making friends with Arganthonios, who ruled for eighty years and lived to the ripe old age of 120. Later Roman writers, including Pliny the Elder, would extend this to an even more impressive 150 years. John thought it possible that this legend of longevity came about because 'Arganthonios' was an official name for a king, as the leader of a silver-trading empire, rather than a personal name. Herodotus describes the Phocaean Greeks meeting King Arganthonios at Tartessos in the middle of the sixth century BC, but he also mentions an earlier voyage of the sea captain, Kolaios, from Samos to Tartessos, in the mid-seventh century BC. It's quite likely that the Phocaeans and Kolaios each met an Arganthonios – but that, with a hundred years between these voyages, it had not been the same man.

Tartessos also became associated with the legend and worship of Hercules – and, in fact, this is why we still refer to the Strait of Gibraltar as the 'Pillars of Hercules'. Writing in the second century AD, Arrian described ancient Tartessos as a Phoenician town, containing a temple dedicated to Hercules (of Tyre). And Tartessos also became part of the myth of Hercules – who travelled across Europe to capture the cattle of the monster Geryon, described by some as king of the Tartessians.

This kingdom, then, was well known in the ancient world, featuring in straightforward histories but also passing into legend. But was it possible to locate it today? Although several classical writers, including the Roman writer Avienus, writing in the fourth century AD, identified the ancient Tartessos as Gadir (now Cadiz), John believed that the site of modern Huelva was a better candidate. He thought that the Roman writers were confusing the much earlier kingdom of Tartessos with the later, Phoenician city of Gadir, which was only founded in the Iron Age. Based on archaeological excavations, Huelva was first proposed to be the site of ancient Tartessos in the 1960s. The archaeological deposits at Huelva date back to the tenth century BC. And broader archaeological investigations have since revealed a more widespread area of Tartessian culture, stretching from Andalusia into southern Portugal, spanning the tenth to the sixth centuries BC.

As our conversation took us back in time, we had spiralled into the centre of Almodôvar, navigating our way through a labyrinthine one-way system, all the way to the Museu da Escrita do Sudoeste, Almodôvar (the Museum of South-western Inscriptions, Almodôvar). There were two small galleries containing a selection of the inscribed stones, or stelae, which had been discovered in south-western Portugal. A stela is a stone slab that is designed to stand upright, forming a marker. Most – perhaps all – of these particular stone markers were gravestones.

On the ground floor, a single room held a collection of nine stelae, every single one with strings of strange letters engraved into it. John made a beeline for a tall stela in the corner. It was a stone he hadn't seen before. It had been found in 1998, and its discovery and inscription had been published in Portuguese, but this was John's first glimpse of it. He excitedly got out his notebook, sat down crosslegged beside the stone, and started to copy down the letters.

This inscribed stela, like the others, would originally have been a gravestone, but it had been reused in antiquity as a door jamb, with a vertical channel carved out towards the right-hand side. Part of the inscription had almost completely been worn away, rubbed almost out of existence by the swinging of the door. Then the stone had gone on to serve another purpose; it had been recycled once again as a grave marker – it had been discovered in a late Roman grave.

John was excited by the chance to examine this particular stela for the first time. But the inscription on it was damaged and fragmentary. In the opposite corner of the room, there was a replica of another, much better preserved stone. This one stood about four feet tall, and its inscription was almost completely intact. Rather than regular lines of lettering, the script snaked around the edges of the stone, then spiralled in towards the middle. The letters themselves were quite peculiar. Some looked like runes. Others resembled Greek letters.

John had finished transcribing the new stone and I asked him about this more complete inscription. It was from a necropolis in Fonte Velha, where several of these stelae were discovered. It was found lying face down on top of the grave, like many other stelae. John thought it unlikely that the stelae had just fallen over in this way – it seemed too much of a coincidence that they were all face down. They were clearly designed to be set upright in the ground, as all of them possessed a blank lower portion. But, perhaps, some time after burial, they were purposely laid flat as part of the funerary ritual. It's another of those archaeological conundrums that we'll never really know the answer to.

'And can you read this one?' I asked John.

'Well, yes. It starts in the bottom right-hand corner . . .'

He pointed to the beginning of the inscription and traced its spiral with his finger: '. . . *Lokobo niirabo to araiai kalte lokon ane narke kak isiinkolobo ii te-ro-bare be tasiioonii.*'

It was like an incantation. It sent a shiver down my spine. John was reading out forgotten words from over two and half millennia ago.

He attempted a translation of the inscription. The first word seemed to be the name of a god or gods – the Lugoves. It was a Celtic name, similar to 'Lugh' in the Irish pantheon and 'Lleu' in Welsh. So the inscription began by invoking the Lugoves of the Neri tribe. Then, *'araiai kalte'* could mean something about ploughed land and a grove – which refer to the necropolis where the stela was found. Or, alternatively, *'kalte'* could mean 'warrior' or 'Celt'. *'Lokon'* is a burial or a funerary urn. John thought the word *'narke'* meant something like 'lies unmoving, beneath'. The next part seemed to invoke 'the heroes' – that's the meaning of the *'isiinkolobo'* word. Then there was a word relating to carrying – *'te-ro-bare'* – which means that the necropolis has received the deceased, who is named as 'Ta[ch]seoonus'.

It was clear that the translation wasn't easy. For a start, the alphabet used for these south-western or 'Tartessian' inscriptions was unusual. The basis was certainly Phoenician – but Phoenician writing had no vowels. So it seems that the Tartessians were doing what the Greeks also did (and they may have been doing it even earlier than the Greeks): basing their written language on Phoenician, but adding in letters for vowels. Looking at the inscription, I could recognize some of the letters were similar to Greek consonants, but they were back-to-front, because Tartessian usually reads right to left. The vowels, on the other hand, were quite different from Greek. The letter drawn like an *o*, looking so similar to little 'o', omicron, in Greek, was actually an *e* sound. For the *o* sound there was another symbol entirely, which looked a bit like a hash: a vertical stroke with two shorter oblique strokes crossing it. It looked distinctly un-*o*-like.

I was interested in how John could possibly know what the vowel sounds of this extinct language should be, given that no one actually spoke ancient Tartessian any more, and with the added complication that the Tartessians hadn't simply adopted an existing alphabet. The Phoenician basis of the written language was, of course, an important clue to the consonants, and later Celtic inscriptions, using Roman script, revealed how words should sound. Finding similar words in Tartessian meant that John could deduce the sounds of the Tartessian letters.

But, of course, being able to read the words, to sound them out, was only the start. This written language may have used the Phoenician alphabet as its basis, but the language itself was not Phoenician. This is where John's linguistic sleuthing really came to the fore, as he'd had to make careful comparisons with other known, ancient languages in order to translate Tartessian – and to elucidate its relationship with those other languages.

There was a recurring string of similar words on the stelae – some kind of formula – which represented a standard form of words relating to death and burial. Although the tense of the verbs and the order of the words were sometimes different, this formula was a helpful clue in translating the inscriptions. The most frequently repeated word in this formula was the verb that appeared on the Fonte Velha stela as '*narke*'. Sometimes it appeared on other stones as '*narken*', '*narketi*' or '*narkenti*'. It looked like it was behaving like an Indo-European verb – and this was important, especially as many scholars in the past had thought Tartessian too strange to belong to the Indo-European language family. Although there didn't seem to be an equivalent word in any of the known Celtic languages, ancient or modern, 'narke' sounded very much like the Greek word 'narco', which means 'to grow stiff, numb, dead', and which gives us 'narcotics' and 'narco-lepsy'. But John didn't think it was simply a borrowed Greek word – instead, he thought that the Greek and Tartessian words were similar because they were both, ultimately, from the same ancestral, Indo-European language.

So John was sure that Tartessian was Indo-European – but was it Celtic? Some linguists have said that, while Tartessian certainly includes some Celtic names, this is a red herring and the names are embedded in a language that is itself non-Celtic. But John's careful analysis of all the Tartessian inscriptions – and there are nearly a hundred of them – turned up more and more words that appeared to be analogous to words in other Celtic languages, ancient and modern. This wasn't a mere sprinkling of Celtic loan-words, but something much deeper. In the end, it was the density of the Celtic words and forms in Tartessian which convinced John that Tartessian really was the oldest attested Celtic language.

In his book about the south-western inscriptions and the Tartessian language, John writes that 'the long-held spell of the Hallstatt and La Tène cultures on [ideas about] the origin of the Celts must begin to loosen.' If Tartessian is indeed Celtic, then it is too far away and too early to fit the traditional idea of Celtic origins in central Europe, in the Iron Age. The Tartessian language cannot have been brought to Iberia by Celts who originated and migrated from around the Alps in the early Iron Age. It seems that some Iberians, at least, were already speaking a Celtic language right at the start of the

Iron Age, and it probably went back much further, into the Bronze Age – and perhaps even earlier than that.

With these stones in Portugal, it felt like I was finally getting closer to understanding who the Celts really were and where they came from. Despite that eye-catching blossoming of Celtic culture in the La Tène period, in central and north-western Europe, it seems that linguistics offers us the best chance of understanding the origins of the Celts because it's language that really did unite these groups of people right across Europe, and through centuries. And here, carved in strange letters on these monumental grave markers, was the earliest evidence of a Celtic language.

Archaeologists in the past might have been tempted to come up with an invasionist interpretation for these stones. Who were these people, arriving in south-western Iberia in the late Bronze Age, bringing this tradition of inscribed grave-markers, and their language, with them? But, in fact, it's only the inscriptions that were a novelty. The stelae belong to a tradition that goes right back into the middle Bronze Age. People in this region had been erecting such stone grave-markers for 1,000 years before they started to write on them. Archaeologists have found around a hundred of these stelae in south-western Spain and Portugal. These earlier stelae don't have writing on them, but they carry engravings of warriors.

Upstairs in the museum, John showed me the 'Aboboda I' stela, which illustrated the continuity beautifully; here, an engraved image of a warrior appeared in a 'frame' containing an inscription. The warrior was a curious little figure, clearly wearing some form of armour, brandishing two throwing spears in his stick-like arms, and with a smiling, cartoon-like face. John translated the inscription as, 'For the hero, Valkos: they are bound unmoving . . . this grave has borne him for the winged one.'

The Tartessian inscriptions emerge within this existing funerary tradition, where the Bronze Age Iberians were already accustomed to erecting stone stelae as grave markers. This was a strong local tradition, and something quite special to the Iberian peninsula. But, at the same time, this south-western corner of Europe was part of a much wider culture. The material evidence clearly shows that the lands of western Europe were linked by maritime connections as far back as the Neolithic, and those networks of exchange continued – and thrived – as the Bronze Age took off. The Iberian penin-sula was an integral part of a well-connected group of Bronze Age societies that faced the Atlantic. All along the Atlantic seaboard, from Portugal to Scotland, archaeologists have found similar artefacts, spanning a period from roughly 1300 to 700 BC. This 'cultural complex' includes socketed bronze axes, leaf-shaped bronze swords, lunate spearheads, V-notched shields and feasting gear, including cauldrons, roasting spits and flesh hooks. The cultural connectivity between these places – modern Ireland, Britain, France, Spain and Portugal – is such that archaeologists talk about the 'Atlantic Bronze Age'.

Archaeology bears witness to the flourishing exchange of goods and ideas along the Atlantic seaboard, but those connections are also attested in historical sources.

In *Ora Maritima*, Avienus writes: '*Tartessiisque in termi-nos Oestrumnidum negotiandi mos erat*', which translates as,

'The Tartessians were accustomed to trading as far as the Oestrumnides'.

The Oestrumnides – the 'western isles' – were rich in tin and lead, and Avienus describes them as lying two days' sailing from Ireland. They could have been Cornwall, Brittany or the Isles of Scilly.

But from around 900 BC, the Iberian peninsula started to be drawn into a cultural change that was sweeping across the Mediterranean, as the Bronze Age gradually gave way to the early Iron Age. Iberia didn't turn its back on the Atlantic, but there was an increased focus on connections to the east. By around 800 BC, that orientalizing influence had become really serious as the Phoenicians started to establish colonies in the western Mediterranean. Trading with the Oestrumnides in one direction and with the Phoenicians in the other, Iberia – with Tartessos at its centre – formed a link between the Mediterranean and Atlantic systems of exchange. Silver, copper, gold and tin from the Atlantic flowed, via Tartessos, into the Mediterranean, while wine, oil, jewellery and figurines flowed into Iberia from the east.

But along with all those eastern imports came something more important than the luxury goods, or indeed any new metallurgy. The Phoenicians brought with them a new technology, which would eventually transform the world in a way more profound than any new metal: writing. And by the middle of the seventh century BC, the Tartessians were using this Phoenician trick to write their own inscriptions, in their own language, on their own funeral stelae.

The presence of a Celtic language at such an early date in Iberia, attested by these inscribed stelae in south-western

Portugal, presents a problem for the traditional story of Celtic origins. It remains a problem even if we've moved beyond invasion hypotheses, if we're still clinging to a central European origin for Celtic language. Before Tartessian was recognized as Celtic, the earliest attested Celtic language in Europe was Lepontic, from northern Italy. And the earliest examples of this language are very short inscriptions, often single words, on pieces of pottery and a few gravestones, dating to the fifth or early sixth centuries BC. The earliest of the inscribed stelae from Portugal date from around 650 BC to 625 BC. And, of course, this is only the earliest date we have for the written language, which already seems to be mature, fully formed. John thought it safe to assume that the spoken language had already been in place for a long time – though we can't be sure how long. But there was certainly plenty of other, material evidence for cultural continuity in the area, and the origins of the Celtic language may go right back to the earliest use of metal, and perhaps even earlier than that.

A Celtic language existing this early – right at the beginning of the Iron Age in western Europe, and probably going back even earlier – certainly doesn't fit with the old traditional story of the Celts originating in central Europe and then expanding, pushing out, and eventually reaching the Atlantic fringe. It's the last nail in the coffin for that idea.

'We need to think again about the origins of the Celts,' said John. 'I think there's been a tendency to ignore the Iberian material, to sweep it under the carpet. And that's because there is a conflict with the standard model if we have this evidence of a very early Celtic presence out in the Atlantic west. We've got abundant evidence for this now, but we've had indications about it for a long time. We already knew that there were probably Celtic languages associated with Tartessos in the early Iron Age.'

Even if we didn't have the inscriptions on the Iberian stelae, there would be good reasons to think that a Celtic language was being spoken in Tartessos during the late Bronze Age and into the early Iron Age. That name of the king of Tartessos, Arganthonios, is itself Celtic. It's very similar to the title 'Argantodannos', found on silver coins from Gaul, from much later. And when the Romans arrived in Iberia, they recorded the existing place names there, many of which contained Celtic words such as -*briga* (hill fort) and *eburo*- (yew tree). But the inscribed stelae provide us with more evidence of this ancient Celtic language – written in stone.

'At this point, we really do need to look at the whole thing again,' said John.

The weight of the evidence stacked up against the standard model is impressive. The model isn't just creaking; it's broken. And yet it still lingers on. In one of his essays on Tartessian, John expressed his frustration at the dogged persistence of this old idea: '. . . despite repeated debunkings and general signs of exhaustion . . . the standard narrative of the Celts still begins in Iron Age central Europe, much as it did half a century ago . . .' In conventional stories about the origin of the Celts, the countries out on the Atlantic edge of Europe – including Portugal, but also Britain and Ireland – still tend to be treated as if they are peripheral to the main narrative.

When invasion theories were all the rage, the map of Celtic Europe showed a homeland in central Europe with black arrows representing the spread of the Celts to the east, south and west. Tartessian cannot be shoehorned into this standard model. It's way too early. And not only is Tartessian too early for the traditional model, but also the Hallstatt and La Tène cultures never made it to south-western Iberia. It breaks any idea of a firm and potentially exclusive connection between Celtic languages and these particular cultures. We could try to modify the standard model, perhaps pushing it back into the Bronze Age, but with the Celtic or proto-Celtic homeland still in central Europe. Did the people of the early Urnfield culture speak a Celtic or nearly Celtic language? Place-name evidence suggests this is unlikely – there are very few Celtic place names in the Carpathian basin.

The persistence of the standard model is puzzling – and yet, despite a paucity of evidence, there are still a few archae-ologists clinging on to it. This perplexes geneticist Stephen Oppenheimer, who has written: 'The current orthodox view of the origins of the Celts is one of the last remaining archaeo-logical myths left over from the nineteenth century . . . If it were not a sincerely held conviction, the Iron Age, central European Celtic homeland story could be regarded as a hoax. There is no clear direct evidence, linguistic, archaeological or genetic, which identifies the Hallstatt or La Tène cultures as Celtic-linguistic homelands.'

The standard model not only linked language and material culture – it linked both of these to a specific group of people. Scientific archaeological techniques are now allowing us to test that link. Isotope analyses have cast doubt on the idea of mass migrations into Italy during the La Tène period. On the other hand, similar techniques are revealing an astonishing degree of mobility among the Beaker communities of the Bronze Age. A study of several Beaker cemeteries in Bavaria, looking at strontium and oxygen isotopes in teeth, showed a high level of mobility: a quarter of individuals didn't grow up anywhere near the place where they were buried. Similar techniques applied to the Amesbury Archer, an early Bronze Age man who lived around 2200 BC, and who was buried close to Stonehenge, show that he probably spent his childhood in the western Alps. Early results from the large Beaker People Project, applying isotope analyses to 250 Bronze Age burials from Britain, suggest considerable mobility, with perhaps ten per cent of people in some areas moving considerable distances in their lifetimes.

These types of scientific technique are allowing archaeologists to get closer to answering a question which has always troubled them – how much is the spread of ideas, in a particular time and place, and evidenced by archaeology and linguistics, related to the movement of people? Genetics provides us with another way of interrogating this question. DNA is, by its nature, inherited, so the DNA of living people holds clues to their ancestry. But it's a very confusing palimpsest. It's very difficult to reconstruct population history based only on this modern data. The ability to decode ancient DNA, if it's sufficiently well preserved, provides us with a window into real genetic diversity in the past, and holds out the promise of answering many more of our questions about mobility and migrations. But this field is still relatively young and, just as with some of the isotope studies, the numbers of skeletons sampled are still fairly small. We need to look at large samples before we can get any real idea of how ancient populations were expanding or shrinking, migrating and mixing.

In the meantime, modern DNA does provide us with some clues. Patterns of particular gene variants, or alleles, may provide some clues about how genes have flowed from one place to another. Y-chromosome data suggests that around seventy-five per cent of British and Irish ancestors arrived even before the first farmers got here, in the Neolithic. In terms of its Y chromosomes, the roots of the modern populations are mostly Paleo- or Mesolithic. In fact, that percentage increases as you move further west, so that the pre-Neolithic proportion of Irish ancestry is nearly ninety per cent. Geneticists postulate that this deep ancestry represents the recolonization of Britain and Ireland after the Ice Age, probably from a glacial refugium in northern Iberia. If the Y-chromosome is anything to go by, this suggests that any later arrivals, even if their languages replaced those of the indigenes, only made a minority contribution to the gene pool.

Trying to date the arrival of genes, and trace migrations, is so beset with problems that some don't even attempt it. But there are geneticists who have drawn tentative conclusions based on current evidence – which can be conflicting. Y-chromosome studies suggest that the Anglo-Saxons added very little to the English gene pool, whereas analyses looking across the whole genome put the Anglo-Saxon genetic contribution to south-east England at somewhere between ten to forty per cent. Even if we take this higher estimate, it's clear that Anglo-Saxons did not replace the existing population of England, even if the English language replaced Brittonic. There is a genetic divide between England and Wales, but this appears to be an ancient divide, not created by the influx of Anglo-Saxons in the first millennium AD. It goes back to the Neolithic or even earlier, and probably reflects the different maritime connections to Britain – via the Atlantic or the North Sea.

Y-chromosome studies appear to rule out the Celtic 'homeland' being central Europe. The distribution of modern Y-chromosome lineages seems to reflect a Neolithic contribution, via the Mediterranean, followed by an early Bronze Age expansion from the eastern Mediterranean to western Iberia, and up into Britain and Ireland. This latter input of genes, which is minor, contributing less than ten per cent to the gene pool, still might represent the people who started to speak Celtic in Iberia, and then carried the Celtic language to the north. Geneticist Stephen Oppenheimer speculates that this might represent a focused migration of specialist copper miners. And indeed it's hard to imagine how a rapid transmission of complex technologies could take place without a spread of the language used to communicate it. As Barry Cunliffe puts it, 'Anyone can carry a pot from one place to another, but to explain how you extract copper from an ore – you've got to talk to somebody.'

This is something that John Koch has also written about. Rather than the new language arriving on a wave of invasion, John has suggested that Celtic language may have reached Ireland, in particular, and spread along the whole Atlantic seaboard more generally, not on the tongues of an invading warrior aristocracy, but via wandering artisans. Koch uses the Irish term *'aes dano'* – 'people of skill' – which probably equates to the word *'kerto'* in Tartessian.

And so we can imagine this class of professional, skilled people, who moved around, helping to spread new technological know-how, but also speaking and spreading the lingua franca of the Atlantic seaboard – a very early Celtic language. Caesar listed the Druids and knights as the two high-ranking classes in Celtic society – all the rest were peasants. But he may have been missing this other, equally important class of itinerant craftspeople. If so, perhaps he missed them because they were, by nature, wanderers – because they existed beyond the confines and social structures within individual tribes. Perhaps those artisans were not as important in the Celtic-speaking later Iron Age societies of north-western Europe as they had been in the Bronze Age – though the transmission of ideas like mercury gilding is easier to understand in the hands of the *aes dano*. I thought back to the Snettisham Hoard; someone had arrived in Britain with that knowledge of how to coat bronze with gold, using mercury from Iberian cinnabar. It was an impenetrable process unless you had somebody to tell you how to do it.

The implications of the Tartessian evidence extend much further than Iberia; it's important to the whole of prehistoric western Europe. It should certainly make us look at Celtic Britain and Ireland differently. Our time frame and geographical focus both shift. We're no longer considering a wave of influence spreading from central Europe to the west during the Iron Age. Now we're peering right back into the Bronze Age, and seeing Britain and Ireland as part of this Atlantic network. Tartessos forms a hub connecting the eastern Mediterranean and north Africa with north-western Europe. Knowledge, skills and language travel up and down the coasts by sea. And so it's in these thriving coastal communities, facing the Atlantic, where we see the earliest emergence of something that, nearly 3,000 years later, we can recognize as being Celtic.

Rather than being an import from central Europe, it seems quite likely that the Celtic languages that survive, right out on the edge of north-western Europe, are the descendants of a language that grew up on the Atlantic fringe. Did this completely turn the idea of Celtic origins on its head? I asked John.

'It does mean we need to take it apart and put it back together again, to get the real picture.'

As a Celtic linguist working in Aberystwyth University, John found it interesting and exciting to be part of this developing new perspective on Celtic origins.

'There's been a tendency – using that standard model – to think of the arrival of the Celts in Wales as being like the railway coming down to Aberystwyth: we're the end of the line; we're the last stop; we got here last and we're still here.

'But the idea might be: look the other way – look at the Atlantic, and maybe that's how it starts. Rather than only being part of that final episode, where we find the survivors, maybe we're right there at the beginning of the story.'

Threads: Where I Wanted to be When I Started

The impact of the Roman Empire on Europe still resonates down through the centuries. The language of that empire, the colloquial Latin spoken by merchants, settlers and soldiers, evolved over time into what we know today as the Romance languages – Italian, of course, but also Spanish, Portuguese, French and Romanian. Eventually, the Celtic speakers of northern Italy, Spain, Portugal, France and Romania fell silent. In Iron Age northern Europe, beyond the Celtic-speaking tribes, there were people who spoke an early pre-Germanic language. In the fifth century AD, Germanic migrants from the continent brought their language to England. The Anglo-Saxons didn't wipe out or replace the existing Britons, far from it, but their language caught on. Brittonic and Latin fell out of use in what would become known as England, as more and more people began to speak English. And yet, in the west – in Cornwall, Wales, Scotland and Ireland – the old languages, spoken there since at least the Iron Age, persisted. They are vibrant, beautiful, living languages, but they are also echoes of a family of languages that were once spoken right across Europe – from those wild, windswept Atlantic shores to the coast of the Black Sea, and beyond, into Anatolia. In our new story of Celtic origins, those languages that persist out on the western edge of Europe were also born here, in the west.

This new perspective on the origins of the Celts, this idea of 'Celtic from the West', is still relatively new, and is certainly not universally accepted. To many European archaeologists, historians and linguists, the standard model is still the orthodoxy. Hallstatt and La Tène are still at the core of their concept of the Celts. And, indeed, no one doubts the existence of those cultures and their spread. What is contested, though, is just how far those cultures spread – and whether the dissemination of a certain element of material culture should be taken to imply a spread of other aspects of culture, such as language, or a movement of people. The evidence for such a neat package of 'Celticity' just isn't there.

The challenge represented by the Tartessian inscriptions is even more profound than its demolition of the standard model of Celtic origins, because it makes us question what 'Celtic' actually means. It destroys any idea of a neat link between language and material culture – indeed, that very idea seems to have been an illusion all along. And it's right to be brutal about this fact: the development of the Celtic language in western Europe has nothing at all to do with the much later Hallstatt and La Tène cultures. Here's a heresy: there's no reason to believe that the people who started making the artefacts that we recognize as typically 'Hallstatt' or 'La Tène' even spoke a Celtic language. They could just as easily have been speaking a language belonging to the northern branch of the Indo-European tree – a Germanic or pre-Germanic tongue.

So where does that leave us? Is it possible to be a Celt, defined by your material culture, by the styles of weapons and jewellery you make, but without speaking a Celtic language? Is it possible to be a Celt if you speak a Celtic language but don't have anything that looks Celtic about the rest of your culture? And what about Celts today? Is this an ethnic identity based only on language – relying on Edward Lhuyd's definition of Celtic languages – without any other cultural or biological connections with extant or ancient Celts? Perhaps we shouldn't be so quick to dismiss language, or indeed, mock attempts to preserve it – it's more important for cultural identity than perhaps any other aspect of culture, or biology.

N

DEVELOPMENT
OF CELTIC
BY 3000 BC

SPREAD OF CELTIC
BY 2000 BC

CELTO-ITALIC
5500 - 5000 BC

A NEW HYPOTHESIS SUGGESTING
HOW THE CELTIC LANGUAGE MIGHT
HAVE DEVELOPED, FROM A BRANCH OF
INDO~EUROPEAN IN THE WESTERN
MEDITERRANEAN, FLOWING NORTH INTO THE
ATLANTIC ZONE, AND LATER SPREADING BACK
EAST, INTO CENTRAL EUROPE
(ADAPTED FROM *BRITAIN BEGINS*, CUNLIFFE, 2012)

INDO   EUROPEAN

6000 BC

None of the ways in which we define 'Celts' map neatly on to one another. There are linguistic Celts, archaeological Celts, artistic Celts, ancient historical Celts, ethnic Celts and biological Celts. But the problem is they don't coincide. There is not a single, coherent Celtic package.

The archaeologist Raimund Karl sees this is a crucial problem for anyone trying to study the Celts: they never existed as a real thing – they only exist as a construct, as something we wish to study. This is 'Celtoscepticism' at its most extreme, and it's a perfectly defensible stance.

So has all this searching been in vain? Did we only go in search of an illusion, perhaps an eigtheenth- or nineteenth-century fabrication, which seems almost to have been plucked out of thin air? Well, even after the iconoclastic revelations from south-western Portugal, I'm not a complete Celtosceptic. I think, in this search for the Celts, we've unearthed something very valuable, because what we've discovered is a real richness, and we've achieved what is surely a much more satisfying perspective on Europe in the Iron Age.

The emerging picture is varied and complex – after all, this is human history and prehistory that we're looking at. It defies our attempts to reduce it, to capture it on a map with neat lines drawn around cultural complexes and black arrows representing their spread. We've seen La Tène art spreading to England and Ireland, but we've also seen torcs and Thames swords spreading in the other direction, back to the continent. We've learned about some migrations from the classical authors, but picking up the evidence of these population movements in archaeology proves almost impossible. The spread of ideas requires people to be mobile, but it doesn't require mass migrations. Genetics is starting to provide some answers, but looking for clues in the DNA of living people is fraught with difficulty. Nevertheless, as it stands, there's no evidence for a wave of new genes spreading from central Europe to the west in the Iron Age. In the future, ancient DNA may help to shed more light on the question of just how much population movement occurred alongside the spread of ideas.

Once we pick apart all those tangled threads, it can seem like that's all we've managed to lay our hands on – a collection of disparate strands, which occasionally get knotted up together, but which are essentially separate. It's hard to join them up in any meaningful way, to look for any wider or deeper meaning. It seems that we've been searching for an archetype – and that this just doesn't exist. There is no one 'Celt'. All of those different ways of being Celtic shift and change over time, sometimes coming together, briefly, but often not. But perhaps this is the deeper meaning, after all – that human society and identity are wonderfully complex and fluid. We can try to spot larger trends – looking at how technology changes, art evolves, or power shifts over time – but we may be seeing patterns that weren't obvious to the people living through them. St Jerome knew the Galatians spoke a similar language to the people living in Trier, but it's unlikely that the Galatians knew or cared about their linguistic cousins in the west. The person who owned that La Tène fibula in Gordion probably had no idea that people made and possessed similar objects right the way across Europe, as far away as Gaul, Britain and Ireland.

By teasing apart the tangled threads of our Gordion knot, we do gain some insights into wider societies, economics and politics of late Bronze Age and Iron Age Europe. For me, it's the threads that represent the lives of real people that really shine out – like golden strands, still glittering after all these years. Teasing them out has been worthwhile in itself.

We've certainly got very close to individuals who lived and died 2,500 years ago, whose mortal remains and grave goods contain clues to their lives and to the societies they lived in. And, of course, we've also got those portraits – which may be secondhand and embellished, but are near contemporary, nonetheless – written by the chroniclers of the Greek and Roman civilizations.

But the question of who the Celts were goes beyond looking at individual lives and understanding particular lifestyles. In the end, it's a question about origins, and that's why Barry Cunliffe and John Koch's hypothesis of 'Celtic from the West' is so important.

Barry Cunliffe started to write about this idea back in the 1990s, convinced that archaeology didn't support the traditional model. His musings were much more than just romantic conjecture. He is no armchair archaeologist: his insights derived from real, tangible, physical evidence. All of his hypotheses started from that point – from the ground up. And he tried to approach his subject without *a priori* assumptions, without prejudice.

Barry Cunliffe's assessment of the archaeological evidence was that it revealed a different story, something completely contrary to the standard model of Celtic origins. He thought that Edward Lhuyd's *Glossography* of 1707 still stood up to scrutiny – as a brilliant piece of scholarship, in fact. But it's also important to realize that Lhuyd hadn't come up with the idea of Celts coming from the east from his study of linguistics. The concept had emerged out of a biblical notion, and Lhuyd sneaked it into the Welsh preface of the *Glossography*. But, nevertheless, this had become the accepted linguistic model of Celtic origins. Archaeology had been practically non-existent when Lhuyd was writing, and, later on, archaeological discoveries were simply fitted to the existing linguistic model, which then developed into the invasion theory. This theory had been roundly attacked by Grahame Clark in the 1960s, but the standard model of Celtic origins continued to enjoy a remarkable hold on the popular – and the academic – imagination.

It's interesting to note how this new model of Celts from the West has been received by European scholars.

'The Germans still won't have it,' Cunliffe explained when I met him. 'The French are quite happy. The Spaniards, of course, are beside themselves with delight.' It's clear that the political implications of the theory went far beyond the Iron Age – they fed into modern concepts of Europe too. 'That's why the Germans are so keen to hang on to the standard model,' Barry told me. 'And people have quite recently identified the modern European ideal with the Celtic Europe. And the Scots were getting very upset with what we were saying – until they realized that what we were actually saying was that they weren't the result of a group of Germans coming across, but a much deeper-rooted indigenous people. And then it all became politically acceptable – in Scotland, Ireland and Wales.'

The varied responses to this new theory of Celtic origins are fascinating. After all, this hypothesis threatened to pull apart the carefully constructed tapestry that represented the orthodox view of prehistoric Europe. It's not surprising that it was more than a little unpopular in some circles. I'd always known that this was a subject fraught with controversies – some people even object to the use of the word 'Celt'. Barry Cunliffe was not one of them.

'You have to be very careful. You have to explain what you mean, and communicate your reservations. But Celts exist – the Celtic concept exists. Some people call themselves Celts today. A lot of people in the past spoke a common language, and some of those would have called themselves Celts, and it's not unreasonable to call that language "Celtic".'

More than any other aspect of culture, it was language that formed the most robust and enduring connection between the Celtic communities of Iron Age Europe and, indeed, that provided us with the best definition of 'Celtic'. But while labels provide us with a way of talking about the past, they can also constrain us. The story of the Celts might be largely an Iron Age one, but it continues through the Roman period – all the way to the present day. And its roots are much earlier. Restricting ourselves to the Iron Age means missing out on that key part of the story of the Celts, which goes back at least as far as the Bronze Age.

There are reasons to doubt the historically attested mass migrations from central Europe into northern Italy, Greece and Anatolia during the Iron Age – and even if mass movements happened, the people who ended up at the extreme edges of the Celtic-speaking world would have been markedly different at the end of those migrations. But there was no evidence – historical, genetic or archaeological – for an Iron Age westwards expansion from central Europe. And, as far as Britain and Ireland were concerned, there was no evidence at all – coming from any direction – for a significant social or technological change in the Iron Age. This was perhaps Barry Cunliffe's biggest problem with the standard model – the major theme from the Bronze Age into the Iron Age was one of continuity.

In Britain, there was much more evidence for change in the Neolithic, and then again in the Middle Bronze Age. And there was always contact in two directions – Britain had a west side story and an east side story – the west side contact was via the Atlantic, and the east side via the North Sea. These contacts saw a flow of ideas operating between Britain and the continent, right the way through history – and prehistory. But even during times of social and technological transition, there was still a major theme of continuity.

Along with the transitions detectable in material culture in prehistory, the Celtic language had at some point reached these shores. The linguistic evidence suggested that the Celtic language originated much earlier than the Iron Age, perhaps blossoming first in south-western Iberia, then spreading up and down the Atlantic seaboard. Rather than being invaded by Celts in the Iron Age, Britain and Ireland probably became 'Celticized' in the Bronze Age, perhaps even earlier. We can reject any theories of mass migration or invasion, but some movement of people had clearly been involved in the spread of language and material culture.

Could the roots of the Celtic language go back even further than the Bronze Age?

'I think it could go back to the spread of the Indo-European language family across Europe – with the Neolithic,' explained Barry Cunliffe. 'One of the arms of Indo-European comes from the spread of the Neolithic along the Mediterranean, where people, with characteristic pottery, spread from Greece, through Italy, into southern France and Spain, and out to Portugal and the Atlantic. There's another stream as well: Indo-European also comes to the west via an overland route into north-western France. But it's the Mediterranean spread that's important here – taking place in a period of just 500 years – a very clear and fast maritime movement of the Neolithic, from the eastern Mediterranean all the way to the Atlantic. When that Mediterranean arm reaches Portugal, it's there that the Indo-European develops into a maritime lingua franca – and that is the basis of Celtic.

'If you accept that Indo-European is reaching the Atlantic zone by 5000 BC, you begin to see how ideas and technologies spread along the Atlantic seaways – you're getting concepts of burial, concepts of cosmology, concepts of art – from the fifth to the fourth millennium BC. And that involves language, too, there's no doubt.'

So, if we're defining Celts as people who speak Celtic, can we really find Celts as early as the fifth millennium BC?

'Well – you've got to ask: what are the roots of the Celtic language?' challenged Barry Cunliffe. 'They are in the Atlantic zone, in the Neolithic period. And this is where the whole of the Beaker spread comes from. Until the middle of the third millennium, there's essentially an Atlantic spread. From the middle of the third millennium, with the Beakers, it spreads from the Atlantic, along the rivers, into central Europe – a spread of people, culture and language.'

Some linguists have contested the origin of Celtic in the west, pointing to the inclusion of words relating to horses and wheels, which surely come from horse-riding steppe cultures. But this may not be a significant challenge – Barry Cunliffe suggests a Neolithic spread of 'paleo-Celtic', followed by the Bronze Age spread of 'Beaker Celtic', which took the language inland. There, around the Rhine, this language may have blended with another stream of Indo-European, picking up words that originated from the westwards expansion of the Yamnaya culture of the steppe – creating 'New Celtic'.

The evolution of the Celtic language, as Barry described it, seemed to be inextricably interwoven with what John Koch has called the 'three strands' of Bronze Age Europe – three areas of innovation that transformed society: bronze, advanced sea-faring and chariots. John also draws interesting parallels between our society today and the European Bronze Age, describing 'the rise of international elites on a tide of new technology with long-distance mobility as a way of life.'

But does the link with our prehistoric past go beyond analogy? While ancient genetic lineages can be teased out of genomes, that says nothing about any folk memory of ethnicity. And perhaps even seeking a link with an ancient ethnic identity is foolish; ethnic identities change over time, and, anyway, how do we make sense of any identity that covers 3,000 years and spans a hundred generations? Ethnic identity is such a complex thing. It can change over your lifetime. You might feel that your recent ancestry feeds into it – I'm sure the background of your two parents is important, here, and perhaps your four grandparents. But what about your eight great-grandparents? It's likely there's already quite a mix of ethnic identities there – how do you choose which ones you identify with? Go back 300 years, some nine generations before you, and you find a maximum of 512 great-great-great-great-great-great-great-grandparents. It's a maximum number because, going back this far, it's highly likely that there will have been some reproduction between cousins, and so the actual number of your ancestors is less. But, anyway – of those hundreds of potential ancestors, which contribute to your ethnic identity?

It's a nonsensical question, because you probably don't know who any of them are. And yet, wrapped up in ethnic identity is often a feeling of a very deep connection with past generations. But that doesn't come from your genes – unless we're talking about a few genes that affect features like hair, eye and skin colour, which might seem somehow relevant. Your ethnic identity has more to do with immediate ancestors – the ones you know about. It is likely to be the same as your parents'. But then it might be different, because it's about place as well as ancestry. If both your parents came from India, but you were born in Britain, you may think of yourself as British. If both your parents and all your grandparents were born in Britain, does that make you 'more' British? That's a tricky one because, as we go back through the generations, you'll inevitably start to find ancestors who came from much further away. It quickly becomes clear that there is no such thing as 'pure' ethnic identity, from a genetic point of view. Our family histories are wonderfully complex and often cosmopolitan. We're all genetic mongrels.

So ethnicity is not a biological phenomenon, even if it might draw on some biological features like eye, hair and skin colour. We construct it based on our recent ancestry, on the place in which we're born, the place in which we live, a particular set of values and rituals – which may or may not be associated with a religion, the language we speak and the stories that we tell. In fact, of all of those strands, it's probably the values, rituals, language and stories that provide us with the deepest, most meaningful connections with the past, and those connections are only very loosely associated with biological ancestry.

Turning to a modern Celtic ethnic identity, we've already discovered that this only really emerged after Edward Lhuyd defined those languages – Scots Gaelic, Irish, Welsh, Cornish and Breton – as 'Celtic'. So is there any meaningful connection between ancient Celtic identities and modern Celtic identities, or are they two completely separate constructs?'

For Barry Cunliffe, the reinvention of the Celts is fascinating, politically and emotionally. 'There are links right back to the time when Celtic languages were spoken more widely. But there's also a fake modern Celtic identity. On the other hand, the folk music and festivals in Brittany represent a musical tradition that is rooted in the landscape, with a long-standing connectedness with the landscape. And it's interesting how old traditions keep going, even if they change their names. So *Tout Saints*, All Saints Day, is actually *Samhain* – and people go to cemeteries and clean the graves. There's a real heritage there – which is not even seen to be a heritage. The more time I spend in Brittany, the more I can understand it. They walk the boundaries, which quite often relate to prehistoric monuments. I do believe in a degree of Celtic continuity. But I don't like Celtic reinvention.'

The Celtic revival has also seen renewed interest in Celtic art, although modern Celtic art often harks back to mediaeval art, which some scholars see as being only loosely inspired by

La Tène. But is it right to see that original, Iron Age La Tène art as quintessentially Celtic? It seems to be a nineteenth-century label which has stuck. In some places, certainly, La Tène art may have been produced by people who spoke a Celtic language. But not everyone speaking those languages made La Tène art. There were many other forms of art made by Celtic-speaking people. In Spain, archaeologists have sought long and hard for this style of art and have found only a few La Tène brooches. And I think the interest in that single La Tène brooch from Gordion says more about archaeologists' preconceptions and preoccupations than it does about any ancient reality. The futile search for La Tène across the Celtic-speaking world reminds us just how tenuous the links are between language and other aspects of culture. And it surely reminds us that it would pay to adopt a more scientific approach – we should be searching for ways to test hypotheses, rather than for evidence to support them.

In the end, it may be much more useful to view Celtic material culture as a complex picture with lots of overlapping zones where discrete collections of specific objects are found. Such 'artefact sets' can tell us more about shared patterns of behaviour – patterns which would vary across the Celtic world. Barry Cunliffe uses the example of feasting gear found in the Atlantic zone in the late Bronze Age: cauldrons, flesh hooks and roasting spits. Although feasting was an important aspect of Celtic society, right across Europe, the Atlantic feasting gear represented a specific type of behaviour that was localized to the Atlantic zone, extending from southern Spain and Portugal up to Shetland. It was a 'community of behaviour' that showed connectivity between these places.

But is that connectivity just something we perceive, with the benefit of hindsight, and with this wide geographical perspective? Or would it have been *felt* by those communities up and down the Atlantic coasts of Europe – did they have a feeling of connectivity and a common ethnic identity? If you look at the *longue durée*, as Barry Cunliffe does, there's a clear tradition of contact going right back to the Neolithic. These were maritime connections – travel and communication by sea was easier – and of course essential where islands were involved – than overland connections. And these connections fostered a common culture along those Atlantic coasts. A member of the late Bronze Age elite from Portugal, going to Shetland, would not have been at all surprised by the lifestyle or the equipment used by people there – it would all have been very familiar.

We can envisage myriad overlapping journeys by boat up and down the Atlantic coasts of Europe: a constant frenzy of voyages, carrying raw materials, manufactured goods, language, ideas, friends and potential spouses. As well as these individual journeys, it's very likely that people would have gathered regularly in a more organized way, on a greater scale. There may have been traditional gatherings at particular times of the year – just as there are in many societies today. What we know of the Celtic calendar, from history, myth and archaeology, suggests that there were significant times in the year, tied to important events in the agricultural year, which undoubtedly provided excuses for festivals and feasting. There was Lughnasa (the Gaelic festival marking the beginning of the harvest season, at the start of August), Samhain (the end of harvest, at the close of October, and transmuted into modern Halloween), Imbolc (the start of Spring, at the start of February), and Beltane (the

Gaelic May Day festival). At these times, we can perhaps imagine that large numbers of people would have been making huge journeys, of hundreds of kilometres, for feasting, meeting, exchanging wives, exchanging news and carrying out their business. Such meetings, festivals, feasts – whatever we choose to call them – would have been crucial to creating and maintaining wider social networks, and to spreading ideas. Such gatherings would also have depended on and promoted the development of a common language. This all reminds me of a festival I'd been lucky enough to visit in Yakutia, in Siberia, where people had travelled in from an area the size of France to the site of a Reindeer Festival – for races, socializing, fun and matchmaking – helping to reinforce the reindeer herders' social network. But we don't have to look so far away to understand the role of the festival in society and culture. Much newer festivals, like the recently inaugurated May Day festival in Oxford, and the round of summer music festivals including Glastonbury, and numerous modern Celtic music festivals, remind us how important these live events still are to us today – even in the era of the internet and virtual communications.

By drawing analogies with the present, it becomes easier to think of those ancient societies as more similar to our own than perhaps we've been prepared to accept before.

It is interesting and wonderful that the ancient languages and stories have persisted in north-western Europe, in the lands we think of as 'Celtic' today. There never was a major migration of 'Celtic' people to these islands, but it may be possible to pick up the traces of some earlier migrants against that more prominent genetic signature of the original colonizers, after the Ice Age. But, most importantly, those (probably Bronze Age) wanderers brought with them a new language, new ideas and new stories – which took root and survived, right through history to the present.

Our drive to understand the past has led us to divide history and prehistory up into chunks, which, while useful in discussion, can be extremely unhelpful. It can mean that we miss the bigger picture; it makes us think of a staccato succession of 'ages'; and it also makes the past – and the people inhabiting it – seem vastly and categorically different and distant from us.

'I try to get away from history as episodic,' Barry told me. 'I look for continuity. The past and the present are not all that dissimilar. There have always been people coming from the continent into Britain. Our concepts of identity are always changing. And so it's always been.'

Talking to Barry Cunliffe, who has studied the Celts so closely for so many years, I felt some degree of resolution. It was now becoming possible to weave together these threads – to create a wonderful tapestry out of archaeology, history, language and identity.

'I do think the questions I set out to study are coming together,' said Barry. 'It gets to where I wanted to be when I started.'

It certainly seems that we've come a long way from the old invasion theories and the attractive simplicity of that standard model of Celtic origins. Even though there are still many questions left to answer, what emerges from the latest archaeological, linguistic and genetic studies is a rich, detailed, complex and *messy* picture of the ancient Celts. It's about discovering a real heritage, not inventing one. And it breathes new life into concepts of Celtic identity today.

EPILOGUE

I met up with Neil Oliver on the wild and windswept west coast of Ireland. We were in Spiddal, County Galway, for a modern Celtic festival: the Traidphicnic music and crafts festival. We listened to some music at this modern Celtic festival and headed down to the beach.

'Did you find them?' Neil asked me.

'It's so difficult. I've travelled right across Europe, trying to grasp these people, and they just keep on slipping through my fingers. But I've realized that's because we need to make up our minds about who they are. Is it a biological definition, a genetic definition, or a definition based on language, on art, or some other aspect of culture?'

'Do you think part of the problem is that we've always been taught that the Celts *appeared* from somewhere – almost as if through a trapdoor in history – when in fact the truth is that they were the descendants of people that had been there all along?'

'I think we've been totally hoodwinked by this nineteenth-century idea that there was an Iron Age invasion of Britain and Ireland that brought Celtic language and culture with it. There were some people who came to Britain and Ireland

– not so much in the Iron Age, probably in the Bronze Age – bringing the Celtic language with them. But they didn't wipe out the people that were there before. They introduced the language and that language took root, and people still speak it here – which is wonderful.'

'I blame a lot of the confusion on the Romans,' said Neil. 'The Romans were the people who wrote about the Celts, and we turn to them again and again to try to understand who the Celts were. But then we have that Roman veneer – they dumped their civilization over the Celts. It's because of the Romans that we can't see the Celts. But – when you come to a place like this, when you hear people speak Gaelic here – is that a genuine echo of the ancient Celts?'

'I think it is. And I do think it's with the language that we get closest to them. And now we think that this Celtic language might have grown up in western Europe – the story's looking more and more as though Celtic started off here, along these Atlantic coasts. And isn't it a triumph that no one speaks Latin any more? But the Celts are still out there, to be heard.'

Further reading

The Celts seem to attract controversy like no other people or concept in history. I know that this is a hugely controversial subject, and I know that there are many opinions which don't appear in this book, and that will upset some people. Having said that, all the experts I've met, and whose ideas and theories are woven together in this book, are well respected in their fields. I am not presenting my own thesis here, merely collecting together the work of many well-recognized experts – archaeologists, linguists and historians. The theories presented here are all published elsewhere, in academic journals, conference volumes and in books aimed at a wider audience.

For a general introduction to the archaeology of the Celts, I would recommend Barry Cunliffe's *The Ancient Celts*, and its diminutive cousin, *The Celts: a very short introduction*. Barry Cunliffe's *Britain Begins* is an extremely accessible introduction to the wider sweep of British prehistory.

I must also recommend Neil Oliver's *A History of Ancient Britain*. Not because I have to, but because it's one of the most beautifully written introductions to British prehistory that I've read.

The relatively new 'Atlantic Fringe' theory is explored in a series of scholarly articles in two conference volumes, *Celtic from the West* and *Celtic from the West 2*, both edited by Barry Cunliffe and John Koch.

Miranda Aldhouse-Green has written widely about Celtic mythology, and I heartily recommend her small but wonderfully detailed *The Celtic Myths: A guide to the ancient gods and legends*, as well as her *Dictionary of Celtic Myth and Legend*. Ronald Hutton has written an epic but highly readable book on the druids: *Blood & Mistletoe: the History of the Druids in Britain*.

Many of the works of classical historians and geographers are now available as translations online, some alongside the original Greek or Latin. It is wonderful to enter the expansive Library of the Internet, and pick up Pytheas, Strabo, Livy, Avienus, Hecataeus or Herodotus to read. This rich archive of ancient literature is surely one of the more enlightening rabbit holes you can hope to descend into.

If you want to plumb a little deeper, then here's a small selection of journal articles you might want to track down:

Bridgman TP (2005) Keltoi, Galatai, Galli: Were they all one people? *Proceedings of the Harvard Celtic Colloquium* vol. 24/25: 155–162.

Clarke G (1966) The Invasion Hypothesis in British Archaeology. *Antiquity* 40: 172–189.

Fernandez-Gotz M & Krause D (2012) Heuneburg: First city north of the Alps. *Current World Archaeology* 55: 28–34.

Hummler M (2007) Bridging the gap at La Tène. *Antiquity* 81: 1067–1070.

McEvoy B *et al.* (2004) The Longue Duree of genetic

ancestry: multiple genetic markers and Celtic origins on the Atlantic facade of Europe. *American Journal of Human Genetics* 75: 693–702.

Richards M, Capelli C, Wilson JF (2008) Genetics and the origins of the British population. *Encyclopedia of Life Sciences*. Chichester: Wiley.

Selinsky P (2012) Celtic ritual activity at Gordion, Turkey: Evidence from mortuary contexts and skeletal analysis. *International Journal of Osteoarchaeology* 25: 213–225.

Scheeres M *et al.* (2013) Evidence for 'Celtic migrations'? Strontium isotope analysis at the early La Tène (LT B) cemeteries of Nebringen (Germany) and Monte Bibele (Italy). *Journal of Archaeological Science* 40: 3614–3625.

I have discussed the problem with defining the 'Celts' in this book, but in the end I have accepted the definition based on language as a useful way of approaching the subject. I find Barry Cunliffe and John Koch's new hypothesis – which includes recognizing the Tartessian inscriptions as Celtic, stressing the importance of exchange networks in the late Atlantic Bronze Age, and suggesting that Celtic may have emerged in the west – to be compelling. But there are many archaeologists who disagree with this model, in particular, John Collis of the University of Sheffield. He is concerned by attempts to seek an 'origin' of the Celts, and describes both the standard model of Celtic origins in central Europe and the new Atlantic Fringe hypothesis as 'incapable of proof and equally flawed'. Collis also takes issue with labelling ancient Britons and Irish as 'Celts'. For the sake of balance, you may wish to read his argument – which is laid out in his book, *The Celts: Origins, Myths and Inventions*.

Acknowledgements

This voyage of discovery took me right across Europe and beyond, and I met a great number of people who generously shared their expertise and insights with me, helping me to understand different aspects of the Celts, as well as showing me a wealth of archaeological finds. I couldn't possibly have written this book without them.

In the repository stores of Stuttgart Museum, I met archaeologist and curator Thomas Hoppe, who introduced me to the wonderful grave goods buried with the Hochdorf Prince, and also showed me archaeological finds from Heuneburg. At that hill fort, I met the State archaeologist for Baden-Wuerttemberg, Professor Dirk Krause, who took me on a tour of the citadel and showed me the recent LIDAR survey. Back at the State Office for Cultural Heritage Management Baden-Wuerttemberg, in Esslingen, archaeologist Simone Stork showed me the human remains and the golden jewellery from the Bettelbühl burial mound. In the Ulster Museum, Belfast, while filming the third series of *Digging for Britain*, the current archaeology series on BBC2 and BBC4, I met curator Greer Ramsey, who let me hold the incredible Corrard torc. And in the British Museum, curator Julia Farley introduced me to the wonders of the Snettisham hoard, while metallurgist Nigel Meeks used a scanning electron microscope to show me details of the Great Torc and evidence of fire-gilding on another piece of torc. In the course of filming *Digging for Britain,* I have been lucky enough to visit Burrough hill fort during recent excavations led by Jeremy Taylor and John Thomas of Leicester University, and to visit the Iron Age 'Durotriges Big Dig' excavations near Winterbourne Kingston, led by Miles Russell and Paul Cheetham of Bournemouth University. At Gordion in central Turkey, I was introduced to the site and the wider landscape by archaeologists Brian Rose and Gareth Derbyshire, of the University of Pennsylvania. On the long beach at Burnham-on-Sea in Somerset, I rode in a reconstruction of an Iron Age chariot, made by Robert Hurford. At Ribemont in France, I was privileged to examine remains from the site of Ribemont and to talk to archaeologist Gerard Leslay du Fercoq, in the Centre Archeologique Somme. At Glauberg in central Germany, I met archaeologist Ines Balzer and her colleagues, who allowed me to get very close to the sandstone warrior statue, and to closely examine objects from the burial mound. In the National Museum of Ireland in Dublin, I met archaeologist Ned Kelly and Head of Conservation Rolly Read, who talked to me about the mysterious bog bodies. Linguist John Koch, of Aberystwyth University, met me in Portugal, and showed me the Tartessian inscriptions on the stelae in the Museu da Escrita do Sudoeste, in Almodôvar (well worth a visit!).

And finally, at the University of Oxford's Institute of Archaeology, I met up with Barry Cunliffe, Emeritus Professor of European Archaeology. His books had been my constant travel companions; his approach to the evidence brushed away the accretions of old theories; his insights cut through what seemed like inextricably knotty problems. And so I got on a train to Oxford, and headed for the Institute of Archaeology, to finally meet him. We went for lunch in a small French restaurant round the corner from the Institute – two modern Britons discussing the Celts over a feast, complete with a small flagon of Gallic wine – undiluted. Barry provided answers to many of the questions that had emerged during the course of my journey, as well as talking to me in detail about the 'Celtic from the West' hypothesis and the archaeological evidence to support it.

I am hugely grateful to all of these experts for sharing their knowledge with me, and for showing me some astonishing archaeological finds, but I should also say that any mistakes I've made in this book are all my own.

I didn't travel alone on this voyage of discovery – this book accompanies the BBC2 series, and so I must thank everyone who was part of this large team, behind the scenes metaphorically, and literally behind the camera on location. Accompanying me on the journey, telling his own strand of the story, was archaeologist and presenter Neil Oliver. Overseeing operations from *Celts* HQ at Broadcasting House were executive producer Cameron Balbirnie, production managers Gezz Mounter and Amanda Robinson, and production coordinators Kathryn Jein and Thu Dinh. My travelling companions on various shoots included series producer and director, Jeremy Hall; producer/director Micky Lachmann; assistant producers Gemma Hagen, Mark Edger and Fiona

Cushley; researcher Ivan Lazic; cameramen Chris Openshaw, Tom Hayward, Patrick Smith and Noel Hines; sound record-ists Andy Paddon-Smith, Kuz Randhawa and Chris Youle-Grayling; and the 'eye in the sky' drone camera operators Nils Keber and Bernd Schoppner in Germany, and Rory Watson and Kevin Lever in Somerset. Special thanks to Micky Lachmann, Jeremy Hall and Gemma Hagen who took many of the BBC photos for this book.

As well as the team of experts I met in the course of filming and writing, and the team producing the television series for BBC2, I have also had an awesome team helping me to make all of this into a book. Jon Watt, my editor at Heron Books, has a clear eye for the bigger picture and has encouraged me to see the wood rather than get embroiled in the architecture of individual trees. Susan Watt has also helped enormously. My copy editor has also been very astute and helpful. My literary agent, Luigi Bonomi, persuaded me that I would be able to write a book to accompany the BBC series to what seemed like an impossibly tight deadline. He might be wrong, but I am grateful for his belief in me. Hilary Murray, of Arlington Enterprises, also seems to delight in setting me impossible tasks.

Many colleagues, friends and family have listened to me harp on about the Celts this year, and some have even been kind enough to offer constructive criticism. Thank you all. Especially Dave.

INDEX

Bronze Age
  Beaker culture 251
  Celtic language 247–8,
    254–5, 265
  evidence of elite 92, 94,
    100–2
  feasting gear 270
  funerary stelae 245, 246, 247
  goldmining 114
  hoards 90–7
  nomads of the Pontic steppe
    79–80
  population instability 93–4
  trade/ communication net-
    works 43, 46, 47, 49, 98–9,
    106, 120, 246–7, 254–5,
    271
  Urnfield culture 47–9, 50, 98
brooches 67, 68, 99
  see also fibulae, Bettelbühl
Brythons/ P-Kelts 103
burials 177–8
  Bettelbühl Princess 66,
    68–78, 82–3, 84
  bog bodies 156, 211–24
  catacomb culture 79–80
  chariot/ cart 17, 18, 79, 110,
    111–12, 166, 195
  Glauberg Prince 109, 197–8,
    208
  Gordion, Turkey 146, 147–8,
    151–7
  Hallstatt cemetery 44–5,
    46–7
  Hallstatt grave goods 44–5,
    53–4
  Heuneburg 59, 62, 66, 67–8
    (see also Bettelbühl Prin-
    cess)

hoards and funerary rituals
    96–7
Hochdorf Prince 15–22, 53,
    66, 84, 99–100
lack of British and Irish Iron
    Age 101
Princess of Vix 66
Ribemont-sur-Ancre enclo-
    sures 184–9
ritual offerings 96–7,
    99–100
Scythian kurgans 81–2
timber-grave culture 80
Urnfield cremations 47
warrior burials 109–10,
    111–12, 198, 205
Bury Hill hillfort 123

Cadiz 161, 239
Caesar, Julius 32, 34, 35, 63, 67,
    119, 123, 162, 163–8, 180,
    182, 211, 254
Camillus 131, 132–3
Camulodunum 169
Cantium 36
Carnutes tribe 191
Carthage/ Carthaginians 52,
    160–1
Cartimandua 195
Cassiterides 37–8
Cassivellaunus 166–7
catacomb culture 79–80
Catuvellauni tribe 169
cauldrons
  burial of Hochdorf Prince
    17–18, 21
  Celtic myths 202–3
  Gundestrop 118, 203–5, 208